The Bigger the Better the Tighter the Sweater

THE
BIGGER
THE
BETTER
THE
tighter
THE
SWEATER

21 Funny Women
ON BEAUTY, BODY IMAGE,
& OTHER HAZARDS OF BEING FEMALE

Edited by SAMANTHA SCHOECH & LISA TAGGART

SEAL

Contents

Stretch Marks: Pregnancy & Other Bum Deals

The Breakdown: Aging & Illness

Introduction

A few years ago, a teacher friend of ours tried an experiment with her eighth graders. This was at an exclusive girls school in Manhattan, the kind of place that produces the Nancy Pelosis and Toni Morrisons of the next generation. Our friend had her students list all of the women they admired for their achievements. Bombarded since enrollment with tracts covering Susan B. Anthony, Harriet Tubman, Sandra Day O'Connor, and Sally Ride, the girls rattled off dozens of names, quickly topping fifty. Next, the teacher had them identify women they admired for their looks—actresses, hip-hop artists, *Sex and the City* girls, and barely pubescent models filled this roster. Then our friend had the girls choose one of all these women in whose footsteps they'd most like to follow, one role model to whom they might be favorably compared when they got to the ripe old age of thirty. Each girl wrote a single name, anonymously, on a piece of paper.

The result: Every single girl, save one lone ambitious student (we wonder where she ended up), chose a name from the Babe List.

These girls were thirteen, sure, so they were most likely at the height of their adolescent angst over their appearances. But they were also no dummies: They knew that looks matter to girls and women in a way that blows everything else out of the water. Even when you're as old as thirty.

It's no secret that American women are obsessed with their bodies. It's not just the dieters and the triathletes who chronicle every dimple, muscle, and hair; it's everyone: the young, the old, the overweight, and the ectomorphs. Even women who would much rather use their minds for something else find themselves considering the way their aging arms swing after waving or pondering what a life in the body of Heidi Klum might be like. Body obsession is like an obnoxious relative: No matter how annoying we think it is, it always gets an invitation to the party.

The statistics are staggering. Eighty percent of American women are dissatisfied with the way they look. Twenty-two percent of college women claim to "always" be on a diet. Americans spend more than $40 billion—approximately the gross domestic product of New Jersey or double what the United States spends annually fighting HIV—on diet-related products each year. Since 1997, there has been a 465 percent increase in the total number of cosmetic procedures performed—what was once reserved for the truly rich or the truly unfortunate is now the choice of millions.

But statistics tell only a small part of the story. Women are simultaneously taught to scrutinize themselves—are our eyebrows arched, our legs smooth, our jawlines taut, our elbows moisturized?—and to feign nonchalance. We are supposed to care whether our jeans make our butts look big, but we all know how obnoxious it is to actually ask if they do. We obsess about the most minute details of appearance, but to speak honestly about our bodies is a rare thing. Most women would rather discuss their sex lives in detail than admit their true weights.

Perhaps the magazines are partly to blame—one week Nicole Ritchie is a dangerously thin cautionary tale; the next week the same rag declares her a fashion icon—but it's not just the movie star–obsessed who feel schizophrenic about their bodies and looks. Smart, funny women—such as the ones in these pages, who are otherwise engaged in life and mostly doing just fine, thank you very much—feel it too. When Jennifer Carsen is diagnosed with a potentially fatal illness, the first thing she looks up is whether or not the treatment is going to make her gain weight. Kim Wong Keltner is kept up at night pondering her areolas. Roseanne Malfucci needs three alter egos and a therapist to make peace with her breasts.

Not that all of our concerns are cosmetic. Many women can still feel acutely the horror of puberty, when their bodies seemed suddenly not their own. After a diagnosis of scoliosis at age thirteen, Adrianne Bee imagines her spine as "some sort of clear, headless snake that dwelled along the ocean floor and had yet to be classified by scientists." Tara Bray Smith remembers long adolescent afternoons spent examining herself in the mirror until she was intimately familiar with even her most hidden parts.

And for those of us who survive adolescence unscathed (ha!), aging, pregnancy, and illness can change what was a nice, comfortable relationship into something fraught and adversarial. As she starts chemotherapy for breast cancer, Patricia Bunin realizes the only hairstyle in the world she most desires is her own doomed 'do. Molly Watson reluctantly enters the world of infertility, and confirms her suspicions that what once had been pretty fun would now be a chore. Monica Holloway wants to age with grace and dignity like Georgia O'Keeffe but something about L.A. keeps tempting her through the doors of the dermatologist's office.

◆ ◆ ◆

This book is not an antidote. It will not cure you of your obsessions or help patch up your relationship with your thighs. It doesn't urge you to practice acceptance or learn to love your love handles. We're not optimistic that this is the year we'll all get comfortable with the size of our breasts, and don't look to us if you want to be talked out of dieting. Beauty and the American woman's quest to tackle, tame, and control her is a far-too-convoluted social knot, one that a single funny book can scarcely begin to unravel.

What we're offering, aside from hilarity and wit and straight-up laugh-out-loud writing, is the solace that can be found in commonality. You thought you were the only one battling pimples and hairs and moles and cellulite and banana boobs? You thought you were the only person ashamed at the depth of your shallowness when it comes to your looks? Well, take comfort. What the essays in this book offer, if they offer nothing else, is proof, once and for all, that you are not alone with your vanity or your ugliness or your concerns. Not even close. We are in this together, warts and all.

The Pencil Test & Other Boob Failures

The Slow Boob Movement

KIM WONG KELTNER

*M*ere hours after I gave birth to a gigantic baby the doctor had dubbed "The Hulk," the lactation specialist said to me, "Oh, you have African American boobies."

This struck me as a weird thing to say to a sleep-deprived woman with an intravenous feeding tube, catheter, and no pants on. But that's what she said, right in front of the team of doctors, nurses, and relatives who had all come to fuss and take pictures of Baby Hulk and my zitty, sweaty, bleeding-from-the-crotch self.

The boobie nurse felt me up like a lusty, somewhat clinical sailor, and all I could do was lie there and thank my maker for the morphine drip, compliments of Brown & Toland. I am very modest, you see, and I am usually reluctant to whip off my high school–era minimizing Warner's within the peripheral vision of my best girlfriends or even my own mommy.

Was the nurse saying my breasts were big or small, or a different shape from what she expected? Having recently had my gut slit open via C-section, I was still reeling from the sight and sound of my amniotic fluid gushing onto the operating room floor. I was trying to think of a tactful way to apologize to my doctor for drenching his Bruno Maglis with my innards, and I simply was not ready to discuss the racial differences of boobies. Nonetheless, lying there, I wondered whether I needed to give a little speech about how I was proud to be a Chinese American. How my boobs were proud to be Chinese American, too.

She pulled my hospital gown open further so that even the janitor who'd come to empty the trash could see my African American boobies. Watching him carry out a bag that said, CAUTION: BIOHAZARD, I was jarred back to my breastfeeding lesson. The lactation specialist then ordered me to "squeeze it like a hamburger." Breasts aren't shaped like Whoppers or Quarter Pounders, but I'm a people pleaser, so I tried to do as I was told. I pinched and compressed my flesh without success. In my anguish, I reminded myself that I needed to feed my infant. Bilirubin buildup was threatening to turn my baby the color of a pumpkin, and she was already in the butternut squash spectrum.

So, I had African American boobies. Whatever the definition, there ain't nothing ghetto fabulous about cracked nipplage, latching on, or pumping and dumping. Breastfeeding is all fun and games until someone gets an eye poked out with a giant, swollen, thumb-length nipple.

Eventually, like many unsung mothers throughout the ages, I finally did figure out how to get the milk out of my engorged breasts and into the mouth of The Hulk.

But still. For the next three years, I wondered about this African American boobie comment. It stuck with me until just recently when I was reading an article in *Esquire*. A guy wrote into the magazine's sex column, saying he's an aficionado of large, dark nipples. He wanted to know how to tell if a woman has them without having to undress her first. As if it would be a total waste of time for him to slip roofies into a girl's drink only to later find that she had miniscule, carnation-pink tittie balls.

The advice columnist told him to try hooking up with African American women.

(Or for that matter, Kim Wong Keltner of San Francisco, California!)

The article went on to quote a plastic surgery specialist with twenty years' experience who said that requests and procedures for areola reductions had recently squirted through the roof.

Well, gee. I always knew that the area on the breast around the nipple had a separate name, but I never remembered it. And now here it was, staring me in the face: "areola." Basically this specialist was saying that gals couldn't ditch their bigger-than-desirable areolas fast enough. Someone somewhere had decided that this was not the "in" kind of boobie to have.

How sad it was to read that the newest fashion in plastic surgery was now making my natural shape extinct. The possibility of this dearth of big areolas and nipples due to elective plastic surgery bugged me. First, the rise of the Itty Bitty Tittie Committee, and now this? I was so disturbed, in fact, I turned to the one person women find comfort in when they feel helpless.

Martha Stewart. How many nights had I lain awake in the past, my large areolas resting comfortably on my chest, reading Martha's magazine articles about the rapid disappearance of the earth's many varietals of heirloom tomatoes, peaches, and good-eatin' chickens? If the emergence of the Slow Food Movement could ensure the longevity of the adorable and quirky Mr. Stripey Tomato, I wondered if, likewise, a grassroots, Slow Boob Movement could gain momentum in this country. Instead of the homogeneity of standard B-cup boobies, all with small, polite nipples, didn't the world deserve variety?

I could just picture it. If the current plastic surgery trends continued, eventually the large, pendulous breast would have to swing the other way. Folks would become weary of perfect little cupcake knobs. Where were the flapjacks, apple fritters, the beignets of boobiedom? People would soon grow bored with pert blandness with nary a hair or inverted nipple to make life interesting.

There would be a quiet uproar. Soon, the B-cup boobie would rank in desirability along with those gray-pink sandwich tomatoes piled high at Albertson's. Meanwhile, slowly but surely, connoisseurs of boobage would catch on to the charms of the lopsided sisterhood, we with our stretch marks and bulging womanliness flowing forth from the tops of our tired sports bras. There could be Take Back the Boob protest marches.

You know how stores trot out the weird pumpkins around Halloween and everyone gets excited? With the Slow Boob Movement increasing in popularity, the savvy public might pause to surreptitiously ogle my boobs at the farmers market, at first merely fascinated by my unique form but then gripped by my breasts' artisinal goodness, doubly valuable because they've been locally cultivated for more than thirty-seven years.

Perhaps I'd start my own publication, *Breasticles Today,* and our maiden issue would spotlight natural areolas. Our readership would realize that everything old is new. Soon the whole world would be clamoring for glimpses of old-school boobies.

If you have ever been unfortunate enough to sit through the entirety of Steven Spielberg's movie *A.I.,* you may recall that, after all human beings have been extinguished from the planet, aliens revive Haley Joel Osment's bloated, robot corpse from the bottom of the ocean, because he is the only half-decayed remnant of a creature who has any memory of what real humans were like. Perhaps if I can resist society's powerful mob yell urging me to reconstruct my breasts to better resemble Jennifer Jason Leigh's in *Fast Times at Ridgemont High,* then I, too, can be revived millennia from now by benevolent aliens seeking a glimpse of African American Boobies. Or maybe the aliens will just choose to reanimate an African American woman instead of me, having used their outer space powers to ascertain that my boobie anomaly does not warrant bringing me back to life, because, based on their records, all indications point to the very real possibility that in my heyday I was a persnickety little twat.

Late at night I think of these things. I think of aliens, heirloom veggies of yesteryear, Jennifer Jason Leigh's nipples while she humps Mike Damone in the pool house, and Haley Joel Osment as a bloated, human cyborg at the bottom of the ocean.

And I sometimes think back to that nurse who said I have African American boobies. As she watched over me like a stern coach, jets of milk finally did spurt forth from my sore little crunchberries. The engorged milk ducts made my breasts feel as if there were marbles under my skin. Up to that point, the words *marble bag* brought to mind men's tighty-whitey underwear, but oh how accurately did they describe my milk-bulging breasts. Back at the hospital, I worried about my stretched-out skin, and, in my morphine haze, I thought a lot about the villain in *Silence of the Lambs* and how he starved the fat girl so he could make a size 14 dress out of human skin. Such were my delirious musings during the early days of motherhood.

My daughter is three years old now. Last night, she reached across my chest and gave me a squeeze.

"I like your boobies, Mommy," she said, patting them. And at that moment my tittilicious breasts were all the bling I needed.

My Life As a Mammal

LAURA McNEAL

*W*hen I informed my best friend almost nine years ago that I was expecting a male child, she said, after a distinct pause, "I can't even *imagine* you with boys."

I couldn't imagine it either, in spite of the fact that I'd been trying to get pregnant for four years and had just conceived with the help of a fertility stimulant. I knew that boys could be and frequently were the outcome of pregnancy. I was just assuming that, given my personality, a boy wouldn't be the outcome in my case.

It's not just that I am ignorant of baseball, basketball, football, and the subtleties of world wrestling. It's not that my main hobbies are baking, knitting, reading, and watercolor painting. I do not camp. I do not ski. I do not surf. But for hundreds of years, women did none of these things and managed to raise boys.

So I think it was something else that my friend was contemplating during that distinct pause. I think we both knew the odds. Certain children are going to run screaming through the house with imitation guns, and certain children are going to sit and move the Fisher-Price people in and out of the toy barn, and we all know which gender is most likely to do which.

I am the sort of person who would do well with a child who wanted to move the Fisher-Price people in and out of the toy barn.

Still, month after month, the doctor studied the quivering black and white lines on the ultrasound and said the baby looked like a boy to him. I reminded myself that Charles Dickens, Thomas Hardy, my father, and my husband had once been boys. Boys could be pensive, bookish, and sweet, like Christopher Robin. As a child, my husband had collected baseball cards and listened to entire Yankee games on his radio. At three, my father had sat beside his mother's stove and pretended the rectangular bits of coal were train cars. Of course, when he got a little older, my father moved on to blowing up mailboxes and shooting hawks, rats, lizards, jack-rabbits, beer bottles, tin cans, and cottontail bunnies.

◆ ◆ ◆

I decided to concentrate instead on the act of giving birth. Giving birth was what women talked about the way veterans talked about war. Giving birth was so painful that it was routine to numb the entire lower half of the body or to cut open the mother as if she were a wolf in a fairytale. Giving birth was what I began to prepare for: how to do it without numbing or cutting.

I tried to assure myself that I was a mammal, and a mammal does two things. It gives birth to live young, and it nurses them. These, along with warm blood, are the two seminal qualities of mammalhood. There is nothing else: not "mammals have two legs" or "mammals live on land" or "mammals like to sit quietly and color." You'll notice, in fact, that men don't even qualify as mammals by this definition. It's the women who certify the species for mammal status, and they are thus equipped, like whales and wild coyotes, to do these things without technical assistance.

This was the working principle of my doula. A doula is a birth assistant, a woman who plays the historical role of the mothers, aunts, and elderly females in the cave who would, I gathered from my reading, help the birthing woman push the baby out while men were out clubbing edible mammals. I was still planning to go to the hospital, just in case, but I knew the doctor wouldn't be there until the last minute and that the nurses would be busy with all the other birthing females. I also knew that if my husband said, during the sixteenth hour of labor, "You're doing fine! Keep pushing!" I would look at him the way I looked at him when he leaned over my shoulder while I was preparing Julia Child's chocolate mousse and said, "Can't you just use egg whites in that?" I would look at him with the knowledge that he had never done what I was doing, and furthermore, he wasn't a certified mammal. How would he know?

My doula, on the other hand, had given birth to live young. She had helped other women push out live young, and if she said I was doing fine, quite possibly I would believe her.

What the doula said to me in the last month of pregnancy was this: You are just like a whale or a wild coyote. You can, if necessary, give birth all by yourself. If you go into labor on a dirt road somewhere, and you don't have a phone or a human being to help you, you can give birth *all by yourself.*

Although I sincerely hoped this wouldn't happen, I found it extremely comforting. I was built to give birth! It was my destiny! I could do it on a dirt road!

Obviously, it's not 100 percent true. I've read enough history to know women used to die giving birth to live young. Frequently. But I had also read *The Good Earth* in ninth grade, and the only thing I remembered about it was that the main character works in the fields for a while, goes in the house, gives birth, and goes right back into the fields, as if all she'd done was take a coffee break.

When the contractions began on April 28, 1998, I started out like a good Chinese peasant woman. I worked all day at my desk. I wrote most of a story about the revival of the Lindy Hop. Then the doula came over, and we walked around in a field. By 9:00 PM the contractions hurt enough to make me say the word *hospital,* so my husband and the doula and I climbed into the car and drove to the hospital so that I could be a coyote/whale/Chinese peasant in a bed, wearing a gown.

For the next seven hours, the doula sat beside me and said, "You're doing fine." She did some acupressure on me, which meant I let her press on parts of my hand so that we would both believe we were on top of the situation. The nurse came now and then to measure and count. At 3:30 AM, the doctor appeared, and at 4:00 AM, I pushed like a coyote, or perhaps a whale. For a moment, it seemed that I was the coyote, and Sam was the whale. But then he emerged. Our baby was alive, human, healthy, and fine. We admired him tearfully for one, maybe two, triumphant minutes, and then it was time for Sam to do what nurses call "latching on."

I had just pushed live young through a narrow and sensitive orifice without painkillers or screams. I was one hell of a mammal, so I was not afraid of the Second Mammalian Imperative. My breasts would fulfill their destiny. The nurse helped me arrange myself for what I preferred to call "suckling," the gentle process of milk passing from breast to mouth that I had observed in Old Master paintings. She handed me my tiny naked young. He opened his mouth, and then he closed it.

This is the moment I began to question Nature and my place within it. In the first place, a "latch" is a piece of metal or plastic that clamps down hard on an inanimate object, such as a window or a gate. In the second place, if you got your nipple caught in the latch of a window or a gate, you would scream and free yourself. When Sam latched on for the first time, it was all I could do to keep myself from screaming and freeing myself. I was glad when the nurse said we could stop and test his vitals.

• • •

All the next day, in a kind of sleep-deprived ecstasy that was quickly turning into primal fear, I admired Sam in his capsule and tried, with the help of various nurses, to become a food source. I had been warned by Lamaze classes and pregnancy books that the worst thing I could possibly do in the hospital would be to let my baby sleep outside my room with the nurses. If I did, they would feed him with bottles. The baby, spoiled and greedy, wouldn't bother to learn the more technically demanding art of breast drinking and he'd be addicted to formula, easy living, and—it was almost guaranteed—heroin later on.

But the nurses studied my breasts with guarded skepticism. They would stand to the side and show me how to pinch my nipple and thrust it into Sam's mouth. "Does it hurt?" they would ask.

"Yes, it does," I would say.

"Then he's not latched on properly." They would have me stick my finger into Sam's mouth, thereby breaking suction, and try again.

"Does it hurt?"

"Yes."

"Can you hear him swallowing?"

I listened. I could not.

"Is your milk letting down?"

How would I know? Nothing had ever happened inside my breasts before. For thirty years, they had just sat there.

"I don't know," I said.

"Well, your milk may not have come in yet."

This was an alarming detail. For the last forty weeks I had been preparing for this baby—signing up with a diaper service, buying a crib, prewashing his layette in gentle laundry soap, ordering birth announcements—and what I should have done *first* was call the breast milkman and make sure I had plenty in there when the baby arrived. What kind of survival plan was this that the mammal's milk would arrive several days *after* the live young?

My doula reassured me by telephone that during the first hours or days after birth, the baby was drinking colostrum, a sort of maternal vitamin syrup. Colostrum was so concentrated that the baby couldn't really chugalug it, so probably things were going just fine. We'd watch Sam's diaper and see. We'd watch for wetness and we'd watch for poo.

The situation made me consider my breasts with the eye of a scientist—all cold, hard evidence. They were not large. They were not medium. They were undeniably, disturbingly small. As a relative once cheerfully put it, I was built for speed. This might mean, I suddenly realized, that I was *not* built for milking. I reminded myself that the pregnancy books and my childbearing friends had specifically and authoritatively said that the size of one's breasts has absolutely nothing to do with how much milk they contain. They all said, in various ways, that it is not like comparing a gallon jug to a one-cup carton.

Still, as I lay in my hospital bed next to Samuel, waiting for him to produce solid proof that my hooters worked, I recalled an alarming conversation with my doula. When I was eight months pregnant, she had casually asked if my breasts had grown. "Have you gone up a cup size or two?" she asked.

A cup size or two? No. Perhaps a demitasse.

"Sort of," I said. Having large bosoms had always been a secret dream of mine, and pregnancy was a guaranteed boob inflater. I couldn't stand to admit that I was so flat chested that not even pregnancy worked.

"I think so," I said. "Yes."

Recalling this possibly important lie, I tried not to worry too much. Sam slept in his capsule, his tiny head soft and round in the knit cap, his body tightly bound in flannel, the incarnation of sweetness and need.

It was at this point that I turned on the wall-mounted TV and watched a spritely educational show about the animal kingdom. The camera zoomed in on a koala bear that had just given birth. "She simply isn't making enough milk!" the zookeeper said, and then the zookeeper described how they were going to give the koala's baby to a different mother. The next image showed the hapless koala, her nipples exposed to the whole world, her baby gone.

I felt a slow, panicked recognition. *Le koala bear, c'est moi!* I needed to avoid zookeepers at all costs. In any case, Samuel was a very quiet little package. Why not just go home? Everything would be absolutely, completely fine.

◆ ◆ ◆

I have a notebook on my shelf that contains phone numbers and interview notes. I was writing a weekly column when Sam was born and the notes go right from questions about turtle gardens and the Lindy Hop to a fanatically detailed account of my time with Samuel from Thursday, May 7, to Wednesday, May 27.

Sam cried when he wasn't nursing, and he nursed nearly all the time. I nursed him until my nipple felt, with each compression of his mouth, as if it were being pierced by a sewing machine needle. I stared out the second-story window of our house at the pink climbing roses. The spring was wet and cloudy that year and the roses trembled in the wind. A pair of bluebirds had nested in a birdhouse I could see from the sofa where I sat hour after hour, nursing, and I watched the father bluebird carry insects to the chicks and then come out again with their droppings in his mouth. *Well, at least I don't have to do that!* I thought.

I took Sam to the pediatrician for his one-week checkup and he was found to be losing, not gaining, weight.

"The thing is," he said, "not all women can nurse. Babies can be fed in other ways. You're probably going to have to supplement."

Le koala bear, c'est moi! I held tightly to Samuel and considered the word "supplement." The doctor meant formula, and it's hard to convey the distaste with which natural-birth people view formula. I'd spent nine months learning that formula is the junk food of the infant world and the loathsome tool of corporate greed, sold to Third World women who have no choice but to mix it with filthy water. Like cigarette packages, cans of Similac contain a small government message. Only this one reads: BREAST MILK IS RECOMMENDED.

I had also read about the legions of sadly misinformed women who give up on nursing because of perfectly fixable problems, such as the failure to latch on properly. Maybe this was a perfectly fixable problem.

So like any sane, flat-chested koala bear, I asked the doctor if he knew a lactation consultant in town, and he sent me to see Lottie.

Lottie was also a children's dentist, and she did breastfeeding consultations in the back room of a building that smelled like mint and high-speed drills. She had a motherly air and, underneath her dentist's smock, breasts much larger than mine. (I suppose only Hugh Hefner is more focused on this part of the anatomy than I now was.)

Once Lottie had me seated in the lactation room, she smiled, admired Sam, and asked me how many times a day Sam soiled his diapers. I said that sometimes not even once a day. Again, I was quizzed: Did I feel my milk let down? Did Sam seem to be swallowing? Did I hear liquid going down his throat?

He did not. I did not.

Lottie hesitated. She said she had become a lactation consultant because breastfeeding was wonderful for her and because she had been surprised to learn, after her own success, that some women had trouble with it. She wanted to help those women. But in my case, she said reluctantly, the doctor was right. "You have to supplement," she said.

It was like a priest telling a supplicant she was going to have to fornicate with the devil. I don't remember everything in the right order after that because of excessive, non–Chinese peasant-style weeping, but I know that I rented a breast pump that looked disturbingly like a car battery. Lottie told me to nurse Samuel and then to give him an ounce or two of formula from a tiny medicine dropper (not from a bottle, because he might learn to prefer the silicone nipple to my own), and then pump my breasts to stimulate further milk production. If he didn't wake up on his own every two hours at night, I would need to strip him, tickle his feet, apply a wet washcloth to his head, and rouse him because he needed to keep eating. He needed twelve feedings a day.

I put the breast pump in my car and drove Samuel to the obstetrician's office. There I was to be checked in the lower region, the region where all had gone well. I held in my arms tiny Samuel, who weighed less than six pounds. There in the waiting room was a woman I knew who had also given birth recently. As Hugh Hefner would have noticed, her breasts were large. Her baby was immense. Thank heavens there was not a zookeeper present, because the answer would have been clear. I waited my turn, clutched my baby, and then took him home to jump-start my ta-tas.

Lottie had told me to keep a log of Sam's feedings and the contents of his diapers, so I wrote down, to the minute, how long he nursed on each breast, how much formula he subsequently drank, and for how long afterward I used the breast pump. Then I wrote down how much milk was in the vial after I pumped. On one giddy occasion, I wrote "lots of swallowing and some actual slurping." The log goes on for many pages, all of them filled with tiny black notations such as Van Gogh probably made right before he picked up the ear knife.

I was not a good dairy cow. I was too self-conscious, for one thing. If you have ever removed your bra, attached a suction cup, and flipped the "on" switch, you know what I mean. Dignified, it was not. It was also not encouraging. Milk didn't flow, pour, or spray from me as the air contracted inside the suction cup. It dripped like rain from an eave after the rain has stopped falling.

A few days later, when Sam still wasn't producing the desired number of soiled diapers or gaining the desired weight, I rented an electric baby scale from Lottie so that I could measure the ounces Sam imbibed naturally. It worked like this: Before I nursed Samuel, I weighed him, and after I nursed him, I weighed him again. Sometimes he weighed two ounces more after nursing. Two ounces is half of a newborn's baby bottle, half of what bottle makers call a "serving."

The bluebirds flew into the birdhouse with crushed crickets in their beaks and flew back out with crap. While they were showing off, Lottie called to tell me that she had found a similar case in a textbook. I had "insufficient mammary tissue."

I'd never heard of this, of course. Not as a biological diagnosis. That self-assessment had come to me many times in the dressing rooms of lingerie stores and swimsuit departments, but not while I was reading breastfeeding tracts.

Perhaps that was why I had needed fertility pills even to conceive a child. All by myself, without the makers of Similac, I was incapable of rearing live young. I was a failed mammal.

I held Sam in my arms and he latched on. It didn't hurt anymore, perhaps because of the lanolin. A chemist somewhere, or maybe a desperate shepherd, had discovered that pure lanolin—the oil found in wool—would heal a cracked nipple without harming the baby. I considered giving up the nursing as I nursed. Unfortunately, Sam was happy in only two situations: while nursing or while in constant motion, as I carried him through streets, stores, fields, and parks. He didn't like pacifiers or bottles or anything except the authentic article, and in this we were the same. When he nursed, I felt like a real mother, like the incarnation of the most sacred idea we have.

For the next three months of Sam's life, I bought formula and mixed it and heated it and offered it to him after the nursing sessions. Often, he cried when I tried to give him the bottle, perhaps because he was full, perhaps because he was sleepy. Once, I was so tired and frustrated, so afraid that he was still going to starve, that I threw the rejected bottle across the room. Bottles are made of plastic now, so not much happened. To give my husband his due, he did the bottle feedings whenever he could.

At four months, Sam refused the bottle so many feedings in a row that I decided to risk it. I decided to go breasts-only. It was the trial of the mammary tissue.

I watched him day by day, hour by hour. He still wet his diapers about the same. He still fretted about the same, but not more. At Sam's checkup a nurse told me that it was okay that he soiled his diapers only once or twice a week (instead of ten times per day). "That's within the range of normal," she said. "The outer range, but still."

I wondered where she had been in the early weeks, when it seemed that if my baby didn't poop enough, he was going to die. Anyway, we went bottle-free. I felt as if I had overcome an addiction. We were on the wagon, by God, and we were doing it the natural way.

Many people are probably wondering, as my own mother did, why I felt so strongly about this. Probably it was egotism: the unwillingness to believe that some part of myself was insufficient. It was also an ingrained aversion to plastic. A man named Eliud came once a week in a Tidy Didy Babyland Diaper Service truck and picked up a sack of soiled diapers and dropped off a stack of snowy-white clean ones, 100 percent cotton. I felt better about those diapers, too, the way they went away filthy and came back clean, as if everything that was wrong could be made right again.

• • •

When I was expecting Sam, I had believed everything I was told about how much newborns slept and how easy it was to feed them. I did not believe this anymore. My husband and I had a name for babies who were Not Like Sam. Usually they were female, but sometimes they were male. They were Sitcom Babies, named after the ones who are held briefly by television characters and then set down in playpens so that the characters can do other things. These babies do not cry when attention is turned away from them.

Sam prompted two diametrically opposed responses from people. If I was out shopping for groceries or walking along the beach with Sam strapped to my chest, his face forward and his legs kicking manically against my hips, he invariably smiled so hugely at the people we met that they said, "What a happy baby!"

If I was in a closed-in space, such as my house or the doctor's office, Sam cried, and people—including childcare workers, nurses, and parents of five or more children—would say, "What's wrong with him?"

I didn't know.

Other mothers seemed to live in harmony with their babies. Their babies slept, ate, or observed the world on their mother's schedules, graceful appendages who needed a lot of time and care but who, when given this time and care, enjoyed their existence.

Sam did not enjoy his existence. If I nursed him at exactly the same times, if I fed him exactly the same ultrasmooth pureed foods, if I carried him or played with him nearly all the time, if I moved from place to place and didn't stop to peel potatoes or study the back of a box of cereal, he didn't cry much. I believed that I had made him this way. Nature or nurture, it was my fault. There was the lack of mammary tissue, which had made him work so hard in the beginning. Furthermore, I was stubborn, controlling, melancholy, and overly analytical. Of course I had produced a baby who could not enjoy a Pat Mat.

Still, we went on, as people do. We walked and we nursed and we tried to arrange our day so that more people said, "What a happy baby!" than said, "What's wrong with him?"

I was still nursing Sam when he turned thirteen months old and I became pregnant. This time, it had been simple biology: no fertility pills, no anxious tests. As before, the doctor did an ultrasound. As before, he saw the unmistakable shape of a little boy.

I was thrilled and I was very, very afraid. I thought of that Sylvia Plath poem in which she says she's a riddle in nine syllables, that she's boarded the train you can't get off.

Plath, of course, lost her mind.

· · ·

While I was trying to be more thrilled than afraid, we hit another snag with Sam. Always too small to be above the tenth percentile on the charts, always smaller than you would expect the child of a five-foot ten-inch woman and a six-foot one-inch man to be, he was still adorably, alarmingly petite. He still ate too little, even though he was now eating solid foods. The doctor called it "failure to thrive," a diagnosis more common for listless babies and toddlers.

The doctor, who had five grown children, two of them boys, watched Sam tear around the examining room, opening every cupboard, tugging at me and the rolling chair and the toys, and he shook his head. "It's strange," he said. "He could take this place apart."

But everything else was worrisome. Why didn't he grow more? The doctor ordered tests.

First we eliminated cystic fibrosis. Then we did an x-ray of his hand to see if he had something called primordial dwarfism.

Fortunately, he was not a primordial dwarf. He was just little, and he was picky.

I grew rounder, and we waited for the baby, whom we called Hank. Sam began to say words. When people saw us out together, they invariably said, "You're going to have your hands full."

As the due date approached, the doctor told me, somewhat strongly, that I should really go ahead and wean Sam before the baby was born. I was nursing Sam only at bedtime and nap time, but I was so worried that Hank would have Sam's feeding troubles that I was essentially calling the breast milkman. We were not going to let my mammaries think they could be empty when the baby showed up.

Nervously, a month before the due date, I weaned Sam.

◆ ◆ ◆

Hank was born on St. Patrick's Day, the holiday of green beer. It is also, for me, a privately religious holiday. It is the day of the Miracle of the Breastmilk, the day when I ceased to be a defective mammal, the day the only person in the world who could have set Sam and me free arrived.

It was like that dream we all have of rewinding the tape and doing it over. I was in the same hospital room in the same season of the year. I was wearing a gown, and I had a newborn baby boy. But this time I knew what I was doing, what to listen for, and how to proceed. Milk was needed, and milk was there. When people weighed Baby Hank, they did not look concerned and afraid. They looked nonchalant. He wet. He soiled. He nursed. He slept. We went home to watch the nesting bluebirds.

For the first two months, he showed signs of the kind of fussing that had once driven me to wish, while driving a speeding car on Highway 76, that I could drive straight into a pylon and hear no more crying, ever again. But either because I stopped eating ice cream, cheese, milk, and yogurt, or because of some mysterious process that will never be known, Hank stopped fussing and became content.

This was the saving of us all. I no longer believed that I was the cause of everything my children did or felt. Sam was a boy. Hank was a boy. We had made them from the same genetic material, I had nursed them both, and yet they were not alike. If we had produced a girl, we would have thought that was the difference—that girls really were easier than boys. Had we produced only Hank, we would have consciously or unconsciously taken credit for his sunny, placid self. But I knew that I had not made Hank that way.

So perhaps I had not made Sam so passionate, either, so demanding, so pensive, so bookish and sweet, so completely unwilling, at the age of three, to move the Fisher-Price people in and out of the barn. Although the nurturing could certainly be laid at my feet, his nature could not. His nature simply is. That he lived, and remained mine, is also a miracle. I think of that sometimes when I see him running through the house with an imitation gun, screaming, or hurling a baseball, or grinning at strangers, wearing boots, his legs as thin as Christopher Robin's. We escaped the Darwinian fate of the unfit and walk the earth as grateful mammals, no longer failing to thrive.

Getting from A to B

SARAH HART

*M*y breasts are lost. The fact that they've vanished into cyberspace somewhere between London and Cape Town, as opposed to disappearing in a physical sense, doesn't make the experience any less distressing. Where are those images? I guess I shouldn't worry, really. Anyone surfing into my headless full-frontal and side-angle upper torso is likely to take pity on my sad, barely A cup, sagging, stretch-marked frontage. Apart, perhaps, from a limited fetish interest, I don't suppose they're of any real value to the wider Internet porn market.

The photos were taken by my sister, and downloaded by her embarrassed, trying-not-to-look husband, for me to send to Dr. D, a South African surgeon who, if the images had arrived, was meant to let me know whether my breasts were good enough candidates for enlargement. Providing you can cope with being squeezed postoperatively into economy class and avoid the elbows of fellow passengers, flying overseas for plastic surgery can cost around half the price.

But Internet failures dashed my international hopes for surgery.

My poor breasts haven't had an easy life. At thirteen, I had a benign lump the size of a golf ball removed from the right, followed a year later by an even larger one in the left. I was lucky to get away with a biopsy when the third appeared. Overzealous surgeons are the darker side of private healthcare. I've been told that a small biopsy for all three would have done the trick. A long scar on each breast before my sixteenth birthday hasn't been easy to come to terms with.

Then came my babies. For almost a year, I breastfed first my daughter and then my son. What a joy it is experiencing a newborn babe's gulps, eyes rolled back, blissed-out before falling off the nipple like a satiated tick, blue-tinged milk trickling down a dimpled chin. All power to nursing mothers, the entrepreneurs of the world's most successful milk bars—but I digress.

For fifteen years, I've toyed with the idea of breast enhancement surgery. By the age of twenty-five, although put to good use, my breasts were rather the worse for wear. Convex on one side through the loss of tissue during surgery, they had the appearance of soft crepe paper and failed the pencil test for droopiness with ease. And I felt sad looking at them. I confessed this to my doctor when I was twenty-six, trying to explain my sense of loss and longing.

His response upon examination: "Well, they're not the worst I've seen." Thanks a bunch.

Now don't get me wrong. Through the years I've worked hard at getting to know, accept, and love my breasts. As with my womb, I've celebrated their life-giving abundance at Goddess in You workshops and had them out for all to inspect during an intensive women's sexuality course. I can tell you that comparison therapy doesn't work, even with gentle appreciations and encouragement from well-meaning, shapely coattendees. I've sunbathed topless on a number of beaches, from Greek islands to Brighton, where even the pebbles on the shore were bigger than my A cup. One hot summer's afternoon after an invitation from the mother of my son's school friend, I even tried to get comfortable walking around naked at the poolside of a local nudist club. I declined the invitation to stay for the adults' pajama party later that evening— by then I was divorced but certainly not that desperate.

Exposure doesn't make me feel better, but neither does covering up. Shopping for a bra is a nightmare. Soft, lacy styles pucker limply across a steep, ski-slope chest. Without volume behind them, molded T-shirt styles run the risk of denting. And don't even think about chicken fillets, or what Americans call silicone inserts—they make empty breasts wrinkle up, giving them the appearance of jam at the correct consistency for setting. Too limp to go braless and tired of struggling to find one that fits—I long for capacity. Not loads; voluptuousness isn't for me. Just one size up from barely an A to a nice B. So why haven't I taken the plunge to create the cleavage I desire before now? Quite simply, I haven't had the money.

But now something has happened. Suddenly, although it's taken me years to get here, I am forty years old, with financial means, and without a man. Has there ever been a more powerful force than a woman in these circumstances? No obstacles, no one to put me off. Here's my chance, while I'm still young enough. Just do it. But now that I can, I find that maybe I can't. Fear, desire, and the moral high ground confuse me.

My internal dialogue goes something like this:

Sulky, whining inner child: *But why can't I have them? Everyone else has got them; I want them too.*

Firm but friendly inner feminist: *It's the continual barrage of airbrushed, breast-enhanced media archetypes that's caused you to be dissatisfied with your body. You've bought into the myth of "the bigger the better." I really think you should go back into therapy to address this.*

Angry inner child: *More therapy! We've had years of going through that hell. You're not taking me back there.*

Inner feminist, getting more indignant: *Can't you see that you're objectifying yourself? Having a boob job is just a way of trying to adapt to a male-dominated society that judges you by your body parts rather than as a person. You'd be letting yourself and your feminist sisters down if you went ahead with this grotesque surgical procedure.*

Some days, the inner child says, *Gulp, you're right.* On others, it's, *Get lost. I want them and I'll have them!*

I take this internal conflict to friends, my trusted inner circle. On the whole I am surprised at the initial response. They smile and ponder a while. They are wistful. I see their gazes slip away from my hiked-up top and the breasts in question as they drift into a fantasy of how silicone would change their own lives.

I struggle to call them back, "So, what do you think? Should I do it?"

And then it comes, a confounding list of concerns: There are health risks ("Think of the dangers of leaking implants."), long-term regrets ("Imagine having to cover up Pamela Anderson's chest when you go to your granddaughter's wedding."), and thin end-of-the-wedge fears ("Once you change a part of your body, you might become obsessed with altering the rest.") And, finally, from my closest ally, comes acceptance: "I'd do it if I were you."

"What do you mean—'if I were you'," I retort, louder and more defensively than I intend. "Are they really that bad?"

She squirms in her seat, rolling words over in her mind, hoping that tact won't fail her. "No, they're not . . . but I can see what you mean—they *have* been through the mill."

What am I doing? My face flushes. I'm ashamed about giving a good friend such a hard time, making her walk on eggshells in a no-win situation. Oh, God, I'm confused and more neurotic than I think.

It is when I find myself dwelling on the question "What will I do if people actually notice that my breasts are bigger?" that I start to wonder whether therapy is what I need after all. Maybe I should spend the money getting to the root of my yearning, examine yet again my anger toward my father, my failed marriage, my low self-esteem.

I arrange to speak to a friend who has gone the other way. She is a dear, slim, slip of a thing of four feet ten inches, who endured twenty years of pendulous double Ds until going under the knife for fabulous resculpture to a neat 30C. I confess my fear that acquaintances and colleagues will do a double take. I'm amazed when she says that only one person remarked that she looked different, asking whether she'd lost some weight. My friend believes that people see the whole of you, not the bits you've changed, and I grab on to her body-transformation experience and her views and kick the terror of objectification away.

I do the maths. The cost of two years in therapy equals a breast enlargement by a reputable London plastic surgeon. Countless fifty-minute hours—tearing away denial, beating a cushion, pouring my heart out *do not* equal a new lease on life with pert B cups.

To hell with cutting costs and flying cattle class to South Africa. I don't attempt resending the photos to Dr. D and instead make an appointment to see a Harley Street surgeon.

Dr. G is welcoming, well dressed, and as camp as a row of tents. I like him immediately. He looks at me from all angles and murmurs sympathetically as he takes photos of my front, my left, and right. I learn that I have perfect, well-positioned nipples. What a boost. He lifts my sagginess between his manicured thumb and forefinger and says that my breasts are prime candidates for an augmentation. Dr. G is enthusiastic, and it's catching.

"Because you have a lot of loose skin, the implant will occupy the space well, not like those women who look as if they have pumpkins stuck on to their chests."

It is two weeks before Halloween, and I can't help wondering whether his expression would be different during summer melon season. I tell Dr. G that I don't want to be huge; my aim is to fill a B cup. He nods and says that the slack will need to be filled; it won't look right otherwise, and this will probably mean a large B.

"The result for you will be a better-proportioned look," Dr. G continues. "You have a small waist and wide hips. You'll end up with old-fashioned curves, a traditional figure that's not so common these days."

Having grown up in Africa, I close down an image of what is considered a fine traditional figure in Botswana and let visions of a less-inflated Marilyn Monroe float through my mind.

I try to remain rational, practical, and serious. I ask about implant contracture (Dr. G: "A fairly rare possibility."), loss of nipple sensation ("A very rare possibility."), and whether I will be able to sleep on my stomach ever again ("A possibility, but probably not.").

I go home to reflect. I think of nothing else. I summon the courage to have a discussion with the three remaining members of my family who don't know about the decision I'm trying to make.

The first is the younger of my two sisters. She is unmarried and works at a feminist library. In 1999 she took part in the anti–Miss World competition protest at the London Olympia. Chanting "Miss World, we're not cattle. We'll shut you down just like Seattle," she threw eggs and flour over the flashy suits of the businessmen running the contest as they rolled up to the show in their limousines.

She is shocked that I should consider such a drastic measure and is dead set against it. "There's no need to do this to yourself. If you're unhappy, try some exercise, lift some weights. That will build your pecs," she says. Apart from walking to the underground to catch a tube, my sister is a sedentary type, and I'm amazed that she's paid any attention to the benefits of bodybuilding. Perhaps I don't know her as well as I think. She's right to some extent, though. In an attempt to lift my droop, my upper-body gym workouts brought me surprised but admiring compliments from a male radiographer as he ran his probe over my pectorals during a breast ultrasound some years ago.

My sister's attitude softens somewhat as I explain how I feel. She understands but draws the line at radical surgery. I envy her clarity of conviction. Her beliefs, lifestyle, and her comely bosom mean that she'll never have to make the choice that lies before me. I also envy the amount of chocolate she can eat without gaining an ounce.

The other person I tell is my seventeen-year-old son. He is the most significant man in my life, and having come through some hard times among happy days, we have learned to communicate well and have a deep respect for each other.

Trying to maintain as much sensitivity as possible for his feelings without losing sight of my own, I explain my reasons. I choose my words carefully, selecting medical terms and avoiding language that is in any way sexual. "Augmentation . . . surgical procedure . . . incision . . . silicone," I say in a sensible tone. I am aware of sounding like a healthcare brochure. As I speak, a look of horror crosses his face. Abashed, I feel my status of "mother" slipping as I voice my pseudoclinical justification.

He looks at me with skepticism and interrupts, "Men don't like fake breasts." I restrain myself from retaliating and asking him why each of the *FHM* "honeyz" he has on his wall appears to have "the pumpkin look" that Dr. G ridiculed. With a stab of pain I realize that we cannot reach each other on this one, and the fear and panic in his eyes almost breaks my heart.

Oh, boy, I feel bad. I can read the subtext beneath his anger. He's embarrassed, and I can't blame him. At seventeen, he doesn't want to think about his mother enhancing her chest. I understand that his hormones act as a radar detector, and I imagine that he processes a range and bearing on breasts everywhere he goes. To have a discussion with me about implants is just too much. And I know he is thinking about the humiliation to be endured if his friends notice that his mother's had a boob job. His eyebrows bunch into a scowl, and his mouth is a thin line of parental disapproval, the preserve of teenagers across the Western world.

After these two responses, I cannot face a conversation with my father.

I'm deflated. The euphoria I experienced in Dr. G's office has disappeared. Pulled hither and thither by the opinions of others, I feel mixed up, guilty, and stuck. Immobilized, I do nothing. Autumn drifts into winter and my breasts hide under sweaters and thick coats. But around Christmastime I start once again to hear a familiar inner whispering. It starts as a little sigh, released while I was trying to bolster a boned, black bustier to wear at a seasonal party. No amount of prodding or padding gives the lift needed to bring the little top to life.

My longing grows stronger within me. Pushing treats into Christmas stockings makes me muse on how it would feel to fill a lacy bra. I daydream about silk basques while basting the turkey. Unfed by lack of discussion and opinions of others, my anxiety shrinks. By Boxing Day I'm ready to surrender. I can no longer fight against what I know I have wanted for years. On the first working day of the New Year, I phone Dr. G's secretary.

• • •

"Sarah, it's all over." I come around from the anaesthetic to the lighthearted chatter of medics that lets you know that you've survived surgery and you're going to be okay. I wake again to the waft of Dr. G, smiling, telling me that it went well and prescribing another dose of morphine when I groan in pain. Four hours later, over the shelf of my chest bound by a mass of bandage, I eat a cheese sandwich with a cup of tea. When I stand up to go to the bathroom, I can hardly see my feet for the layers of padded dressing, designed to support and protect a pair of incubating breasts.

I live, cushioned and top-heavy, for nearly two weeks in a strange twilight zone of "work in progress." Inside my casement I feel twinges and occasional shooting pain. I learn to sleep on my back.

Finally, it's D-Day. Walking down Oxford Street on the way to have my breasts liberated, I'm moved to buy Dr. G a large bunch of red and purple tulips. I'm so excited, I can't wait to see the result that I have desired for so long. Dr. G is thrilled with the flowers and ushers me into the surgery. I lie down on the bed and with great care, his nurse begins to unravel me. My mouth is dry, my heart pounds, suddenly the last layer of gauze is lifted, and they appear, my perfect nipples atop the hills and vale of my chest. A new landscape. And what a view! Stitches removed, I stand in front of Dr. G's gold-framed mirror, and for a moment the three of us survey the scene in silence. They are round and full and perfectly proportioned. I am buxom. Dr. G blushes and giggles at my exclamations of delight and appreciation. I forgive him immediately for his underestimation. My journey from A to B has, in fact, been from A to D.

• • •

"Not another one," growls my teenage son, who, to be fair, is beginning to show signs of grudging acceptance. He's caught me trying to sneak into the house with the third lingerie shopping bag this week. I've developed an obsessive-compulsive disorder that has resulted in my spending more on underwear in just a few months than I have in twenty-seven years of wearing a bra. As a 34D, I'm having the time of my life.

My breast-reduced friend is right. Apart from the handful of people I told, no one appears to have detected a change in my physical appearance, or if they have, they've said nothing to me.

Even my father doesn't notice the difference. Whether others observe it or not, I've changed. I have a visible secret that has transformed my life. There isn't a day that goes by when I don't look in the mirror and rejoice at my new curvaceousness, my traditional figure. The "before" shots might still be at large, but I now have the breasts that have been lost to me since I was a teenager. I've found the way home to myself via A, B, and C.

Chair Work

ROSEANNE MALFUCCI

*I*t's 6:03 PM and I am approaching my therapist's building, late again. I'm aware that my tardiness is costing me, but despite this I take a customary pause before ringing the office bell. These few seconds outside her door are reserved for self-scrutiny; it's the time to hide anything that might betray my less-than-together status. My demeanor overhaul goes like this: Slow down my breathing. Clear my head. Fix my clothes and adjust my baggage. I will enter this office with a graceful poise that masks the many issues requiring me to return for a weekly fee of $75.

My therapist (not a Psychiatrist, but a Certified Social Worker) uses a Gestalt approach—integrating work with mind, body, and spirit into her practice. After initial skepticism, over time I have come to appreciate her variety of techniques, which can vary from traditional listening and reflection to interpretation of gestures and posture. As a loquacious Italian Jewish Brooklynite with scoliosis, I've clearly given her a lot to work with, and her insightful responses make even my smallest head tilt feel relevant (which, of course, I love). However, her measured language and serene composition are sometimes more than I can bear.

Me: I feel like I'm constantly obsessed with what other people think. It's becoming a serious problem.

Certified Social Worker: Why is this a serious problem?

Me: Because . . . I'm so preoccupied with other people that I completely forget myself. I'm always so distracted . . . I can never really focus on what I want to be doing!

CSW: When do you notice this happening?

Me: Like, when I go running. I'm constantly comparing myself to the other runners. I get . . . brutally competitive. It's not pretty.

CSW: What's wrong with being competitive? It can help you to set goals and push yourself. . . .

Me: But this isn't healthy competition . . . it's really bitter. I start scrutinizing everyone around me, and when someone passes me on the track I get so mad. . . .

CSW: You know, we all slip into roles sometimes. Everyone has certain ways of relating to themselves, and to others, that may feel familiar, or comfortable, at the time. It sounds like you might be slipping into a role here.

Me: Um . . . there is nothing comfortable about how I feel when this happens! I feel like I want to hurt the other people! . . . I mean, not like, really violently . . . but just, you know, eliminate them. It's fucked-up! It makes me want to stop running altogether.

CSW: It sounds as if you are slipping into a role that says you have to be the fastest, and when someone else is faster than you that you are worthless. Do you see how this role sets up unattainable goals? Do you see how you can never actually feel happy in this role?

Me: But—never feeling happy is not a role; it's . . . a way of life!

About four years ago my therapist proposed that I address this perpetual feeling of mediocrity by reconnecting to my body through exercise. It took two years before I finally submitted to her gentle suggestions and bought my first pair of sporty sneakers. Then, after a month of subpar psych-ups and hungover false starts, I finally began waking up early to run around the track in my neighborhood park.

This was the first time in my life I actively chose to partake in rigorous physical activity, having previously viewed athletics as contrary to my alt-bohemian image. Sitting smugly in the corner of gynocentric separatism, I had always denounced fitness as dull and macho, a mainstream aesthetic preoccupation that bred competition and anorexia. But once I was running three times a week, I was suddenly gaining positive interest in my changing body—seeing tone, glow, muscle definition. I felt proud of my dedication to getting in shape and relieved that I could finally fall right to sleep without that compulsive backward counting.

At first when I ran, I was in my own world, listening to *Club Jams Vol. 1* on my Walkman and appreciating the greenery around me. Each lap I crossed was a new lease on life.

But recently I've been so distracted by the other runners that I rarely achieve those feelings of accomplishment and release. These days, when a male runner approaches, I immediately try to speed up to prevent him from passing me. If he passes, I feel defeated and hope that at least he sees me as a worthy adversary. When a woman passes me, I am furious. The idea that some little woman is stronger or more agile makes me nuts, and if she is skinnier or prettier than me, I am crushed.

Recalling this aloud, I feel saddened that even my most recent success has been overrun with negativity. Sensing that I am once again engulfed in a disorienting gale of self-critique, my therapist suggests we address the discord through "chair work."

Chair work is role-playing for the emotionally distressed. It's a technique designed to shed some light on internal conflict by giving each of the personalities inside us a shot at center stage. In chair work, you divide yourself into your multiple personas, with each embodying a different set of values and perspectives. Next, you assign each "self" to a different spot in the room, physically separating and defining all those voices in your head.

For me, a few selves make recurring appearances:

Deprived-Dejected (DD) Rose perches in the corner, emitting a desperate sexiness through her exaggerated lounging. She alternates between tasteful poses—crossing her legs, leaning against walls, angling to promote maximum clothing drapage. Disdainfully wrinkling her manicured brow, her moony eyes glance over at me and then flit away. Many do not detect DD Rose's woeful, insatiable nature, as it is expertly cloaked by her overwrought, Stevie Nicks–inspired outfits.

Deprived-Dejected Rose: I feel more attractive, but it seems really fragile. As if I am in some cool club of hot people but any day now they'll find out I'm an imposter.... I feel really scared and hopeless because the happiness is so fleeting. Like last night, I just stared at the mirror from different angles, turning front to back to side, and hated myself for my stomach, and my ass....

DD Rose speaks in warm, lilting tones, pausing frequently to make sure she is being understood. She aims to captivate and would rather withdraw than share the spotlight. DD Rose believes love has no gender, and she demands that all suitors demonstrate their undying desire without compromising her autonomy. She secretly frets about her own inability to really care about others. Angry-Political Rose can't stand her.

Angry-Political (AP) Rose is very dykey. A perpetual college student, AP Rose is no-nonsense: unshaven, bowl cut, bushy eyebrows, corduroys. AP Rose is an anarchistic, outspoken progressive, living with the most equitable of intentions. She claims to reject any practice that objectifies women or pits them against each other, yet she strives for intellectual supremacy in every conversation, demonstrating her knowledge with wry diffidence. AP Rose sits forward, legs a foot apart, arms resting on her thighs. She has no time for this bullshit.

Angry-Political Rose: I can't believe this is happening. You say that you're making "healthy" choices, but you're fucking calorie counting! You're ordering diet soda and then trying to cover it up by saying you can't eat sugar 'cause of your yeast infections! It's fucking embarrassing. You're pitting yourself against other women. Judging other people's bodies, their clothing . . . That's not your business! What happened to you?

AP Rose speaks in even, voluble tones complemented by swift hand gestures. Words fly from her mouth with such conviction that it's easy to agree with anything she says.

Peacemaker-Strategizer (PS) Rose avoids tension at all costs. She has highly developed skills in both precaution and negotiation, honed over years of warding off bullies, authority figures, and other slower-witted foes. When listening to the plights of even her remotest acquaintances, PS Rose tilts her head slightly to one side, makes wide eye contact, and— nodding—responds with thoughtful sincerity to assure that she understands your pain.

Peacemaker-Strategizer Rose: It's really great that you're exercising. It sounds like it's making you feel tougher and more independent. You're getting stronger and starting to put time toward yourself! Have some compassion; this took a lot of work.

PS Rose is mutable and takes great pains to ensure that everyone she meets grows to like her. Judicious, she often prevents conflict with witty and humorous sidetracks. She is quick, but lacking resolve, she makes appearances only when absolutely necessary.

Though in the moment it feels corny and awkward, naming my sides helps me to deal with their associated energies when they emerge later. But while acknowledging these dimensions is empowering, it also seems to be a lifetime sentence of New Age emotional training. Am I so fucked-up that I have to routinely channel my own character traits just to stop them from colluding against me? Shit.

The session is about halfway done (I like to clock the precious minutes so as to prevent my own expository blue balls) and I've decided to move on to the weighty topic of my breasts. This is a direct result of a film I recently watched, efficiently titled *Breasts*. Critics and friends had urged me to see this raw, powerful documentary in which women of all ages—most of whom appear topless—speak about their relationship to their bodies. Knowing that *Breasts* was directed by a woman and filmed by an all-female crew, I looked forward to an uplifting take on the trials of womanhood in a breast-obsessed culture.

Instead, I found that the only woman in the documentary who shared my own concerns told a sad story of unimpressive sexual encounters and censure of her breasts. "Molly," a twenty-two-year-old preschool teacher, joked bitterly about the drooping concerns of older women and yearned for firmer breasts. She smiled nervously as she relayed the painful anecdote of a date who couldn't find her downturned nipple in the dark. Her obviously ashamed demeanor, and the camera's lingering gaze, made this woman's smallish, bowing breasts—breasts that looked a lot like mine—the objects of pity and ridicule.

Demonstrating how she failed "the pencil test," Molly slipped a pencil underneath her left breast. The pencil remained suspended, wedged between her breast and rib cage. As the camera panned down to the pencil and then back up to her sheepish expression, she sarcastically remarked that the evidenced lack of perkiness made her breasts "imperfect."

Despite her mock horror at failing the test, Molly's wistful face betrayed the truth—the experiment's results were plainly intolerable. Having failed this test multiple times myself, I awaited resolution, the upshot when she realized that her breasts were just as good as everyone else's. When was Kirstie Alley going to barrel in to lighten the mood? Alas, this moment never came. It was reconfirmed to me that other women, even feminists, *also* think my breasts are ugly. The bitter aftertaste of the film is still with me as my therapist suggests:

CSW: Can you put Angry-Political Rose in that chair?

I begin placing each self in the seats she's pulled from the corners of the room. DD Rose is perched on the couch, AP Rose sits in the deco-knockoff armchair on the left, PS Rose occupies that dreadful canvas director's chair on the opposite wall. My therapist asks me to substantiate their existence by glancing over the room and taking them in.

I am immediately drawn to AP Rose, who meets my gaze with a knowing scowl. She's been looking forward to this all week. Hunched over her folded leg, her stony expression betrays little, but from her narrowed eyes I can tell she's ready to fight. Disconcerted, I switch over to DD Rose, who is curled up on the couch, kittenish, bored. Okay. I switch over to the other chair, expecting to see PS Rose, but she's not there. The thing is, she's never there. After all this time I've still never really been able to make out PS Rose. Her outline and features are always faint, and though she gleams a vague light of promise, it remains distressingly dim.

I stare harder at the glow in the director's chair, hoping to reveal some truth about this inexplicable being. Squinting, I begin to see a sepia-toned outline, but nothing more. I close my eyes to try to envision the inner essence of PS Rose, but nothing emerges. Shaking my head, I take a deep breath and look back at my therapist. I know what's coming.

CSW: Do you want to go take a seat on the couch and see what's happening for Deprived-Dejected Rose?

How my therapist remembers the names of my various personalities is impressive. How she keeps a straight face while saying their names is unbelievable. She looks me right in the eye, referring to the ghosts of my psychosis as if they're real people sitting in the room with us. I look at her, nodding solemnly, and take a seat on the couch. I settle into the velour and shift a little, crossing my legs. My wrists suddenly become limp.

I direct my words at Angry-Political Rose, who, as usual, commands the most attention.

DD Rose: This movie was awful. It made me hate my body even more. I keep thinking of all of my exes, and what they must've thought of me. All you hear about is having big tits, or a big ass, but no one ever says what kind of big. What they mean is porno, gravity-defying, teenage breasts, not floppy, saggy, old-lady ones. It makes me feel like a fucking freak.

CSW: Is she listening to you?

I look over at Angry-Political Rose, who is listening intently. She has one eyebrow cocked in disapproval. I have to look away.

DD Rose: I can't look at her. She's too scary.

CSW: What is scary about her?

DD Rose: She thinks I'm an idiot for stressing about this.

CSW: How can you tell?

DD Rose: She keeps rolling her eyes.

CSW: Can you ask her if she thinks you're an idiot?

I turn to face AP Rose again, attempting to look her in the eye. No matter how I try, I cannot meet her gaze. Instead, I cheat by looking slightly to the right of AP Rose and directing my inquiry toward the calendar hanging on the wall. Making eye contact with one of two costumed babies snuggled in a hollowed-out watermelon, I ask:

DD Rose: Do you think I'm an idiot for talking about my breasts?

Saying it aloud, I immediately know the answer. I look back at my therapist.

DD Rose: She says no.

CSW: Can you ask her what she is thinking?

I turn back and prepare once again to ask the empty chair a question. I open my mouth, but nothing comes out. I squint a little and try again. Nothing. The whole thing feels weird and wrong in the most awful, postmodern way. I can't believe that this is what I'm reduced to. I can't believe I have so many problems that I pay a dollar a minute to sit and do bullshit theater exercises.

DD Rose: It's too hard.

CSW: Okay. That's okay.

We sit in silence for a few seconds. I try to think of something to say. Silence in therapy is terrible. We both know I'm the one expected to break it, so the intensity of the moment weighs gravely as I try to drum up some clever explanation for faltering. Some evidence as to why my breasts are not worth discussion, anyway. Fortunately this time she saves me with a gentle interruption.

CSW: How about going over to that chair and trying to see what Angry-Political Rose thinks?

I want to leave. I'll get up and just walk out the door. I've made it this far without bringing my breasts to the table. Do I really even need therapy? I can think of so many fucked-up people, maybe even more fucked-up than I am, who don't have therapists. They would never do something like this! Why am I torturing myself?

I look down at the floor and feel tears welling up in my eyes. I watch two plink onto my lap, one just after the other, as if my right eye got jealous of my left eye's showmanship. I think about all the hours I have spent in this stupid office. I think about what was happening seven years ago when I first started therapy and about how much I just want to get better. I catch a glimpse of my therapist, who calmly bears witness to my pain.

Slowly, reluctantly, I stand up and amble over to the deco-knockoff armchair in the right corner of the room. I sit down and shift a little. The back of the chair is stiff and uncomfortable. I lean forward and focus. My fist curls. Suddenly—

AP Rose: I can't believe you are talking about this; it's just sad. You could be spending your time doing so many better things. Those unattainable ideals you compare yourself to; they are not real! This is why women get plastic surgery instead of investing in their lives. . . . It's the myth that keeps us on the hamster wheel! The race you always lose! You are never going to be happy with your breasts.

CSW: Is she listening to you?

I look over at DD Rose, who is definitely not listening, and then back to my therapist.

AP Rose: She never listens to anyone!

CSW: Hmm . . . Why don't you ask her?

AP Rose: What's the point?

CSW: You are talking to her, right? Don't you care if she's listening?

Shit. You can't get anything by my therapist! Her mind is like a steel trap—lined with chenille.

I take a deep breath and direct my attention toward the plush beige sofa. I stare at the antique teddy bear in the corner, which probably masquerades as an absentee father for some other client. Shaking my head, I shift my gaze slightly and stare harder, trying to conjure an image of DD Rose reclining on that couch, and scan her for a response. I look back at my therapist.

AP Rose: She says I don't get it.

CSW: Would you like to see what she thinks?

I sigh again. Musical chairs for the emotionally impaired.

I get up and walk back to the couch. Nestling into the spongy cushions, I feel waves of indignant sadness. I am tired, irritated.

CSW: So, how does it feel to hear Angry-Political Rose say those things to you?

DD Rose: It's really hard. It's not going to change anything. I feel like I'm just wired this way. I have always hated my body, especially my breasts. I can never remember looking in the mirror without feeling disgust, even as a child.

Pausing, I feel hesitation creeping in my chest. It's uncomfortable. Something is not right. I inhale and try to wiggle into character. I start again.

DD Rose: And it's not like anyone's coming along to change my mind. Nobody wants to be with me. I've been single for three years now! I've gotten no positive reinforcement. . . .

This is getting intense. I'm starting to feel nauseated.

DD Rose: Not like it even matters. I can never connect with anyone anyway. Everybody pisses me off. The whole thing is totally hopeless.

The words tumble out of my mouth effortlessly, but inside I'm pleading for it to stop. This flagellation is only making things worse. It's too painful.

DD Rose: My body never brought me anything but problems. Sometimes when I'm working out, I feel like if I go at it hard enough maybe I can just beat it into a worthwhile shape. But even if I feel good afterward, the next day it's back to loathing. My body just feels like an ugly extension of myself that I want to disappear. . . .

Unexpectedly, a calm voice enters the room.

PS Rose: I want her to stop talking. It's excruciating. I feel bad for her.

CSW: Why don't you go take a seat on the chair and tell her that?

I stare at my therapist, feeling torn. I definitely want to escape, but I don't feel like getting up. I'm sunk into the clefts of the comfy couch cushions. Fucking chair work. Why is everything so laborious?

I glance toward the misshapen director's chair and shake my head at its flaccid canvas. It masquerades as comfortable, but I know the truth. I muster the strength to relocate. Venturing over, I wriggle in the seat, its easy compliance offering no real support.

PS Rose: You're being really hard on yourself! Of course this is a struggle. No one feels happy with her body. It's not because you're ugly, or because you're weak, or because you're single. That movie was fucked-up! You're not doing anything wrong.

CSW: Is she listening to you?

I look over at the couch, still indented with my emotive imprint, and try to assess DD Rose.

PS Rose: I'm not sure.

CSW: Try telling her again.

I look back at the couch earnestly.

PS Rose: You're a good person. You're really working on yourself. You're going to figure this out. It's going to be okay.

I catch a profile of DD Rose, who's looking at the wall, blushing. Peripherally, I see the corners of her mouth start to turn. A twinge of acknowledgment knits her brow. She smirks. Then she grins.

It's quiet for a few moments before I get up and walk to the other side of the room to take a seat where I first began. My therapist also rises and, after putting the chairs in their original corners, sits back down, facing me. Our eyes meet in solemn recognition.

I feel awkward, but vindicated. This was a groundbreaking session, and I've definitely made some headway. Feeling strong and proud of myself for tackling such persistent obstacles, I start thinking about their gravity in my daily life.

> Me: I'm feeling blown away by the force of my own criticism. It makes me wonder how much I could really be capable of, if I could just tone down the negativity.

My therapist nods.

> Me: It's making me think about my parents, and my relationships, and how I've spent my whole life just channeling other people's messages. . . . I'm starting to wonder, am I ever truly able to think for myself? Which ideas are really my own?

I wait for her input on my epiphany. She must love working with someone so perceptive and savvy. Now we're really digging deep, really reaching for the next level. I'm anticipating her guidance, the wisdom I've grown to value and trust over all these years. She looks back with careful intention, and says—

> CSW: We're going to have to end soon.

Ahh.

I stand up and collect my things while gazing at the floor. I'm not sure what to say after all this. I want to thank her for listening, to pay respect to all the progress we've made today, and to conclude with some dignity. I try to think of a sensitive summation—something poignant and wise.

Me: Well, uh . . . thank you . . . this is, um, really helpful. I'll remember your check next time. Sorry.

Reduced

NANCY RABINOWITZ

I chose my bra and underwear carefully. Nothing too sexy; I didn't want to look like I tried. Nothing too dingy; I didn't want to be embarrassed. Something flattering and tasteful; I was about to be seen in my skivvies. My mother was taking me to that legendary mecca of discount shopping, Loehmann's.

I had been there before, of course, but only as an observer. Too small to fit into the clothing, I had been forced to sit in the doctor's office–like chairs along the side wall—chairs seemingly reserved for henpecked husbands named Morrie waiting for their bargain-hunting wives. Now that I was in adult sizes, I would join the treasure-seeking throngs rooting through the muck of rhinestone-encrusted T-shirts, Annie Hall–inspired fedoras, and *Charlie's Angels* wrap tops for the chance to hit fashion pay dirt for 80 percent off retail. We knew what we were after: there, under that hideous sweater with the appliqués, a Calvin Klein skirt for $35! Here, buried beneath a pile of polyester pantsuits, an Armani blouse for $29.99. When our arms were all but breaking under the weight of our bounty, my mother and I came to what truly makes shopping at Loehmann's a rite of passage for all New York Jewish women: the communal dressing room.

Inside, a woman in hole-ridden, waist-high cotton briefs stepped out of a slinky evening gown. An old lady plunged her crepe-paper legs into one of those polyester pant sets. Two women in bikini underwear stood arguing over which one of them had grabbed a tiger-striped silk blouse off the discard rack first. And breasts were everywhere. I saw women whose breasts were so large and low they obliterated their belly buttons, women who barely filled the triangles of fabric stuck like pasties over what should have been breasts. Lingerie hung like Christmas decorations on the lithe young bodies in no need of real support. Folds of flesh oozed over the backs of too-tight bra straps. Deep crevasses of cleavage yielded crumpled tissues to wipe brows, damp with the exertion and exhilaration of bargain hunting. One woman's sheer, flesh-toned bra made her breasts look like two little bank robbers with panty hose on their heads. "Stick 'em up," they cried.

I stood there gasping for air, drowning in a sea of cellulite and spider veins, when suddenly a braless woman reached frantically for a top from the discard rack, sideswiping me in the face with her naked breast. I was horrified. How could she let that happen? How could any of these women let their bodies be seen like that? How could they let themselves get like that in the first place? The thought that my breasts could one day be less than perfect never occurred to me. I was a teenager. I was invincible. My only worries about the future concerned things such as whether Kurt Schneider would ask me to the seventh-grade dance. Those breasts were as foreign to me as boys with body hair, the need to wax my mustache, and French kissing. And like all of those things, they repulsed me.

It was the summer of 1979, I had just turned fourteen, and my breasts were like babies: fresh, smooth, round, and screaming for attention. Little did I know that by the end of summer camp that year I would barely be able to squeeze my rapidly expanding boobs into a 38DD. They grew so fast my mother had to send me a care package in which bigger bras were stuffed alongside candy, comic books, and *eau de love* cologne. Before that summer my breasts could pass the pencil test. After that summer I could stick an entire case of pencils under one, a sketch pad under the other, jump up and down, and produce a passable representation of the topography of the Grand Canyon.

My shoulders were rubbed raw from bra straps straining under the weight of my pendulous appendages. My wardrobe choices were limited to what wouldn't make me look like a freak, such as oversized overalls to cover my more generous parts and the (sadly) short-lived and (mercifully) full smock top. When I exercised, I wore two to three sports bras layered one on top of the other; still, I felt as though I would give myself a black eye if I attempted to jog. I admit that some of these memories of my enormous breast size might be exaggerated by the painful memories of adolescence itself. My changing body was alien to me. The frizzy hair, the sudden need for deodorant, the way I felt when Joel Malina smiled at me in the hall. (My interest in Kurt Schneider had ended when he tried to French-kiss me at that dance.) I felt different. I felt other. The sudden appearance of those breasts only confirmed my fears: I really *had* lost control of my body. I had been invaded by enormous, Dolly Parton–size boobs—with neither the talent nor the fame to make them an asset.

During the next few years I got used to them. I became expert in strategic dressing. I could camouflage my breasts while accentuating my more moderately proportioned assets. I had thin legs, and in the early 1980s big shirts with little leggings or miniskirts were in. In those outfits, even I could forget how disproportionate I had become.

I even felt comfortable enough to get onstage in front of hundreds of people to play Hedy LaRue in our school's version of *How to Succeed in Business Without Really Trying*. The part demanded that I be sexy, and I went on a crash diet from a book called *The Woman Doctor's Diet for Teenage Girls*. For two weeks I ate an orange for breakfast, an orange and a hamburger for lunch, and an orange and two hamburgers for dinner. Evidently, the author had a doctorate in citrus, with a subspecialty in chopped meat. It worked, though; I lost ten pounds and easily fit into the tight short skirts and cleavage-revealing tops that suited the part. I felt great. People praised my performance. And then I saw the pictures. My crash diet had only accentuated the disproportionate size of my breasts. I looked like Dolly Parton (big boobs) crossed with Barbra Streisand (big nose) crossed with Bette Midler (big hair) teetering around on skinny legs. I asked my parents how they had allowed me to go onstage that way. They answered that they had thought it was great that I had that much self-confidence. But I knew it was because they couldn't bear to face the fact that I was no longer, in any way, their little girl. My breasts were only the outward sign of my growth from little girl to full-fledged woman. If they didn't acknowledge them, they didn't have to acknowledge that I was growing up.

I pleaded with them to get me breast reduction surgery. They balked. I was only sixteen. Then, my junior year of high school, they were convinced. Through an educational grant, a professional director from Manhattan had come to our school to direct two students in *The Typists*, a play about the failed dreams of two people bogged down by the tedium of menial office work. Why that play was chosen, I cannot guess. We lived in a town where tedium meant going skiing in Gstaad two winters in a row. In any case, the entire school studied the play in English class, and then a boy named Matt and I were chosen to perform the piece in two schoolwide performances.

At one point in the script, Matt came up behind me and put his arms around me. When he did so on the day of the performance, some boy in the back row yelled, "Grab her tits!" His shouts yielded more taunts from other boys, until I forgot my lines and stood there, frozen, not knowing what to do. I don't remember finishing the play, blissfully a one-act, but I do remember refusing to go onstage to take a bow. I couldn't and wouldn't face the crowd. I remember my father's fury at the boys, his insistence that the principal take some action against them, and my fevered pleas for him to please, please forget about it. I just wanted it all to go away.

So that's what I did. I made my breasts go away. The play, the shoulder pain, the promise of back problems, all helped convince my reticent parents that breast reduction surgery was my only way out of a life defined by my boobs instead of by my brains or talent. I think my mother was secretly hoping I'd ask for a nose job; that way I could show up after a school vacation with a piece of tape on my nose and claim—like so many other girls in my high school—that I'd had a deviated septum repaired, rather than an ethnic beacon viciously snuffed out. Though it was as bogus as those new upturned shiksa profiles, people happily accepted this excuse. In the heyday of silicone implants, however, I feared they wouldn't be so sympathetic to my desire for a flatter front.

As long as we were doing it, though, we might as well do it right. We did our research and found the best doctor in Manhattan. We asked about breastfeeding—would I be able to one day? Yes. We asked about pain—would there be a lot? No. We decided to have the surgery the summer between high school and college, so that I would start fresh in a new place. I browsed The Boob Book, Dr. Smith's breast catalog picturing page after page of perfectly perky, round, normal-size breasts, with anticipation bordering on awe.

I didn't want to be too small. It seemed funny to me that I could suddenly be small breasted. Like suddenly being told that no, I didn't look like Bette Midler or Barbra Streisand at all—I looked a lot like Doris Day, actually. Goodbye, Nancy Rabinowitz, hello, Nancy Robbins. I decided to be a C cup. Still large, but manageable, normal. I requested small, even nipples—mine had been large and amoebalike. I was going to have the breasts I'd always wanted. Breasts no one could tease me about, breasts no one would notice unless I wanted them to be noticed. The night before the surgery I stood in front of the mirror in my hospital room and examined my breasts. "You will never see these again," I told myself. "Remember this moment." And I do remember the moment. I just have no memory of what my breasts looked like that night or any night before it.

Dr. Smith cut almost all the way around my nipples, down the front of my breasts, and around the underside of them. He removed nearly two pounds of tissue, about a Cornish game hen, per side. The surgery was uneventful. But I did develop a post-surgical infection on my right breast. It healed, but the scar it left traversed the nipple. The scars on the underside of my breasts healed and became barely noticeable white lines. But the scar left from the infection was something else entirely. It looked as if some pirate had buried his treasure in the center of my right boob and marked the spot with a big X. Initially, the only reason this bothered me was cosmetic. My breasts were supposed to look perfect. No one in The Boob Book had a big X scrawled across her chest. I spent years warning potential lovers and apologizing to actual lovers about my deformity, until I realized that no one seemed to notice or care. As the years went by the scar faded from scarlet red to pale white, and I, too, stopped noticing or caring that it was there. I bought new clothes. I went braless in backless gowns to friends' weddings. I was no longer reduced to being "the girl with the tits." I was just a girl.

But fifteen years after the surgery I found out that the scar was more than a surface issue. It was situated in such a way that my newborn twins couldn't latch on for breastfeeding. I breastfed the tiny babies using only one breast for four months before I gave in to exhaustion. I was left feeling like a failure for not being able to feed them longer and looking like a lopsided version of my former self: one enormous breast that had fed two children and one normal-size one that had not. Dolly Streisand, perhaps.

When I chose my breasts from that surgeon's book of boob photos, I had every reason to believe that they would be as perky, round, high, and proud as any of the unattached-to-a-face breasts on the page. Perhaps postsurgery they were, for a time. But by now, my breasts are scarred and battle worn. They droop where they should be perky, they slope where they should climb. They have been cut open, suctioned out, filled, and then depleted of breast milk. They have stretched out sweaters, worn down the straps of bras and bathing suits, fed babies, and titillated lovers. They have survived a pregnancy that made my breasts swell to a horrifying F cup—who knew they even made F cups?—then back down to a D, where they remain. D cups. After all the embarrassment and surgery, the worry and hope. D cups. Once again, too big to be normal. Once again, stare worthy, only now, surgery is no longer an option. I have too many scars and too much scar tissue for any reputable surgeon to risk cutting into me again.

My five-year-old daughter recently asked me when she was going to get "hanging-down boobies."

"You mean sticking-out boobies? Like Mommy's?" I asked.

"No," she said. "Yours don't stick out; they hang down. When am I getting those?"

It was time for some serious intervention. I needed to hoist those babies up. I had heard that Oprah had named one bra *the* bra. I figured that after all those years of weight loss and gain, Oprah knew a thing or two about saggage, and I went to buy one. The saleswoman, whose name tag read BEATRICE, looked at me and said "36D" before I even told her what I wanted. I imagined Bea at a restaurant: Her waitress says, "I'm Shannon and I'll be your server tonight" and Bea blurts out, "32A!" Or Bea at the dental hygienist: "Excuse me, Lorraine, but could you keep those 38Cs off my chin while you get at those molars?" Bea had the Oprah bra, she said, and yes, it really did the job. I tried it on. If I wasn't Jewish, angels would have sung overhead. My breasts were so high and round in my T-shirt that they almost hit me in the chin. I wanted one in every color. Then I looked at the price tag: $68. I almost gave it back to Bea, but I decided to treat myself to two. After all, they cost less than the therapy sessions I would inevitably need if I didn't do anything about my low breast-esteem.

My daughter's comment, while it cost me $142.75 (with tax), wasn't meant to send me over the edge. She wasn't passing judgment, just making an observation. So I try to do the same. I try to be an impartial observer of my breasts. "Wow, they're elongated now," I observe. "Gee, the pale purple of those stretch marks would be a great color for the powder room walls," I note happily. I try not to care that after all that agonizing, all that surgery, my breasts look more like the balloons that clowns use to make those little doggies than the ones my kids get tied to their wrists at the shoe store. (Though at the rate I'm going, I'll be able to tie my boobs around my wrist soon enough.) I look at young women in their teeny tank tops and think: Just wait. One of these days, you too will need a $68 bra. Just wait. One day you'll need a whole hell of a lot more than just the wind beneath your wings. And I think about Bette and Barbra, who, like me, straightened their hair but never their noses. And I think about Dolly, who still has huge boobs that surely, by now, have succumbed to gravity, and who is still singing. And I think, damn it, I will not be reduced to nothing but a defeated set of tatas. I will not be reduced to shame over what childbirth and years have done to me. If Loehmann's still had a communal dressing room I'd go in there and let it all hang out. I will hoist them high and wear them proud. And, with apologies to Barbra, revel in my misty, watercolored mammaries, and the way they are.

Big Asses, Moon Bellies & Wide Loads

Suburban Hottentot

LAURA FRASER

*W*hen I was eight, my parents thought something was seriously wrong with my spine. My lower back had a dramatic curve, a ski jump at the tail, and Mom and Dad worried it would affect the way I would grow or walk. They envisioned braces, surgery, months in a body cast, physical rehabilitation.

My father is a doctor, so I made the rounds of doctors. The pediatrician examined my back, shook his head, and concurred that he'd never seen anything like it. It wasn't scoliosis, or thoracic hyperkyphosis; it wasn't Scheuermann's disease or hyperlordosis. It was a mystery. My condition was so unusual that when my dad hosted a medical meeting at our house, he hoped to get the collective opinion there of his daughter's strange malady.

To my horror, this meant parading around stark naked in front of a bunch of middle-aged men in the living room. I had to walk around touching my toes, so the doctors could better examine my spine, and I was glad to hide my face, not to mention my private parts. They puffed on their pipes and murmured among themselves about how odd the bend in my back was and what it might mean. I felt like a freak on display. I made one slow circle of the living room and dashed back into the kitchen.

The next day, there were many opinions but no verdict on the strange curvature of my lower back—except that it was indeed strange. My parents made an appointment with a specialist downtown. This doc put me through several exercises, took x-rays, and pushed and prodded the vertebrae in my lower back. After the exam, he consulted with my parents, whose faces were stitched with worry. Finally, he had reached a conclusion. "Your daughter," he told them gravely, "has an unusually large and protruding posterior for a child her age."

I had a big ass. And it was only going to get bigger.

Had I grown up in Brazil or Africa, no one would have noticed; I might even have been considered blessed. Maybe for a kid in Brazil or Africa, having a big ass is like having long white-blond hair in suburban Denver. But this being Denver, my ass was considered a deformity, a congenital defect.

There was little to be done. The doctor had prescribed sit-ups, since I'd need a lot of abdominal strength to help carry the mass. He shied away from gluteal exercises, since he thought overdevelopment might make the problem worse. Had reduction glutealplasty surgery been developed, he probably would've suggested that procedure (little did I know that decades later, physicians would actually be injecting flat behinds with hydrogel to achieve what I came by naturally). And, of course, everyone agreed I should lose weight, just in case that would help. At that early age, I started counting calories, eating small portions at dinner—and sneaking food between meals, since my ass apparently had a mind, and appetite, of its own.

I had no idea how dire my condition was, but I was determined to find out the prognosis. I waited until my father was gone one evening and took down some of his thick medical books, paging through the tissue-thin illustrations of bedsores, leprosy, cleft lips, frostbite, and the man with elephantiasis who had to carry his balls around in a wheelbarrow. At that point, having only sisters, I had never seen a normal pair of testicles, so that particular photo freaked me out about men in general for quite a long time. It also made me wonder: *Would I one day have to haul my butt around in a wheelbarrow?*

I was somewhat relieved when, farther on, in the *S* section, I found what seemed to be my particular defect—not elephantiasis after all, but steatopygia, "excessive adipose tissue accumulation around the buttocks." Bingo. The photo, of a woman with what looked like a VW Bug attached to her backside, scared me to near-anorexic behavior for a week or so. Further research at the local library revealed that steatopygia was first encountered in 1810, when a British ship doctor, William Dunlop, brought Saarti Baartman, a young South African tribeswoman, to Europe. Saarti was a Khoisan woman from a tribe that considered steatopygia a sign of rare beauty. But in England, horrifyingly, poor Ms. Baartman was a curiosity, exhibited naked in a cage in Piccadilly and known far and wide as the Venus of Hottentot. After Dunlop had exploited her all he could, he sold her to a French entrepreneur. She died in 1816 after a sad end of alcoholism and prostitution.

I closed the book, hands shaking. I feared I was going to be a Venus of Suburbia. My butt would grow beyond big to bodacious to something mind-boggling. I would forever be stared at, ridiculed, and humiliated because of my huge backside.

My parents were not the only ones to notice my big ass. It's not the kind of deformity that elementary schoolchildren overlook. Kids on the street would yell, "Bertha Big Butt," before running away. One day after gym class in junior high, Pam Thomas, she of the white-blond hair, approached me in the locker room. Pam was Popular, and I was a geeky straight-A student with a big-A Ass, so I doubted she was coming to say something friendly. She checked all around before spewing her words at me: "You have a big ass!" Though this wasn't a news flash—Pam was never the quickest to grasp things—it did hurt my feelings, and I knew that for as long as Pam reigned, from junior high to senior prom, I would never be cool.

And so my ass grew. I learned to cope as best I could: I sewed darts in the back of my jeans so they wouldn't gape around my waist; I learned to always wear black on the bottom; I scoured women's magazines for tips on balancing a wide behind with horizontal stripes on top. In time, my body grew to fit my bottom a little better, but it never quite caught up.

In high school, I never had boyfriends, which I blamed on my deformity. When I went away to college, I thought I had another chance and went on an extreme diet to coax my big butt back into size 12 jeans. I flirted with anorexia, starving myself until I lost forty pounds. The fat melted like wax off my face, neck, collarbones, and already smallish breasts—leaving them nearly flat—but my butt stayed as big and round as ever. It looked as if all my weight had merely rearranged itself, sliding down off the top half of my body and resting on the big shelf below my waist. I was more out of proportion than ever.

One thing losing weight did for me, though, was attract male attention. Up until college, I had never so much as seen a penis except in my father's medical books. Finally, at age eighteen, I had an opportunity to discover that while testicles are undeniably ugly, they are not elephantiasis-man grotesque. As for penises, they turned out to have fairly cheery, if willful, little personalities.

The problem was the men attached to the penises. While I was looking for my first true love and soul mate in college, all the guys were looking at my ass. No one fell in love with my sparkling personality and then noticed my ass later on. It was all about my ass, pro or con. Early on, I realized that the pro-ass guys were mainly Jewish or African American, and the con-ass guys were usually WASPs. Being a WASP myself, my ass had made me an outsider to my own tribe, which was a bit confusing.

I tended to fall for tall, pale, thin men with dishwater-blond hair who had a dark view of the world, read a lot of philosophy, and seemed to think that a big bottom was a sign of immanence, not transcendence. Who could be an intellectual with such a big butt? Who could be a poet's muse? Those were the girls who were equally thin and pale. I was doomed to be earthy.

Then I found the other guys, the ones who were exotic to me, who thought my big butt was just fine. They loved to grab it with both hands; they gave it playful spanks; they whispered to me under the sheets that they had dreamed about it. It surprised and thrilled me that some men were actually attracted to what had always embarrassed me most. But, in the end, I always felt that men weren't making love to me but to my waist-to-hip ratio. No one seemed to love me for myself. I still felt like a freak.

My senior year in college, I went to New York City, ostensibly for an internship, in reality pining after a tall, thin, intellectual guy who was moving there. My internship was at *Rolling Stone* magazine, which seemed like a big opportunity to meet editors and gain some important writing experience, but which ended up being an extremely dull job, Xeroxing for coke fiends for free. At first I worked in the music department, where none of the cool editors spoke to me except to warn me not to borrow any records from the library. Finally, one of the coolest stopped me in the hallway. Was he going to ask me to help him with an assignment? Do some research? "Why is it," he said, with a truly ponderous air, "that all the chicks who work here are pears?"

I only wish I'd had the wit to ask him why all the men who worked there were assholes.

New York City clearly wasn't my town. After college, I traveled by myself around the Mediterranean, where I was relieved to find that my long blond hair attracted more attention than my prominent derriere. My bottom was nothing unusual in Greece, Israel, Italy, or Spain. Art museums there were full of statues of steatopygic women. Outside the United States, my big butt wasn't a defect at all; it was just normal. For the first time, I met men from different countries who were interested in me, not because of or in spite of my bottom, but because I was who I was, a young, independent woman traveling around the world—okay, with blond hair and an American passport (a plus in those days). My big ass made me a freak at home but a proud citizen of the world.

A half-Brazilian friend who grew up in Africa tells me I have a "bubble butt," the best kind, one that she grew up longing for the way I wanted to be as thin and blond as Pam Thomas. Kids teased my friend for not having enough of an ass (though to be fair, she has a lovely figure). When I recently went to Africa for the first time and danced with some Africans (I long ago realized that I was better off with African and Brazilian dance than ballet and tango), I realized that once again, everyone was staring at my ass, but this time in a friendly, amused way. "You," said one of the gentlemen there, "are very unusual for a white woman." And then he asked me for another dance.

Navel Attire

JENNIFER D. MUNRO

$\mathcal{S}$o my sister-in-law from Ohio decides to get her nose pierced. This is Kara's first visit to the Northwest, and she's discovered that she's liberal, although I suspect it might be a caffeine high. Fortified by visions of tattooed bicycle-delivery men navigating Seattle's concrete hills, she hopes a ring in her nose might broadcast the subtleties of her inner nature, kinda like pheromones. Plus it will piss her mom off.

So far I haven't awed her with my freewheeling alt lifestyle. I use sunscreen even for quick dashes to the car on cloudy days and admonish her to keep up with her Pap smears. I'm ten years older, which is light-years to someone who's just had her first legal beer, but I think I know how to impress her. Cautioning her to inquire as to needle-sterilization methods, I take her to Capitol Hill, a neighborhood where curious heterosexuals can pretend interest in cutting-edge fashion while gawking at latex and leather accessories of dubious purpose.

The collars and leashes at the alternative variety store are more than Kara can take, though. Kent, Ohio, has two vegetarian restaurants and the eternally reserved parking spaces for the slain Kent State students, but there's nothing like this. Kara takes a quick lap around the store displays, eyes wide at the vulva puppets, and hovers near the door. But I'm not so eager to fulfill my stereotype by scuttling away in shock at the horse tails. I mention casual interest in a navel ring while I peruse tattoo designs, mostly to fill the awkward silence as the cashier eyes us. She looks like Pebbles Gone Gothic. Pink hair sprouts pom-pom-like from both sides of her head, and a huge bow perches on the shaved scalp between the ratted tufts. I try not to stare while wondering how she got the bow to stick. Everything else on her is black—including her lipstick—and tight; this Pebbles needs no Bam Bam to protect her. I exclaim in delight over the baby bracelets in the display case. She says, "Those are cock rings."

The piercing lady emerges from the back room and complains that her next appointment is a no-show, so she has an unexpected opening. Kara scrams, calling through the closing door that she's going to go find a margarita.

Next thing I know I'm in a back room with my Laura Ashley dress hiked up, and a woman with white plastic bows clipping back her short blue hair is forking a hollow needle through my abdomen. I expect it to hurt, and it does. Christina tells me I can make all the noise I want, but all I do is squeak. She shifts her weight to get the best aim; her clogs on the tiled floor and her concentrated breathing make more noise than I do.

Christina, who sports chin, cheek, nose (bridge and nostril), eyebrow, and multiple ear piercings, steps back and looks meditative as copious blood pools in my belly button. "Very few people bleed like this," she tells me.

Terrific.

"I think it's because you're a Meteor Person."

"Meteor Person?" I'm a Libra and am vaguely aware that this renders me friendly, cheerful, and well suited to balancing a checkbook. But how can this sorceress with her needled wand tell by threading my fat layers that I was born under crashing skies responsible for the extinction of dinosaurs? I feel vaguely flattered.

"No," she says, pinching more than an inch of her own waist, "a *m-e-a-t-i-e-r* person." She spells it out like a compliment. "Like me."

You have to understand. If I were naked in a dark room you could find me every time by the telltale glow of my luminous round belly, shining white like a full moon. I wear dresses my husband calls "potato sacks" and have never bought a pair of Levi's. I wear a one-piece bathing suit with the little skirt to unsuccessfully hide the dirtiest word in the English language, *cellulite*. I expose my midriff only in dimly lit bedrooms and depressing dressing rooms at the mall, suffering paranoid visions of security guards falling over in laughter behind the two-way mirror at my attempts to zip my O-body into an A-line dress. Kind lovers have told me I have an hourglass figure, and, it's true, my ass is up to the task of balancing out my belly. I've spent my life hiding the part of my anatomy that magazines command me to smash, squeeze, or starve into pancake submission. Usually I wind up with gas instead of anything approaching a washboard.

Not only is my tummy expansive, but my belly button bears a scar, a reminder of my ectopic pregnancy nine months before. An emergency midnight surgery sliced the embryo out of me, the only way to save me from hemorrhaging to death in the most devastating of my multiple pregnancy losses. No other child can pass through the scarred gap the operation left in my fallopian tube. My scarred navel, symbol of my inability thus far to bear children. My belly a double shame, double failure. Swells when it should lie flat. Lies flat when it should swell.

Christina noticed the scar as soon as I, relieved I had recently cleaned my belly button lint, pushed down the waistband of the white cotton briefs I buy in quantity when they go on sale. She didn't question me about the scar's origins. She accepts my blemish just as she's accepted my polka-dot dress, my pumps, my pearls, without comment, needing no explanation or disclaimer despite my intrusion in her world; I doubt my world is so kind to her. Store security would be on her ass in seconds if she infiltrated Macy's.

But she wondered if the scar tissue was too thick to allow a piercing. Ready to slink away, I started to pull my dress down and my underwear up. My body would betray me even in this one desire, would rebel against my small act of rebellion, allowing me nothing that I want. But Christina ran her fingers over the scalpel's carved mark, feeling for the depth of the tissue. I didn't flinch, and the scar cooled under her touch. "No problem," she said, turning back to her sterilized baggies of needles.

Now as I lie waiting for my fount of blood to dry up, making a mental note to take an extra iron supplement, I'm not too excited. I'm just glad the pain was bearable. I used to have a high pain threshold, but bleeding internally does something to a person. Especially when it's the child I so badly wanted who nearly killed me, matricide by embryo. Especially when resilience is what nearly did me in. The nurses I phoned wouldn't believe the extent of my bleeding and pain because I was too calm. The doctor misdiagnosed me because I wasn't curled up in a ball on the floor, screaming. Like most women, I've been taught well and choose to quietly bleed to death rather than make waves. But my husband arrived home in time and drove me to the hospital. "Ectopics don't *walk* through the door," the nurse chided later, so the misdiagnosis was my fault. Ironically, I had thought my stoicism would come in handy when I gave birth.

Instead of learning to scream, I learn to avoid pain. No more pregnancy attempts despite my remaining fallopian tube. I can't bear another loss. I order pamphlets on vasectomy. My husband winces and buys the Super Saver Jumbo box of condoms instead. The dusty box migrates to the bottom of his dresser.

The pain aspect of the piercing didn't occur to me until I signed the waiver. I've done this as a lark, hopping up on the table as a reaction against a recent accusation that I'm not spontaneous. This will be relatively inexpensive yet tangible proof that despite my sprouting gray hair and the fact that I've never seen *Sex and the City*, I'm fun, hip, and have an unexpected wild side. All in all a harmless way to begin a midlife crisis. I imagine I'll remove the ring by the time the Visa bill arrives.

At long last I stop bleeding, and Christina allows me to stand. She hands me a mirror. I hold it up, unaccustomed to looking at myself except when absolutely necessary. The amethyst bead winks at me from its nest of ample flesh. I stare at it, at me, awestruck by beauty. The ring doesn't so much hide my scar as decorate it, directing attention away from what I've lost to who I am.

My dictionary tells me that my navel itself is a small scar. We bring it into the world with us, part of the fact of being born. I marvel that my entrance wound is the same as my baby's exit wound. We share the same scar, that stubborn child and I, and with my twinkling bead Christina joins the gap between us.

Christina worries that she's hurt my feelings by calling me meaty. "Look," she says, "you and I have the same body."

But this can't be. Christina is beautiful.

She hikes up her shirt to show me her navel ring. I should have known she has more piercings than meet the eye. The heavy silver ring and lusty tiger eye growl out at me from the white indentation of her belly button. No dainty jewel to get lost like a fine necklace on a Rottweiler or a single light on a Christmas tree. She says bellies like ours need thick rings with large beads to balance things out.

"How much?" I reach for my wallet.

But she says I can't have a larger ring right away. I have to work up to it through incrementally thicker rings.

I tell Christina I'll be back.

My belly, my shame, becomes a lovely thing, adorned as if worthy. I stare in the mirror whenever possible at my sexy, sensuous stomach. I think about the beauty of the word *belly*. Violins have bellies, smooth, round, and strokeable.

I can't expose it enough. I hike up my shirt for friends and new acquaintances alike at a party. They wince and tell me it looks painful. It is. I bare my abdomen for a friend on a street corner. She's horrified, but I'm nonplussed. Even Kara's impressed. She gets her nose ring that summer at one of those muddy, reenacted Woodstock festivals, and I like to think my influence had something to do with her courage. I resist the urge to remind her to use disinfecting cleanser three times a day.

But it's also my little secret. I cruise through the office in my jumpers, distributing faxes and thinking, "If only they knew who is *really* among them." Mild-mannered secretary by day, belly-shimmying wonder by night. I sign up for belly dancing classes. I write erotica. I buy black lace panties and a pair of 501s. I earn my motorcycle license, after completing the safety course. I crook my finger at my husband.

"*Again?*" He rolls his eyes and looks exhausted but reaches for the nearly empty box of condoms. I tell him to throw them away.

Battleships

JENNIFER CARSEN

No you can't get to heaven
No you can't get to heaven
On Susie's hips
On Susie's hips
'Cause Susie's hips
'Cause Susie's hips
Are battleships
Are battleships.
No you can't get to heaven on Susie's hips
'Cause Susie's hips are battleships
And I ain't gonna grieve
My Lord no more.

*E*piscopalians aren't generally known for their rocking evangelism, but the spirit of song was alive and well at St. James Sunday School. Every week, Mr. D, a good-hearted parishioner, would come down to the church basement with his guitar and regale us with songs of God, love—and fat jokes.

I laughed right along with the other kids, even though at that age we hardly knew what hips were, and the only battleships we'd heard of were the ones in that Milton Bradley commercial (Actor One: "You sank my battleship!" Actor Two: [maniacal laughter]). All we knew was that there was something silly about Susie. The other verses weren't nearly so memorable—I recall some roller skates that rolled right by those pearly gates, but that's about it.

As the years passed, I spent less and less time at church and more and more time obsessing about food. I'd always been what people call a "good eater." My mom's obstetrician must have been one of the first Atkins devotees—when I was born in the early '70s, my mother wanted to feed me pureed bananas and carrots, but he exhorted her to give me meat. "Babies need protein!" was his rallying cry. She took him to heart and dutifully used her food mill to grind steaks and chops into baby-friendly mush. My teething ring was a frozen kielbasa.

My passion for food was matched or exceeded only by my passion for sitting around. I'd inherited Grandma Carsen's dreaded sweat gene, which meant that the slightest exertions left me bright red, breathless, and dripping. I chose to avoid this unpleasant fate by regularly camping out on the couch with a stack of Nancy Drew mysteries at my left and a stack of Pringles at my right.

Unsurprisingly, I grew into a rather lumpen adolescent. My younger brother, Dan, wasn't helping my cause, either—for a stretch of about two years he refused to eat anything but bologna and yogurt, giving him a gaunt, ribby look that was widely attributed in our small town to (a) parental neglect or (b) the chubby older sister eating all of his food. Neither theory really bolstered our standing among the neighbors. My mom, fed up, made a double appointment for us at the pediatrician's office. He predicted that we'd both grow out of it.

As it turned out, he was largely right. Dan eventually expanded his palate beyond luncheon meat and Dannon fruit-on-the-bottom, growing into a tall, slim-but-healthy kid. As for me, various school activities cajoled my butt off the couch, and I got a little taller, too. I wasn't often mistaken for Uma Thurman, but I was a perfectly normal, healthy weight.

At least, that's what the scale said. In my own head, I remained the Blobbo who devoured New England. Once a chubby kid, always a chubby kid, at least in your own head. The final straw was an audition for the high school play, when the drama teacher conspiratorially called me aside.

"We've got a part in this one for a beautiful ingenue . . ."

My heart raced. I'd finally arrived.

". . . onstage in nothing but a slip, and she . . . "

I'd need to start working out more.

". . . Do you know anyone who would be good? Obviously, the part's not right for you, so I thought you might be able to help me think of someone."

I dashed out of the auditorium, desperately trying to hold back my tears until I got home (a mere quarter mile away, but I always drove because of the malevolent sweat gene). Before I made it outside, I ran smack into my friend Sophie in the hall. She made sympathetic noises as I poured out my sad tale to her.

"I can't believe Mrs. Rupert would say something like that to you. There's nothing wrong with how you look."

Amen, sister.

"You're just big-boned."

She headed out to her car, and I found an inconspicuous corner of the band room (okay, so I sequestered myself in a tuba cubby) to curl up in before the waterworks started. I wasn't *that* big, was I? I surveyed my legs, which were folded up like a card table in the cramped space. I definitely had nice ankles. My thighs weren't so bad. And my hips . . . it flashed into my head, unbidden:

> 'Cause Susie's hips
> *'Cause Susie's hips*
> Are battleships
> *Are battleships*

My life swirled before my eyes as my hands frantically sought out the fleshy truth. Good Lord, was *I* Susie? I had become a fat joke embedded in a rollicking Christian children's song! Nobody would ever get to heaven on my hips. It was a Scarlett O'Hara moment for me. *As God is my witness, I'll never be fat again!* The battleships and I unfurled from the tuba cubby and headed home to draw up a plan of attack.

In the next several years, I tried every diet known to woman. Susan Powter made me hostile. Counting Weight Watchers points made me confused. South Beach made me cranky. None of them made me thin. I wish I could tell you that I eventually came to my senses, embraced my battleship-hipped self, and chucked the diet books (and, in homage to my feminist predecessors, perhaps a bra or two) in the incinerator. Any woman reading this knows that things just don't work that way.

Instead, I met a guy. A guy who loved every inch of me just as I was, who (sincerely) complained that models and actresses were way too thin, who encouraged me to stop being so damn hard on myself. He was the dashing Mr. Darcy to my neurotic Bridget Jones, and we fell in love and got married. The End.

Well, not really. Even though I'd found a man who made me feel like a natural woman, even though I started to actively get on board with who I was and what I looked like, it wasn't The End. My particular fairytale continued because my thyroid had other plans for me.

Thomas and I had been married for a few years when I decided to start training for the Chicago Marathon. Thanks to the mandatory PE requirement at our college years earlier—which forced me to abandon my Pringles and Nancy Drews in favor of more active pursuits—I had discovered the chock-full-o'-endorphins rush that only physical activity can provide. I was exercising regularly and had even voluntarily done a few weekend 5k races. The marathon training was going well, and I enjoyed the happy side effect of being able to eat like a horse without gaining weight.

It was only after the marathon was over that things got a little weird. I was still ravenous and eating an awful lot, yet I was actually *losing* weight, despite having reverted to my baseline state of relative sloth. I hadn't really noticed how much I was eating until I went home for two weeks during Christmas and cleaned my parents out of house and home, devouring pretty much anything that wasn't nailed down (my dad later observed that one of my more notable predinner snacks was half a roast chicken and about two pounds of mashed potatoes, washed down with a little tub of gravy).

At first I felt like Superwoman—I was sleeping only four or five hours a night, my senses were on heightened alert, I was eating everything I wanted and losing weight. I was snapping and crackling. Life was good.

But soon life wasn't so good. I started to sleep more fitfully, and my heart would occasionally get a little fluttery. I also got winded just walking up the stairs—*Amazing how fast that marathon conditioning leaves you,* I thought—and I was hot and sweaty *all* the time, not just during exercise. I seriously considered carrying around a sweat rag and just wringing it out as necessary, as Grandma Carsen did, but I'd been hoping to reserve that particular eccentricity for my later years.

I decided to see my doctor instead. She ran some tests and told me I had Graves' disease, which I'd never heard of and which sounded, frankly, rather grave. I learned that the thyroid is a little butterfly-shaped gland at the base of the throat that essentially operates as the body's thermostat, controlling basic stuff such as metabolism, heart rate, and body temperature.

Graves' disease is a form of hyperthyroidism, which means that your thyroid goes a little nuts and cranks out too much hormone, causing you to run too hot, like an overheating car. Your heart rate speeds up, your metabolism speeds up, and you feel warm and sweaty a lot of the time. It can also make you moody, Dr. B told me. I could see this. Recent fights with Thomas about trivialities such as his cat-petting technique made a lot more sense when considered in this context.

It was official. I had a glandular problem. I felt like Exhibit A in a 1950s health textbook. Next thing you know I'd have a social disease.

"So what do we do about it?"

"Well, we'll give you beta blockers to control the heart palpitations and a thyroid medication to slow everything down."

I was no dummy—I had a pretty good idea what "slow everything down" meant. "Will I gain weight?"

"Maybe a little." I immediately saw this for the lie it was. "Just watch your diet and you'll be fine."

Dr. B was a wonderful doctor, but she was also a tiny, gorgeous woman who clearly had never had to "watch her diet" in her whole life. I felt hostile. I considered grabbing a tongue depressor out of the glass jar on the desk and whapping her repeatedly with it, but I restrained myself.

"Eventually you'll want to consider radioiodine therapy, which takes out the thyroid completely, and then we put you on Synthroid."

Takes out the thyroid? Like a mob hit? I started to feel a little sorry for my thyroid. Here he was, working his heart out, doing his job just a little too well—an endocrine overachiever of sorts—and Dr. B was talking about having him whacked. I reconsidered my tongue-depressor whapping plan, but she was already gone, having left me with only my paper gown and two prescriptions to be filled.

As soon as I got home, I went online. Was I concerned about the health effects of this scary-sounding disease I'd never heard

of on my heart, my life, my various bits and pieces? Hell, no—at
least not initially. The very first thing I Googled was "Graves disease weight gain." The news was not encouraging. It appeared
that I was likely looking at a weight gain of at least ten pounds
or so, plus more if I eventually became hypothyroid (a typical
result of treatment for hyperthyroid; it's easy to slow things down
too much). Hypothyroid looked like a good time—in addition
to weight gain, the symptoms were depression, fatigue, and feeling chronically chilly. Graves' disease seemed a relative picnic by
comparison. Maybe I could just chuck the medicine and tough it
out? I searched some more.

If left untreated, Graves' disease can be fatal.

Okay, so that's a no. I also found a fun little side effect that Dr.
B hadn't mentioned: exophthalmos, a Graves'-related condition
that causes your eyes to protrude from your sockets, giving you
a lovely bug-eyed stare. Exophthalmos can happen at any time
around a primary Graves' diagnosis, either before or up to two
years after, and there is no way to predict which lucky Graves'
patients will hit the jackpot. The site I looked at helpfully noted
that exophthalmos is commonly found in certain breeds of dogs,
including pugs and shih tzus.

I laughed at the absurdity of it all, then cried a little, and then
pulled myself together because there were far worse things in life
than looking and feeling like an overweight, depressed, bug-eyed
shih tzu. Once I had come to my senses I did what seemed only
logical. I ate an entire frozen pizza, knowing that my heady days
of consequence-free caloric abandon would soon be drawing to
a close.

Within a couple of weeks of starting the medicine, I was feeling
like my old self again—sleeping well, no more heart palpitations,

and absolutely panicked about my weight. I obsessively checked my eyes in the mirror several times a day to make sure I wasn't slowly turning into Popeye. I dragged Thomas into the madness as well, sticking my face in his at random times, such as when he was brushing his teeth or watching TV.

"Do my eyes look different? Do they?"

"Your eyes look beautiful."

"But do they look *different?*"

"Jen, I love you, and they look the same, *and* they look like they're blocking my view of the Cowboys game. Can you please calm down and stop interrogating me?"

I did gain some weight, of course—my still-prodigious appetite was writing checks that my body could no longer cash, so my linebacker fare (those big football players who eat a dozen eggs and a gallon of milk for breakfast every day are my heroes) went straight to my hips. I grew nostalgic for the fiery, calorie-incinerating effects of untreated hyperthyroidism. The battleships ditty floated back into my consciousness for the first time in years, and I did my best to beat it back.

I thought I was over this, that I'd finally learned to accept my body no matter what, hips and all. But no—I'd actually just learned to accept it as it was when I liked it. The idea of its getting any bigger, in a way that was largely out of my control, was something I hadn't gotten around to accepting yet. Clearly I was nowhere near psychologically ready for the physical effects of pregnancy. (Note to self: Renew prescription for birth control pills.)

I remembered a magazine factoid reporting that something like 54 percent of surveyed women would rather be hit by a Mack truck than gain a hundred pounds. At the time, I'd found that appalling. They'd rather suffer possible paralysis—and *death*—than gain weight? But now I could sort of see where they were coming from; swapping health in favor of looking good no longer seemed like such an outrageous trade. It made me really depressed that this warped view was beginning to look reasonable to me. Maybe it was just my thyroid that was making me depressed. Come to think of it, it was a little nippy in here.

But I really was feeling much better physically, and I was starting to see the value in that. It was refreshing to climb a flight of stairs and not feel winded, to have my innate sweatiness retreat to more normal levels. My heart no longer felt as if it would pound right through my chest and head out for the evening without me. And, at least so far, my eyes did not appear to be making a break for it. It took a while to get the level of the meds right—I swung back and forth from hyperthyroid (manic and unstable) to hypothyroid (depressed and lazy) so often that Thomas affectionately began calling me "Sybil"—but once we nailed it, things calmed down.

My weight gain, and my obsessive thoughts about my weight, also calmed down, even though my baseline weight settled at a point I would previously have been wildly uncomfortable with (and, interestingly, one *much* higher than I ever hit in those dark high school days, when I felt destined to a large, loveless existence in the tuba cubby). It became apparent that while I would never hover on the brink of malnourishment, I was equally unlikely to yank the nearby planets out of alignment with my gravitational pull.

I didn't have a Big Dramatic Moment, like they do in the movies. I did not fire off a snappy string of self-assured zingers to someone who insulted my big-boned self amid a chorus of applause and shouts of "You go, girl!" I did not don a dirndl and twirl around on an Alp, marveling at the majesty of life and my place in it. It wasn't an instant epiphany. It was more a quiet, gradual acceptance of who I was, regardless of the fact that my body had decided to weigh whatever it damn well pleased (the *nerve!*). Even if my thyroid ultimately caused me to blimp out like Violet Beauregarde, I was healthy, and for the most part I was happy. Like a self-centered Sally Field, I realized that *I* liked me—I really liked me.

And that was how I finally managed to sink my own battleships.

Beauty Queens & Ugly Ducklings

More Than Pretty

TARA BRAY SMITH

*T*he summer before I turned sixteen my mother pulled some strings with an old friend of hers from high school and got me a job at Burger King. These were the kinds of strings my parents could pull, alas. I was still too young to work the kitchen and was thus confined to the register, which was fine with me because that was the easiest job in the store, though I wouldn't have minded working french fries. My manager, Lita, and I were always fighting because I'd steal them on my way to the employee restroom, where I would never turn on the light; I would just pee in the dark and eat my stolen french fries, stuffing them into my mouth as if I hadn't eaten for days. When Lita finally caught me, she made me wash the windows of the store as punishment, and I was so angry and ashamed that I called my stepmother on the pay phone outside and cried. I was fifteen and there I was having to wash the Kuhio Avenue Burger King windows in my hairnet and my navy-and-burgundy poly ensemble (with visor). Life was not fair.

July passed. I curbed the french fry–copping habit and moved on to vanilla shakes. Then my other, bigger boss, Randall, told me he wanted me to compete in the Miss Burger King Hawaii contest to represent the Waikiki store. At the time I knew it wasn't cool to work at Burger King. For instance, my boyfriend, Heath, always deposited me several blocks down the street when he dropped me off for my shifts and never visited, though I told him I'd give him free food. So it followed it was even *less* cool to be in a Burger King pageant, since pageants were for horse-toothed girls who weren't as attractive in real life, and Burger King was just lame, no explanation needed. But because of the Lita problem, I was worried about getting fired. Also there was the "special" factor, as in I'd get out of most of August's shifts, with pay. So I told Randall yes. One week later, there I was with all the other burger princesses in a van on our way to VIP Models down in Chinatown, where I would be taught beauty secrets.

We were a dozen glossy heads, twenty-four tilting forearms. We had on our listening faces.

"Girls, you know what's most important when you're putting on your makeup for any occasion? What is it, girls?"

In unison we tried to answer but no one really knew.

"Base!" someone called out, and the auburn-haired lady with delicate skin in front of us winced. She looked too short to have been a model. Anyway, what did we care? In front of our special makeup mirrors we were incandescent. Our teeth shone as if they were made of mother-of-pearl; our eyes were jewels.

"Base!" another person yelled. It was silent after that.

Queenie, our "helper"—fortyish, many stud earrings, can-do blazer—stood in back and looked exasperated. The delicate expert herself folded her arms across her flat chest and set her lips in an uneven smear.

"Girls, what is most important in your own personal makeup regimen is that you wash your face! There's a bowl of water and a washcloth in front of you!"

I was confused by all the people involved with our becoming Miss Burger King and wondered why so few of them had real jobs. We had Queenie, of course; and the auburn-haired, bisque-colored ex-model, now an agent; along with her husband, a shaggy, leering photographer in khaki shorts and a Magnum shirt. The pageant expert was a former Miss Kona Coffee, or Miss Billfish, I can't remember which; the poise and etiquette consultant was from Penney's.

Queenie walked down the aisles checking to make sure that a plastic bowl—were they really dog food bowls, as they appeared?—was sitting in front of each of us.

"Let's first work on the basics!" the ex-model said. "Washing your face! Okay, then! Pick up your washcloths!" Done. "Put them in the water!" Done. "Make sure the water is blood temperature when you put your washcloth under the tap!" Our heads bobbed up and down. "If you need to know what blood temperature is, run your wrists under the water and see if it feels too hot or too cold! If it feels just right, that's blood temperature!"

I would go and feel for blood temperature the very next day.

"This is not soap!"

We sat in four rows. Our backs were straight; our elbows perched exactly at breast level, hands framing our faces. I cast my eyes down at my own face, but only when I was sure no one was looking, because, really, who likes a vain girl?

"Now make little circles!"

Sample-size Shiseido and white washcloths were stacked before us, and we looked in the mirror then, straight on, because we were being encouraged to, at last. It was a regulation stare. It was okay now. Our fifteen- and sixteen-year-old skin stretched over our exquisitely rounded cheeks like bubble gum just before it explodes. Lights reflected in our eyes—the special makeup lights that made smaller lights in the green around my pupils—and I could see my wide broad lips that had the weird lip thing that wouldn't crease right when I smiled, and I could see the clinging soap and my freckles and all of the red spots on my face. The other girls were smooth and caramel colored, split by black eyebrows, brown eyes, pink-brown mouths. I looked in my mirror at the girls behind me looking in theirs and suddenly everyone was in my vision, all of the girls in the room. And I wondered who was prettiest.

Later the shaggy photographer approached me. Me out of everyone. "I'd like to make some swimsuit shots of you," he said. "You've got a great look." I was fifteen and flattered, and he was a real photographer. I could tell because the camera he carried ruggedly with one hand was big and many-levered and made important clicking sounds.

I met him at his studio after my last shift before the beauty contest break, still in my burgundy uniform. I carried my bathing suit in a bag for the shots.

"Relax," he said. "You're gorgeous. You look like Kathy Ireland."

"Thanks," I said, though Kathy Ireland was a tired shill for Kmart at that point and I would have preferred Stephanie Seymour.

"How about a wet look?"

"Okay," and I went to the bathroom to put my head in the sink. He played rock music. "Growl," he said. "Make it sexy." And, "Whoa! Not that sexy!" He shot me on all fours, like a tiger, my wet curly hair hanging around my face. He came at me from behind, from under, and from the front, and he yeahed and uh-huhed and oh, babyed the whole time. I thought it was fun. When he asked me if I wanted to take my top off for some other shots I said no, politely, and he didn't ask again, but of course it got uncomfortable after that. But really, he was pleased. When I came out of the bathroom after I'd put on my clothes he gave me a diet Coke and told me I was a natural.

"Really sexy," he said. "Really hot."

"Wow. Thanks," I said again.

"How'd you learn to look like that?"

I shrugged. Where does any girl learn to work it? From TV. From sisters and friends and men. I don't think he expected an answer.

"From my mom," I said, and walked out into the sun.

Beauty pageants are comical. They are also tragic, because nothing so stupid should ever be taken so seriously. But who can help it? The moist eyes, the sincere wish to be chosen. Those long oiled legs and the camaraderie—who can resist? Many apparently, since Miss America has had a hard time getting televised in recent years. Yet I remain a fan. There is no false talent for worm eating or "it all started in church" preternatural singing ability. What we are talking about is off-the-shelf beauty: canned, a little tacky, not even of *Top Model* quality, but beauty nonetheless, combined with a sincere telegenic charisma. Girls with Vaseline on their teeth tucking their butts under and trying to look slim in a bathing suit, though that last five pounds was lost using Saran wrap in a sauna two days before. It's all a little sweaty and of dubious quality. I like this.

Once I was at The Closet, a lesbian bar in Chicago's Boystown, near the area where Mayor Daly years ago erected that first rainbow arc, and I was seeing whether I wanted to go on a date. I was twenty-six and had never gone out with a woman before, and I was sitting across from one who said she was gay, though she'd been engaged. She told me that she was just like me. I wondered how we could produce friction then. I was curious, semiattracted, but if she was just like me, how would we produce friction?

The bartender was a tough, slightly butch, platinum-haired woman. She played lesbian music videos featuring cute androgynous girls looking mean. Then she switched it to *Miss America* because Miss Illinois, a tall, dark-haired white girl, was in the final three. When she won, the entire bar erupted into applause. We clapped and clapped. Probably Miss Illinois had been on television before—Little Miss So-and-So, Teen Miss This-and-That; you must qualify for these things, after all—but she smiled the smile of someone who was not sure she would ever be on TV again. She was not in preparation, not an actress trying out a role. She had already *become,* right in front of our eyes. It really was never going to get any better than this.

Sometimes, when I want something really badly and I'm not sure I'm going to get it, I picture being onstage in a line, me and whomever I am up against. There's a judge, someone I don't know; and there's a judgment, a decision to be rendered based on a question asked. The question might be: Who is the fairest of them all? Who among these would you want to spend the rest of your life on a desert island with? Who will you marry? Who will you break up with? Who's got what it takes? Who is the most *quality person?* Someone is always judging, sizing me up along with the other Janes, a few on my left, a few on my right, and I am never sure if I will win, even in my own contest. In fact, I don't think I've ever won. There is always someone better. Maybe she's got all the smarts and a better body. Or her clothes are nicer, or she likes herself more. Girls' stuff. Why can't we all sit around in our pj's and braid each other's hair? The comfort of hierarchy, knowing one's place, the easy sexual tension of women, how flippantly we talk about desire, titillate each other. How loose we are with our gestures, our kisses and pets and flirtations. Once we get out under the lights, it's war. And I always wanted to win.

I learned a trick in eighth grade. It was at my best friend Crystal's thirteenth-birthday slumber party, the one at which her dad got drunk and told us all to shut up and then sped away on his motorcycle. Crystal was blond and tall and a little fat. She also had a constantly stuffed-up nose, which she tried to clear every so often in the middle of speaking, like this: "Tara, *[snort]* who are we going to invite to the slumber party *[snort]*?"

Neither of us was very cool, so a birthday slumber party was not so much a celebration as a strategic initiative. Sina, Dionne, Paige, and Davelyn were invited. Davelyn was named after her parents, Dave and Lynn. Sina was Samoan. The other two had cool-girl names, names especially chosen by their parents to look good in a junior high school yearbook, signed in silver ink and surrounded by swirls and exploding underlines. These girls wore their blue eyeliner on the inside of their bottom eyelids, had surfer boyfriends named Chad and Troy, and could make a perfect feather with their bangs.

I was short, white, and had big boobs and hairy arms, which I tried shaving when I was in second grade. This unfortunate combination was enough to make me do essentially anything to be liked. So for Crystal's birthday I learned a trick. In one of my countless afternoons with myself in front of a mirror (I found a mole inside my vagina once), I discovered that if I hunched my shoulders over in just the right way so that my breasts loosened from my pectoral muscles and hung free, I could jog my body up and down and my breasts would circle in opposite directions, like baseballs winding up, or like swinging oranges around in the foot of two socks. *Crazy eyes.*

So I did it for them; I took off my shirt and swung my oversized knockers till Dionne, Paige, etc., fell over laughing. "Jugs! Hooters! What's another word? Knockers, ha ha ha, chichis! Look at Tara's tits; look at her boobs!" I had never been that funny before, never brought girls to tears, never been so much the center of attention than on that sleeping-bag-and-stinky-T-shirt night, standing in a knot of thirteen-year-old girls as they cried, "Look at them! Just look at them, will you?"

Until Miss Burger King.

The pageant was held at Waimea Falls Park, which used to be a supposedly authentic Hawaiian place with crafts and hula dancers but then went bankrupt sometime after the Japanese bubble, so there were just all these lost peacocks roaming around. It was held under a tent, and there were cameras, and the owner of the Hawaii Burger King franchise was there, with his attractive blond wife, the one my mom had known in high school. We drove around back in our special vans, and everyone came from my store, and all my family flew in from the outer islands, and it was *the big night.*

Instead of being escorted out in my bathing suit by a marine, I had the guy who usually works the cold toppings station and we were in matching aloha separates. For talent, I sang a ditty that I wrote in the van one day to the tune of "Mr. Sandman":

> Burger King, bring me a dream.
> Bring me a burger like I've never seen.
> Piled high with lettuce, tomato, and mayo.
> I want a burger that will make my day—oh,
> Burger King, bring me a meal.
> I feel like chicken but I want a great deal.
> I want it now, hot 'n' juicy,
> Those chicken tenders, what a doozy.
> Please bring me my tasty dream,
> Burger King, bring me—please, please bring me,
> Burger King, bring me my dream!

There came the evening gown competition for which we all wore muumuus, and then it was down to me and the girl from Kaua'i who did the Burger King rap, and the tent seemed really close to my head, and under my arms was wet, and I couldn't feel my teeth, and then I won.

I have a picture of me afterward, just one, a Polaroid. I have on a turquoise muumuu and a crown, and I'm smiling really hard and holding all these roses up to my chest just like on all the parodies. The whites of my eyes and my teeth are very bright, like the sash, which reads, MISS BURGER KING HAWAII 1985. No one else brought a camera. And of course Heath didn't come.

I got a $100 gift certificate from Zales and a three-month modeling course at Cathy Muller, in which I never enrolled. A brief item appeared in the social diary of the Honolulu paper. Months passed; I didn't have any official duties. Not even one ribbon cutting. I did get a modeling job out of the whole thing, a Japanese shampoo ad in which I sat on a cliff and watched the sunrise, looking naked while the photographer took a picture of my hair falling down my back. The lady assistant had to tape my boobs together so that they wouldn't fall to the side and ruin the shot.

Sometimes I remind my stepmom about the whole thing, and I roll my eyes and say, "God that was so ridiculous. . . Can you believe I . . . ?," that kind of thing. It's a form of reverse boasting, and I can relive the moment protected by irony. "But you were into it," she retorts. "Into the whole thing. I'm so glad I kept that bowl. Every time you get on your high horse about something I just think of that bowl with your name engraved on it, TARA SMITH, MISS BURGER KING HAWAII 1985, and I feel better."

I feel ashamed. So I repeat the story, as I am doing now. To a friend or a stranger or someone I want to make laugh. I'll sing the Burger King song, and I'll tell about how we had to wear muu-muus, and I'll include the detail about the Burger King rap. I'll feel safe and exposed at the same time, protected in a roomful of flash. It's intended to disarm.

I did end up going out with a woman, though the one who produced friction was nine years younger than me. Somehow in my midtwenties I hadn't gotten enough of whatever I was sup-posed to have gotten at eighteen, so I had an affair with a much younger woman, a freshman at Mount Holyoke. It was exciting and beautiful and sexy, and I was in love. I visited her at college. I smoked blunts with her and I played bus driver and drank Bacardi Limón with Coca-Cola with her friends Jen and Lisi, who lived down the hall. Jen had been a teenage beauty queen, too: Princess Kay of the Milky Way, which allowed her the once-in-a-lifetime chance of seeing her own face carved in butter at the Minnesota State Fair. When she won she got a cow-print sash, and the next day she wore her crown to school. There was a TV crew and everything.

On the door to the bathroom on Jen and Lisi's hall there was a pink circle with a blue arrow attached, made out of construction paper, like a chore wheel. It read: MEN, NO MEN, and WISH THERE WERE MEN. They were supposed to use it to show when they've escorted a man to the bathroom. It was on NO MEN every time I visited. I spent a lot of time in that bathroom, giddy, worried, wondering what I was doing at Mount Holyoke at twenty-seven years old. I'd walk into a toilet stall and sit down without pulling down my pants. I'd decide I'd wait there for a few minutes, and then I'd flush the toilet and walk back. Signs were everywhere: taped to the walls, on all sides, lined up one on top of another like windowpanes. A pink sign was about breast self-examinations and a white one was about the food pyramid, and acne. There were order forms for Mount Holyoke blankets, to benefit the crew team, and reminders about the environment. In front of me when I flushed the toilet was a sign at knee level asking, ARE YOU ABOUT TO PRAY TO THE PORCELAIN GOD? BEFORE IT'S TOO LATE, CALL HEALTH SERVICES. I'd walk to the sink and drink some water. Then I'd smile at myself, a ritual, to check my fake tooth. I had knocked the real one out at a party six months after the Miss Burger King pageant, so stoned I didn't even feel it. My father never got mad at me for that one. He figured losing the tooth was punishment enough. I wondered when I'd have to replace the cap, which always looked a little bit darker than the rest of them, but maybe that was just me.

Pear Apparent

BETH LISICK

*L*unch hour is a big deal for a receptionist. At least it was for me back when I was twenty-six and answering phones in the advertising department at a weekly newspaper. I had recently moved up from being the "assistant to the assistant to the publisher." The new position was okay but considerably less kinetic than the last. I sat, I greeted, I forwarded. I could take no breaks during the workday, save for the occasional sprint to the bathroom, drying my hands on my pants on the way back down the hall. So when lunchtime rolled around, I couldn't run away from those phones fast enough. I'd get clearance from my supervisor and disappear for sixty minutes straight. Always the full sixty.

As the months passed, the hour itself wasn't enough anymore. I was finding it necessary to put greater and greater distance between those phones and me, to physically leave it all behind. The nearby lunching options, places polluted by my coworkers, had long been exhausted: the mediocre deli, the semifancy bistro, the Mexican restaurant run by nice Chinese people. This was my new thing: As the clock ticked down to my impending lunch hour, I would get my jacket on and grab my keys, positioning myself for a quick exit. Then, with the flip of the right number on my desktop digital clock, I would dash out to my car, usually parked several blocks away, and drive to a new neighborhood, hazarding parking fiascoes and traffic tickets, just for a change of scenery.

On one such afternoon, in a downpour, I drove to a French *crêperie*. The food there was delicious, if a bit pricey for my budget, but I reasoned that I *needed* to enjoy such a luxury to maintain sanity. Decades of articles, usually titled something such as *You Deserve It!*, in women's magazines backed me up. I sat down solo at the counter, ordered a sparkling lemonade and a mushroom crepe, and broke out a novel to read. I felt transformed. Instantly it was as if I didn't have a job, or at least the kind of job that required me to repeat the same two phrases over and over and over again, day after day.

As I was leaving, with about eight minutes to get back to the phones, these two kinda fabulous boys approached me. Daniel and Jose. They said that they were students at the Vidal Sassoon salon downtown and were wondering if I would like to be a hair model for an upcoming show. I swear their little gay noses must have smelled it on me. Not only my desperation to be temporarily transported into some other world, but the fact that I had an actual docket as a hairstylist's victim. In the previous ten years, I had done a number of hair modeling jobs, sometimes for a little money, sometimes simply for the free cut and color. Back in those days, I would allow the stylists to do whatever they wanted to me. Bangs, razor cuts, flattops, jagged asymmetrical flips. Believe me, I'd had every dumb, trendy, unflattering haircut and color from Bangkok to Berlin. (That's figuratively speaking, though I was once backpacking around Parma, Italy, a trip financed in part by a hair show, when I was plucked off the street by a small village stylist and asked to participate in a *dimostrazione*. I said *si*.) If it had been possible to go pro with this sort of thing, I would have done it. I loved not caring about my hair, and up against all these fussy, fashionable cut-and-dye jobs, it was a little criminal what puny regard I had for the craftsmanship of the architect. Whatever was left on my head would just gather and grow, mostly unattractively, until another opportunity came along.

The boys gave me a card for the salon, telling me to come in that evening when I got off work. The color and cuts were being done all day, and the show was set for the next night at a nearby nightclub. There were to be thirty models in all and they were still trawling the streets recruiting. I told them of course I'd be there and raced back to my desk with a renewed sense of phone-answering purpose that lasted roughly an hour.

Good afternoon, how may I help you? Can you please hold? Good afternoon, how may I help you? Can you please hold? Good afternoon, how may I help you? Can you please hold my hair while I get sick about how my soul is being harvested by this monotonous job?

Five o'clock finally came. How I adored it like a familiar lover. I darted through the sheets of rain and got in my pickup, heading downtown to what I anticipated would be an oasis of sorts. But it was, after all, a hair salon. Another bustling gossip hut with too many mirrors, too many magazines, and terrible music played too loudly. While I was able to enjoy salons on certain levels—the characters and stories, the scalp massages and free white wine—the undercurrent of anxiety in such places, like at makeup counters or gyms, wore on me quickly. The approval seeking and the grinding desire for self-improvement nearly vibrated under the constant thrum of screeching pop songs. Still, I remained upbeat. It was my nature.

As soon as I walked through the thick glass door, Daniel came bustling toward me. He was so cute, brown haired and a little wiry, wearing a T-shirt that would have been snug on a toddler.

"This is Beth!" he announced. "We met her at the *crêperie!*"

I held up an awkward hand and waved to the assorted stylists and assistants and models who were buzzing around in "let's put on a show" mode. Everyone was close to my age, midtwenties, and representing an impressive range of urban style and acne-free skin tones.

"Let's get you into a chair," Daniel said, leading me by my wrist. "What we're thinking of doing is going light, light, light. Shimmery light."

"That's great," I said, plopping onto the cushion. My hair was in its natural mousy brownish state, but it always bleached up easily. Stylists usually commented favorably on this—how quickly the color could be sucked out by their chemicals. It gave me a hollow pride, as if my hair's ability to lighten was a special talent and I was just giving it a stage to shine.

And so our journey began. The application of bleach, the sitting around, the rinsing, the toning, the second rinsing, the foil-encased low lights, the sitting around again, the third rinsing, the towel drying, the cutting, the blow drying, the product application, the touch-up cutting, the final drying. It was about four and a half hours later that I became the proud owner of, as Daniel called it, "a champagne-colored graduated box bob with cognac-tinted disconnection and baby doll fringe."

It was pretty sweet, I admit, though I knew that after the next night's show, it would begin its inevitable demise. Daniel and I would run into each other on the street in a few weeks and he would be horrified at what had happened to his creation.

Exhausted and hoping to be excused, I was on my way to the dressing room when Daniel informed me that I still had to pay a visit to the wardrobe people. Most of the shows I'd done previously had required me only to sit in a chair onstage in front of other hairdressers at an exhibition, though a few made me "walk." This usually meant putting on a brightly colored shapeless smock or a black T-shirt and jeans and making a pass down a runway, trying to pause and pivot to show off the cut. The Sassoon kids, however, had something more elaborate in mind.

Daniel walked me into the back where a few other girls with fancy new hairdos were trying on clothes. From some of the conversations I overheard, it appeared that many of the "models" were actual models. A lot of them were complaining about not wanting their hair changed too much so the pictures in their portfolios would still be relevant. Discovering they were real models made me feel better. Sure, I didn't look as good as they did, but none of us was getting paid for this. The smug girl inside me felt superior being the $7-an-hour receptionist who dabbled in their world only for the free cuts and color. I didn't actually *care*.

In my late teens, I had thought briefly about modeling. I was sure I didn't have the face or the ambition, but I had a semblance of the body. By some fluke of nature, or perhaps an unchecked thyroid condition, I was tall and thin like the girls I saw in magazines. Fortunately, the hellacious and degrading parts of modeling were apparent from afar and I never chose to pursue it. Just this hair stuff. Hair modeling felt fine because people were judging you based only on what a third party had recently done to your scalp. Plus, we all know what very important thinking organ lies just underneath the scalp. If I squinted, I could believe hair modeling had something to do with my brain. The UC Santa Cruz student in me knew this was all pure sublimation, but I was sticking to it.

I walked over to "wardrobe," a corner of the salon with a rolling rack of clothes, and introduced myself to Gina and Heather. They looked me over and handed me a tight black dress with beaded fringe at the bottom. I could tell right away it wasn't going to fit.

"I think this is too small for me," I said, making a dumb apologetic face. "I'm a lot, uh, wider than this."

"Just try it on and see. You might have to suck in a little."

Suck in? It was my hip bones and butt cheeks I was talking about. Neither were pneumatic.

The other girls were getting changed right there in the middle of the floor, so I dropped my cords, sheepish about the trails of spider veins on my thighs, which were in some places clustered like blue and green bruises. I'd had them since elementary school. At least I wasn't wearing one of my more terrible pairs of underwear.

It was a little saggy, like most of my cotton Jockey for Her pairs, but at least it didn't have holes.

I pulled the dress over my head and tried to squeeze it over my ass. I crossed my ankles, pressed my thighs together, and bent over. After managing to pull the hem down, I immediately wanted to take it off before anyone saw me. It was sausage-casing tight. I shuffled over, awaiting my inevitable shaming. "Oh, boy," Gina said, shaking her head. "Heather, come look at this."

"Yeah, I can't really move," I said. I was doing that thing where I was trying to abort any of her comments by asserting that I had thought of them already.

Heather came over, dragging Daniel by the hand. They stopped about ten feet in front of me and Daniel put his hand over his mouth.

"I'm sorry," he said, looking at them. "Isn't there something else for her to wear?"

Heather and Gina sighed big. It was late. They looked over at the rack and then started sizing up the girls who were already dressed. They looked back at Daniel. Then back at the middle third of my body. At this point, they basically stopped making eye contact with me or addressing me directly. Finally, someone spoke.

"I mean, it's just so *interesting*," Heather said. She circled around me. "She doesn't really present as a pear at first."

Present as a pear? I paused to ponder whether this particular phrase had ever been uttered in all of human existence. And then I was struck because I had always thought I'd known what a pear-shaped body looked like. A particular meter maid came to mind. Perhaps that pharmacist with the wasp waist but the bottom like a bisected basketball? Then again, no. Not the pharmacist. She also had some boobs. She definitely was not, like me, lucky to drop into an A cup at the highest point of monthly blotation. A pear meant that you carried your weight on your ass and hips. It was your center of gravity. You were disproportionate. You were bottom-heavy. Mud flaps and saddlebags, that's what we're talking about.

Clearly, I was halfway down the rabbit hole.

Heather broke me out of it, coming up with a brilliant idea. So brilliant, I could almost see the lightbulb above her head.

"Where's the other pear?" she asked brightly, looking around for another girl with a sack of grain in her undies. "Maybe they could switch outfits, because I think the other one is a bit more, um, narrow."

"I'll go find her!" I volunteered out of nowhere, imagining that we would surely recognize one another immediately and have a lot to talk about.

I scampered through the mirrored hallway of the salon, my eyes trained on every hunk of rump and thigh I passed, curious to find the other pear.

"Here she is!" Jose called. "She says she'll switch with the other one."

I smiled briefly and then dropped my eyes to her bottom half. She didn't look big at all! To me she appeared positively waifish, but apparently everyone else figured that, if an avalanche hit, she and I would be the first two kebabs on the spit.

"I don't think I'll fit in that one either!" the pear said kindly, ripping off her frock and tossing it into my arms.

Was she a blond? A brunet? I honestly cannot recollect what she looked like from the waist up, though her bony haunches will be burned into my memory until my final hour.

I handed her dress to Jose for a second as we attempted to exhume my body from mine. Gina stepped in to assist, grabbing it under my armpits as I bowed toward her like a praying mantis, squeezing my butt in an attempt to make it *that much* smaller.

"Don't rip it!" Heather cried. "Ease it over her hips!"

"Easy . . . Easy . . . " Daniel cooed. "Easy does it."

"Maybe we could sort of roll it up her," Gina suggested.

It was as if they were sliding a condom off a redwood.

I closed my eyes, trying hard not to think about how I was standing in the middle of a downtown San Francisco hair salon in my pathetic droopy underwear while five onlookers determined whether or not they'd just wasted four and a half hours mistakenly grooming an undercover pear. A conniving pear, at that. One who didn't even *present* as a pear at first.

My former dress slid over the other girl's frame without a hitch, while hers clung to mine like saran wrap.

"That's a little better," Heather sighed, running a hand down my hip bone as if to convince herself once and for all it was real. I could have sworn that Daniel looked over at her and mouthed, "Sorry!"

When I had arrived, I was my regular self. Excited. Game for anything. Now I felt defeated. I had wanted to be the girl without any ego, the one who would show up and let them do anything to her hair, the one who would wear whatever dress they gave her, without complaining that something made her look fat or didn't complement her skin tone. For the first time in my life, my body was getting in the way of my plans. It had created a problem. The Great Vidal Sassoon Pear Problem of 1995. I changed back into my clothes and took off out into the rain, thinking how lame this was.

I showed up the next night anyway, prepared for the possibility that they might have found a skinnier girl in the meantime and would want to cut me loose. "It's their fucking problem if they do," I grumbled, shaking my graduated box bob this way and that. My muscled thighs and wide hips and small boobs had always done right by me before, and if these Sassoon people didn't like them, they could just fire me from this stupid-ass "job" that didn't even pay. And honestly, as a white middle-class woman, I was kind of enjoying this mild form of persecution. It didn't happen very often.

"I'm five feet eight inches and 115 pounds, and I'm too big for their show!" I imagined saying on the evening news as the reporter encircled my hips with a measuring tape and women across the country gasped in horror.

But as it turns out, they didn't replace me. As a matter of fact, no one made mention of the forbidden fruit the whole night until the end of the show, when we tried to squeeze onto a long bench for a photo op. There wasn't enough room for all of us, so some girls had to sit on laps.

"Come over and sit on the pear!" I said to a lost-looking nymph with a bird pinned to her updo. "And bring your little pal there. I think I can even hold two."

Fine with This

MAE RESPICIO

The Art of Kissing

Sixth-grade science camp, somewhere in the Santa Cruz Mountains near the Pacific Ocean. I am ten. It's my first time away from home without parental supervision. Five girls and I share a cabin with our counselor, Seacliff Stacey, who's in the twelfth grade and like all of the other counselors has a camp name—there are Hiking Heather, Diane Dolphin, and Bonfire Bruce. In the middle of one night Seacliff Stacy goes out with Compass Curt for a smoke, leaving a handful of impressionable ten-year-olds alone in a damp cabin room. Someone turns off the lights and we sit in a circle, Indian-style on the cold wood floor. Each girl shines a flashlight onto her face and we start by telling spooky ghost stories, which don't last but a few moments before they turn into kissing tales. One girl has seen a French kiss. Another has two boyfriends, both in the seventh grade, although she hasn't touched lips with either. The final, a redhead in braided pigtails and braces, says, lisping, "I kissed someone at the tide pools yesterday." She describes it—wet, salty, a little gross. The redhead goes on to say that she's kissed a lot of boys.

For the first time, I think about what kissing might feel like and wonder which boys might find me pretty enough to kiss. Seacliff Stacey—now *she's* kissable, agree all of my new friends.

That entire week we watch Stacey, memorizing her hairstyle and makeup, observing how the boy counselors follow her around during lunch like members of a cult. She is who we aim to be with her feathered bangs, neon hoop earrings, and frosted mauve lip gloss. In the mornings we wake early to see if we can curl our bangs to match hers, even though it's too misty near the ocean and Aqua Net doesn't hold our hair up. On the last day of camp, Sea-cliff Stacey lets all of the girls in our cabin try out her gloss. I have never worn lip gloss. I watch the others before carefully squeezing a dime of it, shimmering and mushy, onto my pinkie and then smearing it onto my lips and telling myself I won't let my parents know. I think I might look older with it on but it's hard to tell. It feels foreign, like jam I forgot to wipe off. My cabinmates and I pose for each other with our high bangs and made-up faces, all of us puckering in the mirror.

Miss (Asian) America

Each year, I am allowed to stay up late to watch my favorite annual television show, the *Miss America Pageant*. It's the sparkly dresses that I love, the way the contestants cascade shiny and perfect down the stairs during the evening gown part. The talent competition is a kind of wondrous joy; I hold my breath during performances of my favorites, such as Miss Tennessee's stirring, jazzed-up electric guitar rendition of "Für Elise" (she's wearing a tuxedo!) or when Miss Georgia juggles batons, blindfolded while walking backward.

Right along with the fifty others I practice my S waves, gracing my hand softly across my collarbones before waving it again in a move called "touching the pearls." Sometimes, during commercial breaks, I wonder why none of the pretty ladies look like my mother—when she's the most beautiful one of all. None of them have black hair. None of them have dark skin. Does that mean I'll never be Miss America? I practice fake crying while mouthing *Thank you! Thank you!* The contestants onstage glitter and blow kisses to the camera.

The History of Smooth Legs

The first day of seventh grade is terrifying, especially at a new school with no friends. It is lonely sitting at a table solo, hoping that no one will notice but that someone will sit down, maybe to talk about Trapper Keepers. A girl approaches and introduces herself, says, "I saw you at the bus stop."

Julie is also Filipina. She has a dimple in each cheek and super-straight teeth. It is a California summer, the sun and the wind cool on our arms, and I am proud of my new yellow Esprit shorts.

Julie bites into her sandwich and asks what subject I have for homeroom. I'm about to tell her when her eyes take on an unreal roundness. She runs a hand down my leg. "You're hairy!" Julie says, and she begins to laugh. "Don't you shave?" she asks.

Shave? I've never thought about shaving before. You're supposed to shave your legs before the first day of middle school? How am I supposed to know that?

That night, I steal my dad's razor and in the shower shave my legs for the first time, not really knowing how and not knowing about things such as razor burn. Despite a few patchy lines and the fact that I haven't yet asked my mother's permission, my legs feel silky and I feel grown-up, how I'm pretty sure the models in *YM* and *Teen* magazines feel. The next time I wear those shorts, I make sure to tell my new friend.

Magic Tricks

It is the ninth grade—I still have not kissed anyone. I have crushes on boys at school and on Joey McIntyre from New Kids on the Block, but I don't share these thoughts with anyone. Mainly I just look at myself in the mirror, wishing my hair were blonder or my body more developed. I am the only one of my friends who has not yet experienced a growth spurt.

One crush is Brian, a kid with skate-punk hair who wears worn-out checkered Vans and is someone everybody likes. He's geeky but cute in a hipster-before-his-time sort of way that later in college will work on girls to his advantage. In homeroom he likes to play "magic trick." That's when he taps on my shoulder and says, "I have a magic trick for you." He'll turn his back and when he turns around again he has stuck a pencil up each nostril. "Magic trick!" he shouts, and for some reason, the whole class loves this. Every day in the hallway Brian smiles at me and says, "Hey." Sometimes he hangs out at my locker during breaks asking stupid questions, and whenever I glance at him he quickly looks away, as if he's been watching.

At the end of the year, lots of freshmen huddle in the courtyard to sign yearbooks. Brian is there and he scribbles furiously into mine; I can't wait to read what he's written (maybe he's asked me to a dance?). I'm about to write in his when Sarah, a tall pretty girl with freckles and golden hair, grabs his hand. Brian takes his yearbook from me before I can think of something pithy, maybe tenth-grader-like, to write. A few minutes later, from across the way, I watch them kiss.

I get home and flip open to the page where Brian has signed the same thing as everyone else: "Have a great summer. Don't break too many hearts."

Why does everyone write that when I've never been so fortunate?

You're Welcome

Jimmy Lopez is the resident baseball player bully who sits in the back of sophomore English chewing Skoal, making fun of fat girls, saying how much he wants to bang the teacher, and generally getting all of the cool crowd to laugh. Every one-liner Jimmy offers is reinforced by hyenalike laughter, even from the nerds who want only to fit in.

During class, Jimmy takes a bottle of Keri lotion from his backpack, pumps a few squirts into his hands, and hurls it toward the front of the room when the teacher's back is turned. The bottle lands on the floor and the white lotion explodes, splatting onto a student's head and across the chalkboard. The teacher raises a fist, demanding angrily, "Who did this?" No one snitches. Then she looks at me, her straight-A student who could read all day if she had the chance. I point at Jimmy Lopez and immediately the teacher assigns him detention without letting him defend himself. She knows he did it. He's done other things.

For a moment, I consider that I may have forever ruined any chance of a decent prom date. Everyone stares at me in shock; my peers may have the same thought. It doesn't matter if this will affect my social life. I don't go out drinking on weekends along Jahant Road. I am class secretary/treasurer and a member of the speech and debate team. Other girls wear lipstick and talk about what sex feels like, but these aren't elements of my tenth-grade existence. For some reason I don't wish for them to be in the same way that my friends do.

When the bell rings, Jimmy Lopez whispers in my ear, "Thanks a lot, ugly gook bitch." This takes me by surprise. Is this what I am? Ugly? Asian? A female dog? Jimmy doesn't make this statement public, just says it loud enough, his voice joking and serious, to make the hair on my neck tingle. No one else hears what he says or notices the smile on his face. For the rest of the year, he'll say this to me each time he passes.

City of Angels

I am twenty-one and freshly graduated with a journalism degree. For the first time I live on my own, a five-hour drive away from overprotective, religious Filipino parents of an only child.

Los Angeles is a strange bubble with commonplace clichés, all of them true. There are the older men, their trophy wives hooked onto their arms as they get into red Ferraris. Traffic loads every street and freeway. Strangers are not friendly unless you're a producer or director or someone who can advance their careers.

What's most noticeable are the women. High school prom queens from across the nation have moved to L.A. to become famous actresses. They are tall, thin, and well styled with balloon lips, halter tops, and big confidence. These women have no inhibitions. They love themselves, love to talk about themselves, and every five minutes will check out their reflections in a window or apply mascara in the rearview mirror (while driving). These women have porcelain skin and angled jaws, and I am told by billboards and big screens that this is called beautiful. Never before have I seen them—so many of them—in person, this kind of airbrushed charlatan beauty. They can be found in the Valley or on the Westside, in restaurants (both patrons and waitresses), at bus stops and malls, down the tampon aisle at Vons. They are who the sixteen-year-olds in Idaho wish to be, and they are everything I am not.

All Those Men

After college life, I begin to realize that I do have something physically appealing to offer, since I get hit on in bars with my girlfriends, down bookstore aisles, while stuck in gridlock on the 405, or during Mass in church. Some of these men include Mr. I Only Know How to Talk about Myself; or Mr. I Have a Handicapped Parking Placard That I Illegally Use (Even Though I'm Not Handicapped); and Mr. I Talk about Ex-Girlfriends on First Dates. I also attract Mr. Asian Fetish Man. ("Are you Filipina? My last girlfriend was Filipina." "Are you from Thailand? My last girlfriend was Miss Thailand.")

"Why is that a pickup line?" I ask my girlfriends.

There's also Mr. Car Boob Man. "Boobs aren't important to me. They're like cars. I'm happy with my crappy car, but if I had a better car, I wouldn't mind. Like breasts on women," he says.

"Oh," I say.

He calls a lot and I don't return any of his messages.

Speaking the Truth

On a Southwest flight home to visit my parents, I choose an empty seat next to a boy about eight or nine years old, traveling by himself. He looks at me up and down and with no humor or sarcasm asks, "Are you a midget?"

"No," I tell him, almost mad. "I'm five feet two inches. And a half."

The little boy moves on to his next question. "Want to help me color?"

For the rest of the plane ride I help him make paper bag puppets and he forgets about his non–politically correct height comment. Has this little boy read the studies that explain how tall people make more money and are smarter? For years afterward, I am traumatized by his perception. Aren't kids the ones who just tell it as they see it? From that point on I scrutinize every photograph of myself to determine just how short I look. While standing in line at the grocery store I measure the height of my shoulders against others.

Naturally Asian

On the local news is an Asian anchorwoman. She's definitely anchorwoman like with the deep voice, the careful pronunciation, and the helmet hair. Only one thing is wrong—her helmet hair is blond. If I have one pet peeve it's Asian women who dye their hair blond. "It's just not natural," I tell my Asian friends, trying to rally them around my belief that blond Asian women are denouncing their ethnicity.

A few months later, a girlfriend convinces me to splurge on an expensive, fancy haircut at the famous José Eber Salon in Beverly Hills. The place is unbelievable. The staff offers espressos to clients, and actress types strut around shaking their glossy hair like in Pantene commercials. First comes my cut: The stylist takes nearly two hours to meticulously shape each strand. Color comes next.

The stylist says, "How about a couple of blond streaks? It's the newest thing. You'll look fab."

I nod and say okay.

Favorites

During the next few years, I develop a list of favorite actresses. They include Julia Louis-Dreyfus, Heather Locklear, Lea Salonga, Natalie Portman, Jennifer Love Hewitt, and Sarah Michelle Gellar. It's not necessarily because of their thespian wiles but because in newspapers, fashion magazines, and *Entertainment Tonight* interviews they reveal that they're all petite women, five feet three inches or shorter. Hooray for short girls!

I study them on-screen and what they are wearing. Do they look short? Is that how short looks? Could they possibly be considered midgets while walking down the street? Or boarding a plane? On-screen, it's hard to tell.

Dating an Asian Women Does Not a Gay Man Make

A girlfriend tells me a story about a male friend of hers who has this theory: Men who date Asian women are gay. His reasoning: Asian women are androgynous looking—flat chested and boylike—so men attracted to Asian women must be gay. My girlfriend laughs. She says, "Isn't that hilarious? He thinks they're *gay*." What she really means is that I am one of her only two Asian friends so I get to hear this joke.

At first I think about explaining that not all Asian women are tiny lotus blossoms. Some are naturally voluptuous. Others are tall. I want to tell her that of course not all Asian women look alike. Instead, it's easier to fake-laugh and say, "That's *way* too funny." Later, I regret laughing along.

How to Know Him Better

After several years of dating I meet Mr. The One. He is an entire foot taller than I am, even when I wear my sexy black high heels. Considering the others I've dated, he is smart, handsome, and surprisingly normal—by L.A. standards.

This is what I ask about his last girlfriend: "Did she have large boobs?"

He doesn't say anything.

"Well?"

He nods. "Does that matter?" he asks.

"Just curious," I tell him.

How to Look Your Age

At Trader Joe's, when the checkout guy rings up the case of two-buck Chuck from my cart, he says, "ID, Missy." At first I think, *Well, shit. I deserve the respect of being treated my age. I'm in my midtwenties. I'm an educated professional woman who's accomplished a lot for her age. I should no longer be treated like a child.* I hold up my ID to his eye level and he studies it. Then he's begrudging, as if he doesn't believe me: "Okay . . . I guess," he says.

The Next Step

A few years later I've fallen in love; I've married Mr. The One. Now there are marriage responsibilities. We own a house. We share income. One of us does the dishes and the other mows the lawn, and it no longer pains me to say that it's me wearing the yellow rubber gloves with the apron tied around my waist. Despite the feminist in me, at the age of twenty-seven I've realized that I hate taking my car to the shop, killing spiders in bathtubs, and opening jars.

As a legally bound pair, we officially possess reproductive potential. When asked by anyone when we're having children, the mutual answer is a shrug, a no, or a shudder. Excuses include how we both want to travel more, fix up the house, plant a herb garden, and enjoy a quality of life that doesn't involve diapers, spit, and mashed yams.

One afternoon, I visit a friend, a new mother, who is burping her perfect tiny newborn on her shoulder. I tell her I'm sick of Filipino family parties because cousins, aunties, and *lolas* won't stop nagging my husband and me about having children. Every time one of them asks, my defense is now to simply walk away. She reminds me that ten years ago, we both used to say that the only reason we ever wanted to have children was so that our boobs would grow from breastfeeding.

"And do they?" I ask. "Do I at least have that to look forward to?"

"They leak, too." She reveals more changes: bigger boobs, leaking boobs, less sleep, no sleep, less money, more fights with her mother. She says she could go on. "The greatest experience of my life," she tells me, in a way I know that she means it.

The tiny person on her shoulder finally lets out a huge one, like a beer drinker, and my friend holds her up to show me. "Good girl," she says, smiling.

Milestone

Two weeks before I turn thirty my husband asks: "How do you want to celebrate?"

I say, you and me for dinner, no gifts, a quiet fall night.

Dinner is small with four friends downtown, in comfortable L.A. weather best for jeans with sandals. A fancy restaurant with dark paneled walls and old Hollywood in its tone. Shared appetizers—prawns still in their shells. A thirty-year-old's wish: "Let's not mention birthdays. Tonight's simply a nice dinner, no cause for celebration."

Still, someone has to ask, a kind of trap: "How does Three-O *feel?*"

My year has built to this question. All of my girlfriends the same age are considering: What have we not achieved in ten-plus-twenty years? Do we look like thirty-year-olds? Do we look better than we did at twenty? What do thirty-year-olds look like, *feel* like? I remind them that in the fourteenth century there was this saying: Comparisons are odious.

By the dinner's end our waiter brings out something round and chocolate, a single candle dug into its middle. He looks at me—apologetically—and says: "Sorry, but you don't want to hear me sing."

I say to him, "Today I turned twenty-one."

The whole table laughs. The waiter says only, "Well, then, let's buy you a drink!"

Things about Her

It is early one morning, still dark outside. My husband lies next to me, asleep. The alarm blares in a high shrill buzz and I press snooze, edging my way into the nook of his arm and wondering more about what's to come. The week before we both visited my ob-gyn, who explained that once a woman is off the pill, pregnancy could happen right away or it could take as long as a year.

I am married to a man I trust and love. My favorite things about marriage include spooning, cooking together, having secret jokes, continuing to learn about each other, and teaching each other. We are at a point of both feeling ready to take a next step. This surprises me.

Whenever I think about having a baby, I think about the baby in the third person and always as a female pronoun. Already, I know this about her: She'll be mixed, part brown and part white—*hapa*—like a large group of children born in the near future will be.

I can see her, the tiny head of dark hair, her dark eyes and soft skin, those pretty features. These she may later question. When she reaches puberty she'll probably develop small breasts. She'll hate me for it. When she's in high school, the boys may or may not be interested. She will or will not feel crushed. Perhaps she'll cry often, questioning her appearance in the mirror or wondering how she fits into the world outside of her family, what it means to be from two cultures. Probably she won't share any of this with her mother, because when she's a teenager she won't want to talk to me about such things. At times she may hate the shape of her nose or the curve of her eyes. She might say things such as "If only I didn't look like you." I am sure she won't always feel this way.

She'll have questions about men. She'll wonder what qualities she needs to attract someone who will love her in a way that leaves her without doubts. She'll ask: "What things qualify me?" On her list: a Filipina American, a woman, a daughter, a partner, and a friend. Small breasted, just her height, perfectly her age. And she'll be fine with this.

The Ugly Prize

LAURA CATHERINE BROWN

*W*e had a family incident at a lake in Maine one summer long ago. We had never been there before. My mother was driving a borrowed station wagon, fearfully, distrusting her abilities. The decision to stop might have been spontaneous, a road sign spotted on a hot, humid day.

The lake was picture perfect. Evergreens surrounded a sandy shore cluttered with families. The sky was brilliantly blue, wisped with clouds. A lifeguard ensconced in a high, white throne presided over the water where red buoys on yellow twine squared off the swimming zone. An enticing wooden platform floated just inside the ropes. Kids were diving off it. People were sunbathing. Sun glimmered on the water like smiles. It looked delicious.

But we didn't have our bathing suits.

You don't need bathing suits, my mother said. You have your birthday suits.

My older sister, Bridgit, was probably nine, which put me at eight, Alexis at six and a half, and Julia, two years younger. No one was allowed to see us nude, not one another, not my mother. We dressed and undressed covertly, sliding in and out of clothes while draped in nightgowns, changing furtively in dark closets, or under the covers in bed, emerging, ta da, fully dressed. We knew my mother knew this.

Don't be silly, she said—a common directive. Your underwear can be your bathing suit.

Stripped down to our underpants, no bikini tops to cover our chests, trembling, we huddled by the trees, pine needles underfoot, on the edge of the beach. All the other children were in bathing suits that, unlike underwear, didn't turn transparent when wet.

No one's looking at you, my mother said. If you make a run for it, you can get to the water before they even know you've gone by. Then you're home free.

But even if we made it to the water unseen—debatable—we wouldn't be safe. What about boys with snorkeling masks? She didn't know there weren't any. And we'd have to come out of the water eventually in our soggy, see-through underwear.

We clamped our palms over our nipples and refused to move.

Why are you doing that? You don't have breasts! You're children! She became a force of nature, grabbing randomly, pushing us toward the beach. You wanted to go swimming! Well, swim! Swim!

People were glancing up from their blankets.

I don't know what's the matter with them, my mother said, allying herself with strangers. They don't want to go in without bathing suits. Can you believe it? They're children. They think they have something to hide.

Who started crying first? My little sisters? Me? We were all sobbing by the time my mother herded us back to the borrowed station wagon: uptight children, lacking spontaneity, refusing to accept the fun my mother offered.

We must have been, as babies or toddlers, naked, un-self-conscious, and happy in our skin, proud of our belly buttons. But I have no memory of that paradise. What I remember is the terror of being seen.

My father was an actor; my parents were immersed in the theater, art, and culture. Okay, my father was often unemployed and my mother worked as a substitute teacher, but they believed in Art, capitalized. They had rejected the bourgeois notions of propriety and conformity they'd been reared in. We were allowed to grow our hair long and go barefoot, as our more conservatively brought-up Illinois cousins with their identical bobs and mandatory slippers and bathrobes were not. We were supposed to be free.

What's the matter with them? our parents asked each other for our benefit. Why don't they run around naked like other kids? Why are they so pathologically modest?

We hid our nudity in closets, under beds, behind armchairs, beneath desks. To us, naked children seemed heedless, verging on imbecilic and deserving of contempt. They might as well have been wearing leashes.

Maybe we were self-conscious because we were (and still are) white. Until I was twelve, we lived on 153rd Street between Broadway and Riverside Drive, a Caucasian anomaly in an African American and Hispanic neighborhood. This was the era of black power, of the Attica riots, of Stokely Carmichael, and of James Brown singing, *Say it loud, I'm black and I'm proud.* When we went anywhere as a family, whether it was to and from the library on 148th Street and Amsterdam Avenue, or to church on 153rd Street, or school on 155th, we invariably provoked hissing and muttering from someone hanging out on a stoop: honky, whitey, white pussy, cracker. The comments seemed to drift past my mother and father, unheard, unacknowledged. They snagged on my sisters and me. We bowed our heads, carrying on our shoulders the ignominy of whiteness, the color of slave owners, Klansmen, the establishment, The Man.

At night I prayed that I would wake up black. No one would look at me twice on the street except to admire my cornrowed hair. My straight, slippery, white-girl hair transformed in my pious reveries into resilient, nappy hair capable of holding a braid without a rubber band. Best of all, as a reborn black girl, I'd be separate from my sisters. For we swam in our sameness, a primordial sister soup, locked in competition despite my parents' claim that we were a noncompetitive family.

The implicit contest was to be the most beautiful and best loved, but that would have been too crass to acknowledge. So the explicit contest manifested itself along opposite lines. Who was ugliest and most grotesque?

As kids, we pulled at the skin of our bellies, proclaiming our fatness, as if this would make us thin. We plucked the flesh of our upper arms, saying, Ew, jiggly. We noted how our thighs shook when we stamped our feet. Jell-O, which my mother sometimes made for dessert, we called "fat thigh" and refused to eat.

When Alexis was declared "underweight" by a doctor, we were all jealous. I couldn't go near her without punching or pushing her, like a reflex. We sucked in our cheeks and stomachs. We played a game we called "poor people" in which we pretended we were starving, foraging for food outside our ragged hut, which was the bunk bed, a blanket tucked under the top mattress and draping over the bottom bunk.

I was the biggest of the four of us, a dubious honor. Heavy things were saved for me to carry, twist-off lids were presented for me to open, mean bossy kids were threatened with I'll tell my sister and you'll be sorry. My anxiety that I'd be required to beat someone up was constant, and I still have an Amazonian sense of myself that is at odds with reality.

Julia's hair was the thinnest. In a family of thick-haired people, the distinction induced an envious schadenfreude in the rest of us.

Alexis had the roundest face, despite the underweight diagnosis. Looking down made her chin go double. When she smiled, a dimple would appear under her right eye, misplaced, a mistake, where no one would want one.

With the encouragement of my mother, we would sit with our fingers poking into our cheeks while we read or studied to give ourselves proper dimples, but never a full palm along our jaws because that could make our teeth crooked.

Bridgit, the oldest, was also the littlest. We were forbidden to call her Bridgit the Midget. She harbored a fantasy that a growth spurt would push her up to five feet seven, at around age fifteen or so. When that didn't happen, she upped the age: sixteen, seventeen, eighteen. Thirty.

My mother, who was also cursed with shortness, though not with thin hair, was an enthusiastic participant in the ugly wars. One of five fat-battling siblings, she bore the cross of plumpness, evidence of gluttony and moral failure. She was never obese by any scientific definition. Chubby, maybe, though she'd say "chunky" for its uglier connotation. She dieted constantly. She didn't want to hide her weight or adapt to it or accept it: She wanted to lose it. She spoke with contempt of the muumuu-donning Peoria cousins. Were they delusional? Did they believe they were disguising the truth of their lumpy, overweight bodies? She wouldn't be caught dead.

"Figure flaw" was the ultimate condemnation she used in assessing herself and others. A figure flaw—thick ankles, piano legs, big hips, small breasts, a pear shape, a short neck, a receding chin, thin lips, small eyes, scanty hair—couldn't be altered. You were cursed for a lifetime. To dye your hair or undergo surgery was to make yourself not merely flawed but pathetic for trying so hard.

On rare days, when my mother was feeling less bad about herself, she'd quip, I turn a good ankle, pointing and flexing her foot. Or she'd declare, My clavicles are good. We would all then anxiously point and flex our feet, or touch our collarbones. None of us got necks, she'd say, and advise us against wearing turtlenecks. Keep the clavicles visible so they'll know you have some bone structure. Unfortunately, none of us got cheekbones, she pronounced sadly. Or eyelashes worth a damn.

My father was terribly thin. He ate three enormous meals a day, prepared and served by my mother, and never gained weight. After dinner, he ate big bowls of ice cream drowning in chocolate sauce, with a stack of Ritz crackers on the side for the salt/fat/sugar combo, and still he couldn't gain. He never wore short-sleeved shirts because of what he called his Mickey Mouse arms. He did stomach crunches and pectoral exercises of the we-must-increase-our-bust variety during his more disciplined periods. I am, unfortunately, he said, more ninety-pound weakling than Mr. Atlas.

We kids were somewhere in between, neither fat nor skinny. We were awkward girls, sturdy limbed, long legged—I, slightly knock-kneed—with large rib cages. Maybe you were awkward, Bridgit says, I was never awkward. And that's true. Bridgit was the tiny girl in the front row at the children's community class offered by the Dance Theater of Harlem. She was doted on and exclaimed over because she was so little, while I was the tall, clumsy white girl in back, the one without grace or balance, a lost cause, envying my other two sisters for their luck in being too young to attend.

I'm an endomorph, my mother would say angrily, and that is my fate. Your father's an ectomorph. You're all probably mesos. We understood the hierarchy: Ectomorphs ruled. Maybe I'm an ectomorph like Dad, Bridgit tendered. Not a chance, my mother snapped, you take after my side of the family. She handed triumph to the rest of us. If we all couldn't be ectos, none of us could.

The absence of my father from our daily lives was unremarkable back then. Better an absence than an intrusive, critical presence. Because critical he was. On the few weekends he took care of us, my father wouldn't permit us dessert, candy, second helpings, or snacks. He assumed—since he didn't know the rules—that we would take advantage. He didn't want us getting fat on his watch. I would sneak candy, envious of friends whose kitchens had candy just floating around in cabinets and drawers, candy they didn't think anything of, candy I coveted.

My father found my hidden stash of allowance-money-purchased Milk Duds and confiscated them. He was trembling with rage when he asked my mother in a low rigid voice, What are we going to do about the duds? He called them duds, as if he had to speak in code. My mother seemed to think a dinner without dessert and my apparent shame were punishment enough. My father insisted that was letting me off too easy.

His anger seemed disproportionate, even then. Was he furious because I broke the rules? Or because I was a pig? Even as my mother won the punishment argument, I imagined myself chained naked to the bedroom radiator, filthy and starving to death, my eyelashes falling out, justice served.

On holidays, when eating indiscriminately was allowed, we kids became depraved, drowning ourselves in an oral orgy of sweets, gorging until we got sick. Alexis suffered diarrhea. Julia once threw up. I got heartburn. Bridgit would hoard some of her Halloween candy all the way until Easter so she could gloat in our presence and savor her chocolate, white with age.

My father made his living as a character actor. When he was in a show and we would visit backstage, the people he introduced us to, from makeup to wardrobe to cast members and stagehands, were incredulous that he was not only married but the father of four. He kept us hidden away like a shameful secret.

If we had been prettier, more talented, thinner, more special, less greedy, might he then have carried photographs and bragged about us? We were mediocre and plain; there was no other explanation, no other possibility.

Julia and I had big, crooked noses. Alexis and Bridgit had chronic rash, sensitive skin. We'd argue about which was worse. We'd compare: Who had the smallest, beadiest eyes? Who had the flabbiest belly, the biggest thighs, thickest ankles, stick-outest ears, meatiest arms? Stupidest-looking smile? Me, me, and me, we argued. We vied for the ugly prize.

In the summer of 1973, my parents separated and my mother moved with my sisters and me to a little house in the big woods, as she put it. Pioneers, we would rally together with courage and love, braving wilderness, weather, and isolation. We'd do it without a Pa.

This was the Catskills. No longer defined by our whiteness, we were invisible in a crowd. Everyone was white. Our house was secluded. It was also small, with paper-thin walls. Privacy was not to be had. You need to cry, you go in the woods, my mother said.

Built to be a summerhouse, the place had several sliding glass doors that reflected us back at ourselves in the dark and, more chillingly, exposed us to whatever ax murderer might be lurking in the woods, waiting to unleash nightmarish violence. Our sense of being watched and judged magnified. This was the crux. See yourself and recoil. Be seen by someone else and die a grisly, deserved death.

Strengthened by feminism, given permission by her consciousness-raising group, my mother began going naked around the house. Determined to transcend the limitations that had been inflicted on her by society, religion, and conditioning, she renounced Catholicism, gave up shaving her legs and armpits, threw away her makeup, and stopped curling her hair.

Naked, she practiced yoga in the living room. I can see her now, the pale skin of her back, her buttocks, and the backs of her thighs, inhaling her arms out and up, gaze following palms, exhaling with a sigh, folding over her legs. The bumpiness of flesh in the twilight. If I don't do yoga, I will die, she said. I mean that. I will kill myself.

Right around this time, Bridgit and I started shaving our legs, plucking our eyebrows, curling our hair, and wearing makeup. Once, in the interest of efficiency and exhausted by the endlessness of the work, I simply shaved off my eyebrows and drew them in with pencil. You look like a weirdo, my sisters said.

When Bridgit's breasts began to grow, I overheard my Illinois grandmother chuckling with my aunt over Bridgit's "walnuts." Appalled, I developed a fortresslike slouch and wore baggy T-shirts. My walnuts would not be mocked.

The summer I turned thirteen, my mother, as part of her life-expansion path, resolved to learn Spanish. She insisted that Bridgit and I accompany her in a lesson from her interactive workbook.

We sat on the porch, my mother stark naked, with Bridgit on one side and me on the other, fully clothed. She held the workbook open on her lap, covering the shameful nest of hair that was our destiny and our origin. She drew the book closer and higher until her breasts were resting on the open pages. The breasts trembled as she sounded out the Spanish words.

Bridgit and I exchanged nasty looks over my mother. We began to play a silent game, passing a mutually hostile glance at my mother's naked form, grimacing as if to vomit, and turning away when laughter threatened. When we regained control we began again: look of disgust at my mother, pantomime of spewing, silent hysteria. Each cycle grew more dramatic, the laughter more bottled up.

¿Dónde está la ventana? My mother's voice rose. She pointed to the sliding glass door. Her breasts quivered. *Aquí está la ventana.*

We erupted. We snorted. We choked. I fell off the porch bench.

My mother flew into a rage. She hurled the workbook on the ground. Then she dissolved into a fit of weeping.

She put her clothes back on for good when she caught Julia shuddering at the sight of her. But what did she expect? We were set in our ways. We hadn't liked being naked as children. We needed privacy from each other's scrutiny, not from the outside world. The outside world wasn't interested.

My mother's consciousness-raising group unloaded its rejected cosmetics on us, a bonanza—eye shadow, foundation, blush, mascara, eyelash curler, eyeliner, lipstick, nail polish—to fight over. Alexis and Julia were too young to bother with makeup but they participated because, as sisters, it was their right to claim part ownership. I have the smallest eyes; I should get the eyeshadow. I have the thinnest lips; the lipstick's mine. I need the blush because I have the pastiest skin, and so on. Ugliness is not infinite. The same claims and arguments circled year after year, embedding themselves into our psyches.

Share, my mother ordered, guaranteeing constant warfare. Except over the eyelash curler. My lashes were too stubby to fit into the clamp. You might say I won that round.

As teenagers, Bridgit and I suffered a never-ending misery with acne. When vitamin E, Clearasil, benzyl peroxide, and positive thinking exercises—such as the one my mother suggested in which we'd gaze into the mirror, chanting, I am a magnificent human being, nothing can undermine my magnificence—didn't work, she finally took us to a dermatologist. She had to borrow money from my grandmother to do it.

The dermatologist told my mother, If I can have their skin looking as good as yours, I'll consider it a job well done.

She threw a fit. Are you kidding? My skin's like oatmeal! You can't do better than that, you shouldn't call yourself a doctor.

I remember sunlamps, acid treatments, antibiotics, and a strict diet in which only two pats of butter a week were allowed. Nothing worked. I outgrew acne in my thirties, when I began to notice wrinkles.

Who had the worst skin then? Me or Bridgit? She had rash on top of acne. She slathered her hands in lotion and wore gloves to bed. Alexis also had terrible, painful eczema on her whole body that nothing but cortisone steroids would diminish. Julia's hair was falling out. We were a family of lepers. Any action to improve or heal was futile. Oatmeal skin was the best we could hope for.

At around age fifteen I began to sweat, all-out, extreme, full-body drenching. To hide the wet stains around my armpits, I stopped moving my arms. To say I was uncomfortable inside my skin is to radically understate. I wanted to die. Open declarations of self-condemnation become habitual, an addiction.

In high school, I used to declare—I thought this was funny—that some people have good days and bad days, but I have bad days and hideous days. As a joke I used to say, When God was handing out noses I thought he said hoses and said give me a long one.

One morning before school, Bridgit put her fist through the bathroom mirror. She hated how she looked. Now *that* I understand, my mother said. She tells the story to this day, proudly recounting the drama of smashed glass, leading up to the climax of the anecdote: the depth of her understanding.

Alexis (the underweight one) got chubby when she was fourteen after living for a summer with my father. He was unctuous with apologies. He hadn't been paying attention. I'm sorry, he said. I'm so, so, sorry, as if it were a tragedy to gain a little weight, as if she had come back grotesquely deformed.

We called her bubble butt and made her cry. They called me strawberry nose and made me cry. Pizza face reduced Bridgit to tears. When Julia muttered about how stupid her older sisters were, we shouted at her, You're ugly, too! Don't think you're not!

Just as I prayed when I was a child that I would become black, I prayed as a teenager that I would get anorexia. I envied one girl at school, a year ahead of me. When her boyfriend broke up with her, she turned skeletal. I can see her with a lollipop at the high school basketball game, solemnly explaining how she would allow herself to suck for ten minutes. Then she'd wrap it up for an hour, maybe more, before she'd let herself have another ten minutes of sucking. That lollipop—a large one, but still—had lasted her all day, the only food she had eaten. I stood by the bleachers at halftime, arms wrapped around my chest, miserably sweating, wishing, longing, to have such control, such—as I saw it—nobility.

I tried to induce vomiting after eating but it was difficult and ultimately made me feel more fat, bloated, and worthless than merely overeating. Try two fingers, not one, a friend suggested. That wasn't effective either. So much work to regurgitate a small, slimy trickle, a fraction of what I had eaten.

The more I resolved to give up eating, the more, it seemed, I ate. Ice cream was the great narcotic. A gallon between us after a meal was not unusual. I'd go through a family-size package of Oreos in a couple of days, all the while imagining myself emaciated. I attended an Overeaters Anonymous meeting with my mother—she was convinced she had to submit to a higher power to control her sugar addiction—and came away gratified that at least I wasn't as fat as the other people there.

It was threatening when Alexis became popular at sixteen—even with her bubble butt. She lost her virginity before I did, an embarrassment. Sexy Lexy, her pals called her. She flaunted her body as if she'd forgotten she was ugly. She stole my boyfriend. An aunt commented to me that Alexis had nice "gams." They're not that nice, I said. To compliment one sister was to insult the others.

There is a photographer, Nicholas Nixon, who has photographed his wife and her three sisters over twenty-five years. Simply titled *The Brown Sisters,* with the city and the year, the series reveals moments of human connection that extend beyond the individual photographs. Their simplicity is powerful. Along with the aging process, they display familiarity and love. One of the most notable aspects of these photographs other than their romantic beauty is the linking of the sisters. Always, arms are draped over shoulders, fingers intertwined, in some form of connection. The Brown sisters appear to be allies.

We're four sisters, just like them. Why weren't we allies? Well into our twenties and thirties, we undermined, belittled, and mocked each other and ourselves, united only in unsightliness. I found comfort in the idea that even though I was ugly, I wasn't alone. My sisters were just as unattractive. We were alcoholics of ugliness. Ugliholics.

My father died several years ago of cancer. He was no longer ashamed of us by then. He probably didn't have the energy. In what I thought would be one of those deep moments of communication one is blessed to experience with the dying, he whispered something to me. As I leaned in close to hear, he said, I credit your mother that you girls didn't grow up fat.

Why did it matter so much about fatness? The shame passes down from parents to children, projected, denied. Perhaps it is our very appetites, our desires and needs that shame us.

The irony of our obsession lies in the photographs that have accumulated through decades. For the past fifteen years or so, when the four of us are together for any event, we get a picture of the sisters. More snapshots than the carefully composed portraits of Nicholas Nixon, those pictures and the many before, from childhood and adolescence, reveal that none of us was ever even slightly obese.

Examining them now, I don't see a family of fat, ugly, sweaty, pimply, pathetic excuses for human beings, but a family of girls and women going through some awkward phases. Bridgit's fake practiced smile, developed as a teenager and used for years thereafter, looks wooden but not disastrous. Dyeing my hair black twelve years ago was misguided but not tragic. Alexis, with her exaggerated, slit-eyed smile and theatrical pose projects utter disconnection, but that was how she felt. Julia's solemn demeanor, with her chin tucked toward sternum, accentuating the diagonal slant of her nose, was not flattering but not a calamity. Not grotesque, only human.

Our preoccupation with our flaws was as disproportionate as my father's anger about the Milk Duds. Of course, the usual trick of the mind convincingly claimed that if we let our guards down, we'd balloon instantly. If we allowed a letup in the criticism, we'd open ourselves to attack from the outside world. We had to remain vigilant. Nothing like self-hatred to keep your appetites in check.

What I didn't know when I was a child, a teenager, a twenty-something, a thirtysomething, is that, even in the awkward years, youth unadorned shines with beauty. I have to remind myself that twenty years in the future, I really will be old, invisible to society at large, looking back at who I am now and concluding that I looked pretty good, too bad I didn't know it. I have to learn to appreciate what I've got, if only to placate my inner senior citizen.

Becoming friends with my sisters happened slowly through the years, an evolution requiring each of us to surrender our claim that we had it worst. We still scrutinize and pass judgment at family gatherings. I'll glance up and catch one sister or another assessing with narrowed, judging eyes, and I know she's surveying me for evidence of the jiggle or the pimple, or the hair-sprouting mole, the gray hairs, sagging jowls, or chin wattle, evidence to compare herself to. I'm doing the same, an old habit to reassure myself that I'm not as bad as all that.

But sometimes, since the flaws are already in focus, already examined and deconstructed, I take heart by looking for the beauty in my sisters.

Bridgit and I have had facials together, the squeezing points of pain still visible afterward when we go out to dinner. Her face glows in the restaurant light. My pores are bigger than yours, she says. Yeah, I say, but you don't get lumpy, painful, red cysts under your skin, do you? I trump her.

When Alexis and I went skinny-dipping in a swimming hole in Ithaca fairly recently, I noted her nymphlike qualities. But my boobs, she said, droop like bananas. Thanks for pointing that out, I said and dropped all muscular effort at holding my belly in, letting it distend and bloat until I looked seven months pregnant. That's what happens when I just let go, I told her. We both ducked underwater and remained submerged until it was time to dash out and hide ourselves in beach towels.

My mother, on her seventieth birthday, led us all on a ten-mile hike in Bear Mountain State Park. She'll hike thirty miles on a weekend. When she and a friend trekked Glacier Mountain in Montana, strangers took their pictures, two elderly women, as prized as a bear sighting. I turned to the side, my mother said, so they wouldn't see how big my hips are.

Julia and I have soaked nude in natural hot springs in Colorado, bits of algae clinging to our skin. She rolled over to demonstrate how her belly flopped. But I thought she looked like a mermaid. Our noses, we agreed, are similarly crooked so that we really do have a "bad side" for photographs. What a great picture, she said she hears all the time, it doesn't look anything like you.

She confided, I always thought you were ugly when we were growing up, but I don't think so anymore.

I was hurt she hadn't seen through the scrim of self-hatred. We were all waiting for the ugly fairy to sprinkle beauty dust on us. Proclamations of ugliness were supposed to illuminate our loveliness. So ass-backward. Why did we assume that feeling good about ourselves meant we were conceited?

The one method my sisters and I have discovered for banishing the inner uglies is exercise. None of us were athletes growing up. (Not just unattractive, but no abilities either!) But you don't have to be an athlete to enjoy moving your body. Vapid bromide it may be to say that exercise makes you feel better about yourself, but the truth is in experience. On the way to the gym I'm dragging my fat, sagging, hopeless body, a middle-aged potato sack in the aesthetic abomination of my sneakers. After a workout, I strut home, slim, youthful, resilient, foxy, and feeling good. But not too good, cautions the ugly mesomorph inside.

Maybe I don't take the merciless internal commentary for truth anymore. But I still feel naughty eating Milk Duds. The jiggle of Jell-O on a plate, I admit, is still repugnant.

The Clearasil Years

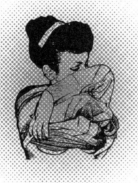

Feels Like Teen Spirit

MARIE "RIESE" LYN BERNARD

I started sweating during the summer of 1994, between seventh and eighth grades. This development, which was clearly an Adult Thing, was entirely incongruous with the rest of my Ascent to Womanhood. I was sweating, but I did not have my period or breasts or a boyfriend.

"Is this like when you said you needed a bra?" my mom asked when I added deodorant to our Kmart shopping list.

"I wanted a bra just for under *white shirts,* Mom," I reminded her. "So that no one can, you know—see through—when it rains . . . "

"When I was your age, I was already a B cup," she told me. "It was terrible."

One of my favorite things about being thirteen was comments such as that one. Other favorite things: boys who were three to four inches shorter than I was, passing notes, spreading rumors, braces with rubber bands, Kurt Cobain and his big fat flannel shirts, Lurlene McDaniel novels about girls who were dying of fatal illnesses, Christopher Pike novels about girls and boys being chased by dead people. And sweating.

◆ ◆ ◆

My decline in middle school potential-girlfriend appeal (which correlated closely with my Personal Happiness) started with The List. My parents had made the wise move of sending me to a small private school for "gifted" students just outside our hometown of Ann Arbor, Michigan (surely public school would have eaten me alive, look at what happened to Dawn Weiner in *Welcome to the Dollhouse*), which meant the number of semiattractive boys who did not play *Magic: The Gathering* was extremely limited. My group of girlfriends was forced to fight over these minibachelors like contestants in a sadistic preteen version of *The Bachelor*: thirteen pretty girls, two cute boys, stay tuned for catfights and tears, tears, tears! The List set me back, and I never recovered.

During the sixth-grade trip to Washington, D.C., my friends and I made a pact to wear T-shirts over our bathing suits for the Pool Party, and at first everyone did: We descended into the glowing blue-green water lightly as a group, and one by one our shirts bubbled up like silky inner tubes, like jellyfish hugging. This physical restraint wasn't any more cumbersome than our decapitated egos, which often seemed so fragile I could hardly get out of bed in the morning.

I thought: *Here we are in our shirts. This is okay.* I smiled at my beautiful blue-eyed boyfriend, scrawny in his bright orange trunks. He was in a protective circle with other sixth-grade boys. I couldn't penetrate the circle because I was a girl, although my breast size suggested otherwise. An older boy at summer camp had told my friend Alex and me: "You're a carpenter's dream, flat as a board and never been nailed!" I'd wanted to tell him he was fat and ugly, but he'd already stolen my voice with one weak metaphor.

Then Amy took her T-shirt off. "This is lame, you guys. It's like, I'm sinking," she said, revealing her sizable chest, and then everyone changed her mind about the pact.

"Yeah, what's the big deal?" Adrienne asked. She had gotten her period in fourth grade. I couldn't imagine anything being a big deal to someone so truly gifted.

My friends, it seemed, were actually not people with souls but sheep: Ronit, Katherine, Olivia, and Sydney followed suit. Or, rather, desuit. Call it deshirt.

I left my T-shirt on but I also died.

That night in the hotel room, the boys (including my boyfriend) created The List, which ranked the girls of our class according to breast size. I wasn't on it. I was dead.

♦ ♦ ♦

My boyfriend, who I was certain was the love of my life, broke up with me a few weeks later. We got back together for about two weeks in seventh grade, broke up again, and that was it. By eighth grade, every single one of my girlfriends was popping glossy blue Midols and ever-so-indiscreetly sneaking to the bathroom with Tampax in the back pocket of her Quicksilver jeans. I shrunk inside my body of bones and ghost-white skin and sweated.

I mean that literally, of course; I was sweating through T-shirts by then, though the peak of my life of perspiration was a few years off, when I achieved the unthinkable: I sweated through an allegedly water-resistant Patagonia fleece jacket in ninth-grade biology (though I suppose Patagonia hadn't tested its resilience to the inner storms of my armpits, rather choosing more likely and common liquid disasters such as rain and snow from the sky).

"Are you Sure?" Adrienne joked at basketball practice, trying to sneak her attack-fingers under my arms, quoting the insidious television commercial that we somehow found unbelievably hilarious. "Marie, are you Sure?"

I squealed, sealed my arms to my sides.

"Or Unsure?"

I pulled down her pants. She chased me around the carpeted gym until I fell and skinned my knees, but I didn't cry. That kind of pain didn't make me cry.

I was clumsy and tall and skinny and I didn't have breasts or my period and I still had braces and I didn't have a boyfriend and I wasn't on The List and I was dead but I was still sweating.

♦ ♦ ♦

Sydney, my best friend in middle school, whose chubby face and pink-rimmed glasses had once denoted her the less attractive member of our pair, developed these really remarkable breasts in eighth grade. They protruded, Pamela Anderson–style, like independent creatures that preceded the rest of her body, leading her into a room, announcing her delicious sexuality, preparing the audience. All the boys were in love with her. They liked watching her run.

I simultaneously wanted to touch her breasts and cut them off. I hated her. I hated her and was her best friend at the same time, because we were in middle school and that's what we did.

Sydney used Secret. At Target, I asked my mom if I could get Secret.

"Will that make you feel better?"

When she said such things, I could feel my intestines tie knots around each other and scream, press out, push at me from the inside, and then try to escape through tears. I couldn't tell her how much I hated myself and my body, and I couldn't tell her how much I was sweating right then. I couldn't tell her anything.

I pulled out my baby-powder stick of Secret in Sydney's basement and put it on before basketball practice. She smiled at me. "We have the same Secret!" she said, hugging me. She was always nice to me. I felt her nipples on my flat smooth plane of chest, I felt her nipples on my rib cage; it gave me goose bumps.

We don't have the same secret, I said to myself. *We don't have the same secret at all.*

♦ ♦ ♦

Sweating is gross. Sweating is dirty. When your teacher takes the chalk and lifts her arm and you spot that wet rim in her armpit, it's okay to giggle and whisper. Sweating is weakness, sweating is nervousness, it's hot and humid Midwestern afternoons, it's being shy in a room of strangers, it's being dirty, it's needing a shower, it's being fat, it's being fat and dirty and a man.

Nice women don't sweat. Maybe they do—when they are running, all greased lighting and spandex through the glossy pages of magazines, or on television slinging tennis rackets with long hard arms, hitting things, muscles wet and absorbing the sun.

Richard Nixon sweats. Basketball players sweat, big drops of sweat that drip to the ground. Men in suits in the humidity in the subway sweat. Cokeheads sweat. Heroin addicts sweat. Club kids sweat.

Sometimes when I was thirteen I would imagine what my life would be like when I was grown up and famous. *Will I still be sweating, then, too?* I wondered. *Will I be on television, my arms glued to my sides, in a black tank top?*

"You'd look beautiful in lavender," Oprah would say. "Isaac, get her something in lavender."

"I can't do pastels," I would say. "I just can't do pastels!"

♦ ♦ ♦

"You shouldn't hide yourself like that," my grandmother told me, picking at my giant Stüssy T-shirt. "It just makes you look skinnier. Why don't you wear shirts that fit?"

"I don't like them," I said, sweating.

In ninth grade, I got my period. It was a relief but also it was one more liquid I had to control and absorb. I felt as if I were exploding everywhere. My father died that year, a sudden heart attack, and my shrunken heart was working overtime to hold all my bones in constant arrested tension to keep me from dying too. I hated that now I was just blood, sweat, and tears, like the band. I was a woman under siege, I was a thunderstorm and a swamp and a trap of quicksand all in one.

◆ ◆ ◆

Oh, the Internet! If only you'd been there back then, I could have found others like me—these clear-faced children with stock photography smiles who offer comfort on the International Hyperhidrosis Society website, these "communities" who could have reassured me that extreme sweating could be "embarrassing, uncomfortable, anxiety-inducing, and disabling," that it could "disrupt all aspects of a person's life, from career choices and recreational activities to relationships, emotional well-being, and self-image"!

The IHS has a newsletter, a support group, and a Q&A with a Miss Teen USA contestant named Frances Rivers who recently treated her hyperhidrosis with a combination of Botox injections and iontophoresis. Three percent of the population is—and was— just like me!

Teen Sweat 101 (which offers a workbook by the same name) claims to have "the 411 on sweat—what's normal, when too much sweat can be a medical problem, and how to kick embarrassing sweatiness to the curb." OMG! Where were you, World Wide Web, when I needed you? What were you doing so far away from me in Virginia, Frances Rivers?

It wasn't until I found an advice column in my cousin's *Cosmo* and tore it out and carried it with me that I even knew that my condition had a name, that I wasn't overreacting, that possibly the right antibacterial soap would not make all the difference, that possibly I needed something real: a Treatment.

"I could never wear cute tank tops or fun colors. I always wore bulky black clothes and jackets," Frances tells "Kelly," a teenager who is afraid to tell her doctor. To the girl "whose mother won't take her seriously," she says, "The next time your armpits drench a T-shirt—show her." Oh, Frances, if only you'd been there for me! What would I have asked you? Where would I have begun?

• • •

Cosmo column firmly in hand, I considered my choices.

The column suggested Certain Dri and a few prescription options. I wasn't ready to tell my doctor, so I took the bus after school to Meijer's—a big box, Super Wal-Mart–esque acre of retailing delights that sat on the outskirts of town by the highway—and I didn't tell anyone where I was going. Everything was so embarrassing then, absolutely everything!

The testimonials on the Certain Dri box were like people exploding into beautiful dry sunshine, wholesome as powdered milk. It said to rub it on before bed. I did that.

By this time, I was in tenth grade and still sweating, and I was also still a virgin. I liked boys who didn't like me back, which was all of them. I didn't have a body yet, but my bones were five feet nine inches tall.

Certain Dri gave me a rash. Things were getting serious. I wore only men's Hanes white V-neck T-shirts, and I tried to ignore the advice of friends on how to "show off my body," which seemed a little dumb to me. Why would anyone want to show off her body? Everyone wanted to give me a makeover, wanted to dress me up.

So that's when I decided to talk to my doctor. Unfortunately, she turned out to be a heartless bitch. *Oh, Frances, what now?*

"It's a normal part of adolescence," my doctor told me. "It will pass."

"It's awful," I sobbed. "I mean—I can't wear *anything* . . . " I cried, and I sweated.

I wanted to clamp her head under my arm and sweat all over her face. Instead, she wrote me a prescription for Drysol. Drysol turned my armpits to red craters, molten lava of skin, which meant I couldn't even wear tank tops anymore.

The sweat still found a way to escape through the cracks of my skin and exist. It was more or less unbearable. Itchy, sweaty, all the time. It helped me hate myself.

We shot a movie, an After School Special directed by my film teacher, under hot lights. I wore a long-sleeved shirt and a T-shirt, and I sweated through both of them. So then I threw on a sweatshirt to cover the sweat stains on the long-sleeved shirt, and I sweated so much that sweat poured down my arms and dripped onto the desk. Luckily my scene was cut, though I can't say why.

◆ ◆ ◆

These are the worst colors: light blue, heather gray. The best are black and white. Stripes are nice. Fitted women's button-up shirts are somehow the worst, though big roomy men's shirts are perfect. Formality makes me sweat. Boarding school was perfect, because even though we had light blue uniform shirts, I could fit an undershirt beneath them and change often—my room was right there!

I started eleventh grade at a boarding school for the arts in northern Michigan. I also began developing my relationship with the black tank top and the zip-up hoodie. I sweated in cold rooms, in hot rooms, on the phone, in the hall, home alone, at a party, with a boy, with a friend, doing my homework, in class, outside, inside. There was no rhyme or reason to this madness. It was just sweating.

However, my body was finally shaping up to be all right. As the year went on and I got a boyfriend and friends and confidence and started writing and smiling, I Became a Woman. I was tall (five feet ten inches) and lithe (130), my face had filled out, my braces came off, I went on the pill and grew perfect perky breasts and a sizable ass for my figure, and I realized that everyone was right after all! Aside from the sweating, all that bad stuff had just been an adolescent phase.

Because I'm a girl, my period of complete self-acceptance lasted for about two months, in late winter of my senior year of high school. For about two months, I liked my body just the way it was. I didn't think about what I ate (not trying to gain or lose, just being okay) or think about exercise or how certain light looked on my skin. I ate Hot Pockets and Cheez-Its and Cheetos and Pepsi and ice cream and entire pizzas and had the muscle mass of a baby bird.

Then, one night in May I was watching the senior dance recital and was struck with a sudden bout of self-loathing, mostly centered around the small belly I imagined growing like a virus from my Ortho Tri-Cyclened body. I asked my boyfriend, a thin and muscular actor, "What would you do if my stomach got really fat?" When he responded, "It sort of ... already ... is," I knew I had to hit the StairMaster. At a school where such habits were reserved for the willowy ballerinas who turned green from not eating and the superficial actresses who belted show tunes in the hallways, my sudden fitness fanaticism was rare. In fact, the StairMaster was our school's one and only piece of gym equipment, and it was in the drum storage room and it smelled like sweat.

"I can't believe you're really doing this," my best friend said after my third day of exercise. No one could. It just wasn't my style. But it became my style.

I bought my first *Shape* magazine and discovered that one of the main culprits of "belly bulge" was liquid calories. *Liquid calories? I thought we peed those out.*

That's when everything changed. No more Coke, Dr. Pepper, or french vanilla cappuccinos to power me through a nine-to-five course schedule. It was time for Diet. It was time to become a Woman. Diet Coke is a common point of reference for American women. Zero calories. Zero! You know how many that is? None! Like lettuce, but even less! Liquid calories. *I thought I could sweat those out.* I was grown and exercising and drinking Diet Coke and I had a boyfriend and I was still sweating.

◆ ◆ ◆

I thought the sweating would pass.

It never passed.

"I've never noticed you sweating," Rich said to me. He was my boyfriend for a minute, when I lived in Manhattan in 2000. He sweated sometimes, but he was a guy, so it was okay. In the morning, I never liked the way he smelled. I hadn't told him the whole truth—I wouldn't tell anyone the whole truth until I met Morgan later that year—I just said I sweated "more than most girls." It wasn't really working as a conversation. "I've never noticed it at all; you're crazy."

"That's because I cover it up so well!" I explained, sweating. I did! I was so careful. I never wore things close to my armpits. I blow-dried my armpits. I changed clothing about once an hour. I avoided social functions or jobs that required outfits I would sweat through. "See—feel it!"

Rich didn't want to feel it.

Rich got a nose job. When he was stuck at home with dried blood and bandages on his face, I came over and cooked meat loaf and baked brownies and then pretended to blow-dry my hair but instead blow-dried my armpits and then I had to give Rich a blow job. I closed my eyes so I couldn't see his gross bandaged face. That was one of my better moments.

It was made possible by sweat. Sweat would always hold me back, I knew. It would hold me back from working in restaurants with T-shirts as uniforms rather than the big billowy white button-up shirts I could hide inside. It would hold me back from wearing things that looked good on me, of ever feeling comfortable going out for an entire day without a change of clothing, of ever shopping for clothing without the additional concern of my armpit sweat on top of the already urgent concern of my faltering sense of self.

My self-esteem, like most women's, is so fragile that it needs everything it can get. I didn't think I could handle any more problems than just the sweating. I couldn't be sweating and fat, I couldn't be sweating and pale. I had to be perfect in every other way so that the sweating was the only thing—not my ass, not my white, white legs, not the eczema on my elbows—I had to think about when I chose how to present my physical self to the world, what to hide and what to reveal.

Women aren't supposed to sweat or to ooze onto things. I felt like a busted fountain, leaking everywhere. For how scrawny I was, the amount of liquid my body was capable of holding for excretion was pretty remarkable.

◆ ◆ ◆

One night during my first week at the University of Michigan in August of 2000, I was getting ready to go out, wearing a black tank top and jeans, and I was sweating. I'd come back from my New York adventures to be sensible and attend U of Michigan for in-state tuition. I watched the other girls get dressed to go out in skimpy faux-vintage T-shirts they probably bought for $50 at the Greenwich, Connecticut, Abercrombie and Fitch; I watched the other girls slather on deodorant as if it were a product that did things. I smelled Spring Breeze and Baby Powder and perfume and hair spray and hope, and I put on a black tank top and sweated. *We don't have the same secrets.*

I couldn't stand it. I couldn't stop sweating, so I called my mom and asked her to pick me up—and then I told her everything. I cried; I said I felt like a sweaty freak.

She took me to Bill Knapp's Family Restaurant, because I loved it and it reminded me of being a girl, like back before I started sweating. Bill Knapp's was always air-conditioned to feel somewhat arctic, and I ate too much food (cheeseburger, fries, Diet Coke) and swelled with salt and said I couldn't go back to the dorms until it got more temperate outside. I couldn't make a first impression with sweat all over my face and my hands and my body. My hair looked like shit.

"I had it when I was your age," she told me. She gestured to her back. "I'd be soaked. My whole back, just soaked. Now I just use Mitchum."

"I tried that," I said. "I tried everything. My problem is worse than yours."

"It'll get better," she said. "It did for me. It took a while, but it did."

I stabbed my chocolate cake. "Mom, it's never getting better. Never."

◆ ◆ ◆

A week or so later, I made an appointment to see a surgeon at the University of Michigan Hospital. I was dressed in a paper gown, which I realized was actually more sweat conducive than anything I had ever worn before. I felt my (imaginary) belly sitting like a package on my thighs. I felt sweaty and naked and cold.

Four doctors entered the room.

"When did you start sweating?" one of them asked, and the other three lifted their clipboards, as if I were the guest lecturer in their class.

I told them my story, and they nodded.

"Can we feel?" they asked. They took turns feeling my armpits.

"Yes," they nodded, gravely. "You are sweating." The main doctor turned to the other doctors. "The hyperhidrosis patient sweats under any and all conditions. This is not a hot room, this is not athletics, and she is sweating still."

They told me my options; they could remove my sweat glands. They told me how the surgery worked while I sweated. They told me about the possible side effects.

"Some people lose control of the muscles in their face," they said. "Some people have compensatory sweating. Most do. Most have compensatory sweating in their inner thighs."

"So it will look like I've wet my pants all the time?"

"Sort of."

"Sort of?"

"I mean, you could sort of say that's what it looks like."

I scowled. I wanted to cry, but instead I just sweated.

◆ ◆ ◆

Michigan, the third or fourth week of school: In Morgan's room, we drank from a big jug of grocery store wine, and I noticed that Morgan was also wearing a black tank top for the third day in a row. Morgan was thin and casually cute like me, sarcastic and smart, but she was gutsier, I think, and prettier. I may have had a crush on her, but I mostly liked boys then. I had a lot to prove.

Then I saw it: just one little droplet slid down Morgan's armpit and dropped off at her forearm.

"Ew," she said, lifting her arm, revealing a wet spot that rivaled my own. "Sweaty McPitts!"

"Oh, my God," I said. "Do you have hyperhidrosis?"

"What?" Morgan asked, wrinkling her nose. "It has a name?"

"Yes! I have it too. I sweat through everything!"

Like sweaty hummingbirds, we couldn't stop talking. We talked about it for hours. But I was surprised that Morgan wasn't

ashamed. All her friends knew, it was a joke, she had two unapol-
ogetic dresser drawers stuffed with black T-shirts, black tank tops,
and sweat-stained items of other colors. We talked about all the
things we sweated through. I told her that I didn't own any
T-shirts (it's true), just tank tops and zip-up things to take on
and off over them. We talked about sweating onto tank tops,
about sweat forming rings down the sides of our bodies, about
sweating so much we thought we might be losing all the water
in our bodies. I felt happy after that. I wasn't alone. It wasn't
Teen Sweat 101, but it was what I had. It wasn't Frances Rivers
but it was something.

◆ ◆ ◆

"You should wear tighter T-shirts," Patrick told me as we tore
through Mervyn's like animals. He was my boyfriend in 2002 and
a Very Serious Bargain Shopper, which was one of many things
that made me think he was insane. (I also love a good bargain, but
I don't take it quite so seriously.) He also would call every pizza
place within delivery range before we ordered to see who had the
best deal (we lived together, we had an apartment and a dog, and
it made me feel validated/lost and compromised/safe). "You have
a really nice body, Marie."

"I don't have boobs."

"You have perfect boobs."

"They're small, though."

"They're perfect. They are small and perky and perfect."

"But I have no cleavage."

"You would still look good in tight shirts," he said. "Like that
one low-cut tank top you have."

"The black one?" I joked.

"Yeah, that one," he said, serious. When he wasn't looking, I did
the quick underarm swipe. I was sweating.

I didn't think I had anything to show. That conversation? That one right then? That was the only time he complimented my body, and we dated for sixteen months. Mostly he talked about his ex-girlfriends, about breasts as big as cantaloupes, about girls who could wear heels and not meet him eye-to-eye.

After I left Patrick, I moved in with eight other ridiculously attractive women, all but one a member of Kappa Kappa Gamma. I was trying to do girl culture. Then I found Seth, and Seth told me every day how perfect I was. He worked at the gym. I could see him watching me and it made me feel beautiful and firm. I started realizing, on my own terms, how good I'd look in tight shirts, how totally decent my pseudocleavage actually was. But then there was that one thing, that one nagging thing.

I started letting my guard down with women and telling the truth about the sweating. It got easier as we all grew up. I saw them, too: taking their Lexapro and crying during *The OC* and falling down the stairs after too many drinks and leaving under-wear in the living room and bleeding through super-plus tam-pons and sporting un-made-up forehead breakouts and binging on someone else's ice cream at 3 AM. For example, I could say, "I know you think I'd look great in this shirt, but you'll kill me when I leave the bar after thirty minutes because I've soaked through the pits, and likely also there will be a small pond at the base of the waterfall known as my cleavage" and not freak out that I'd said too much and made myself ugly and vulnerable.

At first, people think they can relate. "Oh, my God, I sweat constantly too!" And for a moment, I take the bait; I think I have found another companion on this misty path. Then as the conver-sation proceeds, I find that we have nothing in common after all. They don't sweat through every class or in cold rooms or alone. Before long, they retreat. We have differences: They can live with what they have because it's circumstantial and vacillating; I can't because it's constant and overwhelming.

"I guess it's like my laser hair removal," one friend suggests. She claims that she once sported copious amounts of facial hair. Sure, she *could* forgo laser hair removal, she could go out into the world with a visible mustache and peach fuzz on her cheeks—but it would inevitably prejudice and repel and she didn't want that, just like I don't want this.

My friend Diane got new breasts. "I work so hard for this body," she said. She worked out every day, was training to be a personal trainer, ate healthy food. "But still—there's hardly anything I can wear to show myself off, because my breasts are like, nonexistent. They're like, nipples." That's true. They were. She saved money and got new breasts, and I thought maybe her breasts were like my armpits. No matter how happy I was with what I saw in the mirror, my gaze would eventually drift to my armpits and the small smudge of sweat that would grow and grow until it became a big circle.

I was about to graduate from college, move to New York. I would perhaps be getting "a job" (this didn't happen quite so smoothly as I imagined, and I still haven't been on *Oprah*), and I would be going on "interviews" for these hypothetical jobs, and I would have to wear a button-up shirt. I also might not be able to change my shirt ten times a day.

So when I saw in a magazine that doctors had begun using Botox to treat hyperhidrosis, I decided to go for it. It wasn't FDA approved until July of 2004, and *The New York Times* published "New Treatments Turn Off the Tap for People Who Sweat Too Much" in April of 2004, discussing the medical advancement. Almost everyone who knew me forwarded me the article. But by then, to me, my armpits, and probably to Frances, it was old news.

◆ ◆ ◆

Women are supposed to know how to dress to look good, and if you don't, you obviously just don't care, which is the worst attitude a woman can have about her body. You need to be in control of your image. Wear clothes to flatter your figure. Do you know what to wear? If you don't, here are some magazines. Here are some things you can buy. Why are you sweating? Is it hot in here? Why is there a waterfall in your cleavage? Is it me?

Stop sweating. Here's a towel. Here's a Secret. Stop bleeding. Here. Stick this up your vagina. There. Better. If you're hot, take off that Patagonia fleece. You are going to die in there. You are going to just burn up in there and then you are going to die.

◆ ◆ ◆

I saved up, like a girl with her piggy bank. I went to my consultation in December of 2003, a few days before my last week of final exams ever.

"This has really been a godsend for people," the head surgeon told me. He was much nicer than the doctors from the place that wanted me to get thigh sweat. "Can I feel?" he asked.

He felt. His intern felt, too. She had nice kind eyes and blond hair, and she nodded when I told my story. I observed with pleasure that she took a note every time I mentioned a particular symptom or situation that fell in line with the diagnosis she had studied. I was a model patient!

And so they covered my armpits in something made of iodine that turned blue under the lights, revealing where the sweatiest spots were. They told me that I had hyperactive nerves, that my nerves were firing too often and incorrectly. This seemed very right.

"Most people get signals to sweat when it is hot, when they are playing sports," the doctor said. "But your signals just go off all the time."

So they took a needle, and for $1,000, cut off communication between my overactive signals and the fountains under my arms.

Three days later, I was no longer sweating. I kept checking, swiping my underarms, because that's what I did. I was used to that. But no—no sweat. It had been so easy. I've gone back every six to ten months since then, even when it was financially impractical; it remains desperately worth it. It has changed everything. I have one less thing to hide, one less secret. Sometimes I think it's helped me to accept all the other things you can't tell just by looking at me, all the other secrets that come bubbling to the surface when physical insecurities vanish.

No sweat.

Around the Bend

ADRIANNE BEE

*M*y crookedness was discovered in seventh-grade gym class. It was Valentine's Day at Mark Twain Junior High. An action-packed day filled with cards, candy, and scoliosis screenings. My mother, careful reader of all administrative memos, dropped my swimsuit into my backpack before I left. "For gym class, scoliosis screening," she said with a smile. As I walked off the bus and into school, I thought nothing of the screening. My spine was simply a spine that morning—it had a small supporting role in the story of the body, nothing more.

At the time, I thought mainly about my hair. In the morning, while my *Thriller* tape blasted from my boom box, I parted my tresses down the middle and carefully crafted each side into a wing with my curling iron. I raised the top layer of my bangs and curled them backward, fluffing them into a tall plume that shot high above my head like a fountain. Then, unaware of the harm I was inflicting on the ozone layer, I pushed the button on my industrial-size can of Final Net, sending millions of CFC molecules into the air.

For periodic touch-ups, I used a mini travel-size hairspray that lived inside my wooden-handled, monogrammed purse. I kept my finger over the letters, worried that someone might notice that ABM, my initials in monogram order, could stand for "a BM," as in Bowel Movement (my mother always used official medical terms). "Don't worry," my older brother, John, had told me before my first day at Mark Twain. "Most people say 'shit' and don't even know what a BM is."

I also was careful that no one saw Kyle Cooper's initials, which I had written in ballpoint pen on the soles of each of my tennis shoes. This was a ritual performed by a junior high girl who was "going" with someone, but Kyle and I were not going together. I had never gone anywhere with anyone, a fact that was proven by Missy Fox, a girl who was alleged to have gone many places with many boys. She had called me at the beginning of seventh grade and posed a series of questions about a classmate named Marty Jenkins, who was attractive in a scruffy, leather-jacket-wearing, failing-seventh-grade kind of way. Missy asked me three questions one by one: "Would you kiss Marty? With tongue? Let him feel you up?" I answered: yes, yes, and no. The answers, I thought, left me in a good middle zone of virtue, somewhere between Holly Hobbie and Missy Fox. After giving my third answer, I heard Marty's voice on the phone: "Hang up."

Missy explained that Marty had asked her to make a "three-way call," whatever that was, so he could find out "what his chances were with me." Before I could exact my revenge, Marty was sent to juvenile hall for stealing car stereos, which he'd cleverly stashed in his school locker. So that was that.

Kyle Cooper was no Marty Jenkins. He made good grades, served as captain of the debate team, and wore carefully pressed shirts with mysterious crests on the pockets. His older sister, Caitlin, was president of John's high school class ("Outta my league," I'd heard him describe her on the phone). People expected great things from Kyle. I watched him from afar, like a crazed fan, and imagined our future together. Only my best friend, Ellen Schmidt, and my tennis shoes knew that Kyle and I would be wed and have two children, a boy and a girl, twins named Keith and Karen.

I wanted Kyle to notice me. I paid careful attention to the ads in *Teen* magazine and bought new shampoos, conditioners, rinses, glazes. I sprayed my head with Sun-In and sat in the back yard for hours. I ironed and curled my hair until it smoked. To accommodate makeup and wardrobe, I was looking at a good two and a half hours of primping each morning before school. If I could go back in time and remove the *Teen* magazines from my bedroom, who knows what I could have accomplished during junior high—won regional science fairs, learned foreign languages, or started a thriving nonprofit organization.

In spite of my efforts I did not come close to *Teen* model perfection. My short stature required me to shop in The Children's Place, a store smack-dab in the middle of Springfield Mall, the main hangout of the Mark Twain Junior High set. I hung my head low as I entered the store with my mother. While I tried on clothes, I could hear the high-pitched giggles of small children as they flung themselves into a large bin of plastic balls next to the dressing room. My mother would wrinkle her face as I zipped up each new pair of pants. "Stand up straight," she'd say. "And tuck your bottom under." I was never sure how to execute the last command. I would try to rearrange my body's musculoskeletal structure, but no matter how I'd stand and suck in, the three-way mirrors reflected the same three versions of me. All looked short, slightly hunched. Each butt stuck out a little too prominently.

◆ ◆ ◆

When faced with physical disadvantage, one could compensate with great intelligence, wit, a special talent. John had taught me this. Although he was the smallest person in his class, my brother had a large presence. He landed the lead in school plays and eventually a proud place in the school superlatives. He was voted "Most Talented" and stood in the yearbook next to Caitlin Cooper ("Best Dressed" and "Most Likely to Succeed"). John was able to step into a new league. But what about me?

My only talent was reenacting the climactic scene from *Raiders of the Lost Ark*. At family gatherings, John would encourage me. "Do your melting face!" I would suck in my cheeks and roll my eyes into the back of my head before staggering to the ground as if I had seen the mystical wonders inside the Ark of the Covenant. My family thought it was great but it wasn't enough.

I knew that my melting face would not win me the kind of love and adoration enjoyed by my beautiful and talented best friend, Ellen Schmidt. Ellen had broken all of the swim records at Highland Park Pool. Breaststroke, freestyle, butterfly. Her name was everywhere. Ellen Schmidt. Ellen Schmidt. Ellen Schmidt. Cute lifeguards, including Kyle's cousin, Collin, waved hello to her from across the pool, threw her in the water, and gave her free Mars bars at the snack bar. As for me, people often remarked that I was . . . nice.

◆ ◆ ◆

On Valentine's Day I remembered something very important. Kyle Cooper had liked me in third grade! He did! He had sent me a valentine emblazoned with a smiling rabbit that declared I LIKE YOU BETTER THAN CARROTS. And how could I have forgotten the kick-ball game in which Sammy Friedlander had screamed, "Adrianne, Kyy-le liiiiikes you! He wants to marrr-eeee you!" The suppressed memories of Kyle's love came to me as I walked to homeroom. I paused in the bathroom to respray my hair and relive them. The two eighth-grade girls sharing the mirror beside me were, it shocked me to hear, whispering about Kyle. "He's a fox," one of them said. *Indeed,* I thought, as I sprayed and fluffed. And *he liked me in third grade.*

I walked to my locker with new hope and noticed a table surrounded by students in the hallway. The table was filled with buckets of carnations and staffed by a group of cheerleaders. A sign explained that the white carnations were for friendship, the pinks conveyed admiration, and the red ones were reserved for love. SEND A FLOWERGRAM TO SOMEONE SPECIAL TODAY! Sure, I could have simply sent a white carnation to Ellen and signed it "BFF" and been done with it. But some strange force—perhaps part hormonal, part *Teen* magazine–induced—propelled me to this table. I paid $3 and signed my name to not one, but three, heart-shaped cards tied to three red carnations, each destined for Kyle Cooper's homeroom. I felt incredibly brave as I slipped the flowers into a large heart-shaped mailbox. The urge to throw up quickly followed. Did I have to send *three*? Did I have to use a big heart for my closing on each one? I reassured myself quietly. *He liked you in third grade.*

◆ ◆ ◆

At the scoliosis screening the other swimsuit-clad girls ahead of me went through the line quickly. They touched their toes in front of Mrs. Anderson, who swiped her fingers down their spines and dismissed each girl to play volleyball. At my turn she swiped and then reswiped several times with a big sigh. It reminded me of the frustrated cashiers forced to deal with my mother's frequently demagnetized credit cards. Mrs. Anderson handed me a small piece of paper. I read the two possible outcomes: NORMAL SPINE CURVATURE and POSSIBLE SCOLIOSIS, PHYSICIAN EXAM RECOMMENDED, which had a check next to it.

I was in no mood for volleyball. I threw on my Mark Twain–issued PE sweat suit and rushed down the hall toward the girl's restroom. I needed a mirror. Perhaps this had been a mistake. After all, Mrs. Anderson was not a licensed physician. She knew a lot about square dancing and could solve our Rubik's Cubes in less than three minutes, but this was a medical situation. I wanted immediate confirmation of the condition, a prognosis. I wanted to shout, "Is there a doctor in the house!?"

But no doctor was wandering the halls of Mark Twain Junior High, only Kyle Cooper. Before I reached the sanctuary of the bathroom, I saw him approaching, flowers in hand. Kyle's eyes met mine and then quickly looked away. He glided behind a row of gray steel lockers. I followed, keeping a careful distance, and watched him toss the flowers into a trash can. I remembered my brother's words: "Outta my league."

I was sad but not sad enough to cry. So I conjured other embarrassing moments from my past. I thought of my failed campaign for vice president in sixth grade. How I spent the afternoon of my defeat tearing down my posters of Mr. T from the walls of the cafeteria. I had spent weeks carefully drawing him on each poster. I dressed Mr. T in his trademark sleeveless camo shirt; a chunky gold ring on his outstretched finger pointed to passersby. A big balloon from his mouth told them: I PITY THE FOOL WHO DON'T VOTE FOR ADRIANNE. I had yet to cry but thinking of Mr. T helped. I was getting there.

I moved my crooked body to the refuge of the second-floor restroom, where Ellen and I met between third and fourth periods. She bounced in after me and grabbed my shoulder, "So-o, did you hear from Kyle?" When I told her the sad sight I had witnessed in the hallway, she sighed. "At least you don't have scoliosis," she said. "Now, *that* would totally suck."

◆ ◆ ◆

The first doctor, at Children's Hospital, studied my spine x-rays with stern disapproval. "Surgery," he said. "And right away." Then he asked if I wouldn't mind stepping outside into the waiting room while he and my mother "had a little chat." I shuffled outside and took a seat right next to his door. I stared at the back cover of a *Highlights* magazine and pretended to focus my attention on a search for the ten items that did not belong. I circled a toaster in a tree while I listened and picked up key words through the door: metal rod, long recovery, complications. It was not the cutting itself that disturbed me but the idea of a foreign object being placed inside my back. Could it rust? Set off metal detectors? It was like the toaster in the tree. It did not belong in my body.

During the final months of seventh grade my mother and I carried the x-rays of my crooked spine to other doctors and specialists. Inside each new office we opened my portfolio of spine shots. Like models or photographers, we leaned forward in our chairs, waiting for a positive response. We wanted someone to tell us that doctor number one had been mistaken; there was no need for surgery.

We traveled to hospitals and office buildings inside our '73 Gremlin, a car that resembled a giant blue whistle. My mother, who had great fear of driving on highways, clutched the steering wheel tightly and refused to take her eyes off the road—not even to check her mirrors. As her knuckles turned ghostly white, I did my best to keep the mood light. I'd tilt an imaginary cigar to the side of my mouth and say, "Kid, with the right person in charge, your spine could go straight to the top."

"Get it?" I'd say. "Straight to the top?"

"Yes, it's funny," my mother said. "Just tell me when it's safe to switch into the right lane."

• • •

The doctors blurred and merged into one mean man in a white coat with the same receptionist who asked me to put on a paper smock that tied around my neck. "Take off everything except your underpants. Shirt opens in the back!" After they shut the door behind them, I'd remove my training bra, shorts, and T-shirt and slip into the paper smock in ten seconds flat to avoid the possibility of someone walking in on me midchange. Then I waited, clad only in the paper shirt and a pair of days-of-the-week underwear, on top of a paper-covered table. When the doctors arrived they instructed me to stand. "Stop right there," they said, approaching from behind as if to cuff me. They asked me to touch my toes—a test that caused the paper smock to flap open at both sides and fall over my head.

I was not as comfortable with my body as Missy Fox was with hers. Instead of touching my toes, I bent at the waist while holding my arms stiffly at both sides of the paper smock, trying to protect my small chest from exposure. "Arms in front," the doctors said, tilting me back down again. "Like you're diving into a pool. Slowly, no slower, *slowly!* Let's try this again." They tilted me back upright and down again as they traced their fingers down my spine from the base of my neck to uncomfortably close to the crack of my behind. "No need to be such a shy Sarah," a doctor with a white bushy beard said as I hung upside down half-naked in front of him, the tip of his beard tickling my exposed back.

One kind receptionist reminded me that I had moderate curvature—there were many worse cases out there. But I knew the truth—I was hideously disfigured. I began to feel my spine twisting and turning as I walked to class and ducked into restrooms for quick checks using the mirror inside my ABM purse. I became convinced that my spine curved one or two more degrees sideways each night while I slept. Sometimes I dreamed that my spine had moved to other regions of my body, slipped down into my right leg, or wrapped around my neck.

♦ ♦ ♦

The first two doctors agreed that surgery was the best option. The third recommended something called a Milwaukee brace. The fourth said we could go either way, and we weren't sure what that meant. The fifth opinion came from Dr. D.

Dr. D was a chiropractor. His office was tucked into a small space in a strip mall between a shoe repair shop and a dry cleaner. There was no one else in his waiting room and there was no receptionist. Just Dr. D.

My father had warned my mother and me that chiropractors were pseudodoctors, quacks. "Dr. D's Chiropracty?" he said, when my mother mentioned our plans to pay him a visit. "Not the guy with the jingle." My mother and I feigned ignorance although we knew the song by heart. "Threw out your back? Injured your knee? . . ." We had been singing it together in the Gremlin when we decided to give him a shot. "What are you waiting for? Call Dr. D!"

Dr. D was not from the paper-smock school. He had told my mother I could wear a swimsuit. Upon meeting for the first time he seemed happy to see me. "Adrianne!" he said enthusiastically, as if we were close friends reuniting after years of separation. While my mother sat in the waiting room, Dr. D walked me to his office. "Now let's see what we have here." He removed the spine images and slid them into a lighted viewing screen.

I had looked at each disk and vertebra many times in other doctors' offices. I no longer thought of the spine as a part of my own anatomy. It seemed to be a strange creature that operated on its own, without the assistance of a human body—some sort of clear, headless snake that dwelled along the ocean floor and had yet to be classified by scientists. Dr. D smiled. "You don't need surgery."

"Whew!" I said. It was the same sound my mother made each time she changed lanes or merged successfully.

"I like to start at the beginning," he said. "The *how*. How does someone come to have the condition we call scoliosis, you may wonder." I did. Perhaps my mother had attempted a difficult yoga move while I was in utero or my crib had lacked adequate lumbar support.

"There are quite a few causes," Dr. D continued. "Tumors, spinal muscular atrophy, muscular dystrophy, cerebral palsy, spina bifida—terrible things like that. One could be born with a spine deformity. Other times it happens during adolescence. A lot of cases are idiopathic. That's Latin for 'I don't know,' by the way. But I have a feeling I know the culprit of your condition." With a swirling wave of his right hand, Dr. D smiled and motioned to a long leather table and I hopped on.

"These other doctors. Did any of them measure your legs?" I shook my head. "Well, that was pretty silly of them, wasn't it?" I wasn't sure. Dr. D stretched a measuring tape down from my left hip to the bottom of my left leg. He wrote a number on his notepad. "Okay. Now let's look at the right side. *Umm-hmm. Umm-hmm.* Just as I thought. Your right leg is nearly an inch shorter than the left one!" Dr. D looked immensely satisfied. Then his smile faded. "I need to ask you a question that I'm afraid is rather personal." He looked out his office window at the empty parking lot and then back at me. "Have you had your period yet?" I stared at a pigeon that had landed in the windowsill as if to hear the status of my menses. I felt my cheeks flush as I shook my head from side to side. Dr. D's smile reappeared. "Well, that's really quite good to hear. It means you're still growing. Now, what do you say we call Mom in and share our findings?"

My mother entered and sat beside me as Dr. D began drawing diagrams on a dry-erase board. Like the pediatrician and orthopedists, Dr. D rattled off a stream of numbers. "It's important that we move now," he told us. "Puberty is approaching; there isn't much time." I envisioned puberty wearing a cowboy hat, traveling through the night on horseback with a pouch of Midol, tampons, and razor blades, and galloping toward me at high speed.

My limb-length inequality, as Dr. D called it, was connected to my crooked spine and tilted pelvis. I had a mild case of lordosis, a fancy word for a swayback. As with the shorter right leg, I had not been aware of this before, but yes, now that I looked into Dr. D's full-length mirror, I could see the tilt quite prominently. The swayback pushed my pelvis forward, way forward, as if I were beginning the first step of a dirty dance with Patrick Swayze. No wonder Kyle didn't like me. I shot my mother an I-told-you-so look but she was focused on Dr. D's dry-erase board. *Stand up straight, indeed!*

Dr. D recommended biweekly visits for "backwork." He guaranteed that he could reduce my curvature by five or more degrees by the end of the summer or the whole treatment was free. But he couldn't do it alone. I would have to work with him, perform a series of exercises every night. *Every* night, he repeated. My mother said she had to discuss this with my primary physician and my father. Dr. D nodded. "Yes, of course. I understand. But remember, there is always resistance to new ideas."

Before we left Dr. D announced he had a gift for me, whether I returned to see him or not. He riffled through his desk drawers for several minutes and produced a small latex heel lift—0.98 IN. was stamped upon it in thick black letters. I exited the office with my mother and walked to the Gremlin 0.98 inches taller, at least on the right side of my body.

◆ ◆ ◆

From my deck chair poolside I watched Collin Cooper close off the diving area for a game of Marco Polo. The other lifeguards jumped in and Collin motioned for Ellen to join them. I feared he knew I had stalked his cousin. Worse, I feared Kyle would appear on the scene. Ellen motioned for me to join her as she grabbed her goggles, chased after Collin, and dove into the chlorinated depths. Marco . . . Polo. Marco . . . Polo.

After the scoliosis diagnosis, I kept on my oversize *Thriller* T-shirt at the pool. I did not reveal my body. Or swim. I stayed in my deck chair, scrutinizing the smiling models inside my *Teen* magazine "June Swimsuit Spectacular!" I was scanning each willowy figure for a pelvic tilt when Ellen returned, breathless and excited. She dripped water all over my magazine as she leaned in to whisper: "Collin asked me to go with him!" She pointed to Collin's gold serpentine chain, which was newly fastened around her neck. It caught a slant of sunlight and shimmered.

"That's great," I said, trying to smile as I felt my spine twist half a degree.

◆ ◆ ◆

My father was sold on Dr. D's money-back guarantee, and soon I found myself at his office twice a week. I would lie on my stomach while Dr. D did mysterious things to my back. I listened to the snaps and creaks. Sometimes he put on soothing music. Sounds of the Humpback Whale. Babbling brooks mixed with classical violin. I closed my eyes and imagined emerging at the end of the summer completely different. Each time we parted he reminded me that I must be vigilant in my "backwork" at home.

And I was. Every night after dinner I retreated to my bedroom and closed my door to the world, much like the frazzled woman on TV: "Calgon, take me away!" This was time for me. I put on my swimsuit and carefully unfolded Dr. D's map of back exercises, a series of stick-figure drawings with little arrows around their arms and legs indicating proper movement. I laid it on my floor and dropped the needle on my Cyndi Lauper LP. Mimicking the stick figures, I stood very straight in front of my bedroom mirror and pushed my arms skyward and out to each side to form a T. I leaned to my right and then my left. I moved to the floor and did something like the backstroke.

◆ ◆ ◆

Dr. D and I were partners like Ellen and her swim coach were. We had numbers to meet, a goal. While Ellen dove into the pool every afternoon to improve her time, I paddled about with equal determination on my thick shag carpet. Each time I began my regimen, it took only a few moments to feel lighter, happier. I was becoming someone new, someone stronger and more powerful. After several weeks I began extending the exercise routine to incorporate a few of my own moves. I waxed on, I waxed off. I pretended I was Jaime Sommers crushing a tennis ball in one of my bionic hands.

Each day I faced my body in the mirror and made an effort to focus only on the proper alignment for my exercises. Instead of looking for my own shortcomings, I began making a mental list of Kyle's flaws.

I decided that Kyle had a square head and there were no exercises to fix that. But most of all, he was mean. I envisioned our twins handing Kyle gifts, perhaps finger paintings they made at school, only to watch their cruel father lob them into the trash. I had to forget about Kyle, I decided, if only for the sake of Keith and Karen.

◆ ◆ ◆

There were those who doubted Dr. D. My father, my mother, Ellen's parents. Mrs. Anderson. Basically anyone we told about my "backwork," including my pediatrician. "I'll be damned," he said one August morning when he was forced to confirm what Dr. D had told me. "Your curvature *has* decreased by six and a half degrees!" Dr. D had given me a high five when he shared the news and also told me I didn't need my heel lift anymore. Still I kept it tucked inside my shoe for just a few more days.

At the end of the summer I cast off my Michael Jackson T-shirt and dove into the pool with Ellen. I stood a few millimeters taller and Kyle's initials on the soles of my shoes had worn away almost completely. I was ready to turn and face whatever fresh horrors awaited me in the eighth grade.

The Freak in My Pants

LISA TAGGART

*I*n first grade, I was diagnosed with terrible vision. No one was surprised, since I'd had a hard time reading the chalkboard from the first row in class. It was bad: I couldn't see much beyond the reach of my arm, and my astigmatism had an astigmatism. My vision never improved, so it has always been easy for me to exist in a world of denial and dismiss anything farther than five feet away. Take off my glasses, and most problems disappear.

But at the age of eleven, I got confirmation that there was something fundamentally and terribly, awfully wrong with me, and it was too close to ignore. I learned at that tender age that I was a freak of nature.

At that time, like many young girls, I was supremely fascinated by and fearful of my body. At night after I'd brushed my teeth and kissed my parents, I would stand in my underwear in front of the full-length mirror in my bedroom and study my shape. I was short, stocky, flat chested. I'd turn left, to see if the adjectives changed from the side. They did not. I'd turn right. More of the same. I did this most nights before getting under the pink and black flowered comforter on my twin bed. I was anticipating the day when I'd discover some kind of hourglass figure on the girl staring back at me. I wasn't entirely sure what I was looking for, but I knew that, to get Tommy Dantello or Chris Snodgrafft to notice me, I needed something . . . *more* than what I saw. I needed to be taller and thinner. Or I needed to learn to make jokes that got everyone in class laughing like Traci Peterson did.

But the odds of my becoming funny and quick seemed remote. I could barely speak up when I needed to talk to the teacher. So, instead, I hoped to bloom into a silent, brooding, absolutely irresistible beauty. That, I thought, would be easier than developing a personality.

One night during my evening inspection, my profile caught me by surprise. I noticed a curve not of the sort I desired. What was that lump? There was a bump in my white cotton underwear, like half a Ping-Pong ball on the right side of my crotch. I pushed it in; it didn't hurt. It was sort of soft, somewhere between muscle and fat. It disappeared. But after I stepped forward, looked away long enough to examine my forehead for pimples, there was the lump once more. I pushed it back in, but then somehow, there it was again. It popped back when I wasn't looking, like that gopher in the arcade game you never see coming.

I dropped my underwear—no lost Ping-Pong balls there, just a newly grown patch of wiry hair, my biggest accomplishment so far in the maturation game. No wounds either, but, yes, definitely, a bump. I pulled up my underwear. I studied my shape some more. I clearly had a lump in my pants.

I drew the obvious, logical conclusion: I had developed a testicle. A ball. *A nad,* as Tommy D liked to say, as in "I stacked on my dirt bike and totally wrenched my nads."

The lump wasn't exactly in the right place, but then the rules for testicle location on eleven-year-old girls were probably not firm. And honestly, I wasn't entirely certain of where those things went anyway. Clearly the ball had lain dormant, waiting for puberty and now, with my new pubic hair, my current obsession with Chris Snodgrafft, and the breasts that I hoped would burst forth any day now . . . the testicle's moment had arrived.

I studied myself in the mirror. This was a desperate circumstance. I was the only eleven-year-old girl in Marin County, in the state—or maybe even the country—who had a wayward gonad lodged in her lower abdomen. I thought two things:

I was a mutant.

And

No one must know about this.

What could I do? I couldn't, I figured, change my genetic code. I reasoned the only time I was likely to be discovered for the mutant that I was was in a bathing suit. My parents were members of an exclusive health club in Larkspur, which had an indoor pool that scored me all kinds of points with Traci Peterson, my best and only friend. I wasn't about to give up my greatest selling point. Rather, I reasoned, what I needed to do was, when in a bathing suit, *keep moving.* Using the deeply flawed but all-too-common logic that my way of seeing the world was everyone's way, I figured that others would have a hard time seeing the lump too. Especially if I didn't hold still enough for anyone to focus.

"Do you want to go in the deep end first?" I asked Traci the next time we showed up at Mt. Tam Racquet Club's indoor pool. It was Saturday afternoon and the place was full of kids; a handful of women in one-pieces attempted laps in the far lanes.

"Let's just sit on the steps for a while until we get used to the water," she said. Traci was slender and blond, about my height but willowy and graceful everywhere that I was muscular and dense.

We dropped the towels we'd wrapped ourselves in for the walk from the locker room. Traci had a bright blue two-piece that tied at each hip with beaded strings; I was in a black, high-necked Speedo.

"How about we play tag?" I slapped Traci's arm and dove in. When I came to the surface, she was sitting delicately at the pool's concrete lip, only her feet and half her calves in the water.

"Maybe we should lie out in the sun and warm up before we swim," Traci suggested. Outside the glass doors we could see older girls in bikinis, lying on deck chairs and glistening with oil.

"How about we race to the other end?" I asked. I pressed myself against the pool wall, flattening my deformity. I pulled my wet hair over my face and then carefully rolled it back in a fat curl on the top of my head. "Look! It's the latest style. All the ladies are wearing it this season . . ."

Traci sniffed and then tossed her head toward the Jacuzzi, where one of the lifeguards was taking a break in the bubbles. He was about sixteen, with tanned shoulders and a wispy, triangular patch of chest hair.

"Let's go in the hot tub!" I climbed out of the pool and ran over, hunched, jumping into the hot water with a splash.

"C'mon, Traci!" I waved my arms at her. I saw her wince. She turned her head away, as if studying the sunbathers outside. I took a breath and went under. When I popped back up, the lifeguard was gone. Traci padded over and dipped one foot in. "How can you stand that?"

"What?"

"Isn't it too hot?"

No, it hadn't occurred to me to worry about scalding myself. That was a small matter of momentary discomfort and flushed skin—nothing compared to avoiding a shake-up of the entire human genome.

• • •

My mutation was my parents' fault. I knew that much about biology. I knew they had wanted their second child to be a boy. My dad would have liked someone to teach baseball to, someone to take fishing—things he'd done with his dad and three brothers.

He would have liked someone to roll his eyes with when his wife and eldest daughter talked shopping, as they often did.

The desire to show my dad I could be as tough and fun as a boy was probably what prompted me to take up softball the spring that I discovered I was a mutant. At the first practice I ran to center field to learn how to catch fly balls. Five of us girls lined up. The oldest one, who had played before, went first. The coach yelled, "Ready?" and swung his bat. The girl stepped forward, took two steps back, and scooted right. The ball landed neatly in her glove as she carefully cupped it with her right hand for safety.

When my turn came, I stood in the grass, legs bent, weight on my toes, at the ready—just like my dad had showed me the night before. The coach swung his bat. I heard a *ping*. I looked up at the blue sky. It was bright and seamless, a beautiful clear blue.

I heard a *whoosh* over on my left and then the *thunk* of the softball in the grass. I ran, scooped it up, and threw it toward the plate.

"Let's try again," shouted the coach. Again, the *ping*, the entirely empty blue sky, a *thunk* behind me.

"It's hard to see the ball once it leaves your hand," I tried to explain to the coach afterward, as we were loading the bats into his car.

"Do you wear glasses?" he asked.

"I'm supposed to," I admitted. "But I never do."

The coach moved me to infield. And I made a positive discovery: When I could see what was happening on the field, I wasn't too bad at sports. I was quick; I could run faster than the other girls. And I was fearless. The coach let me try pitching, and here is where I excelled. I could really see things from the mound. I could throw hard; some of the girls were scared to bat against me. "You're a natural," my dad said after I struck out the final batter to win our season-ending game.

I flushed with pride. And a little bit of guilt—I knew I shouldn't gloat. It wasn't really fair. The mutancy, it turned out, had some good points. I had a little extra something the other girls didn't, a nugget of male power to use for my own purposes. How could they compete? I was a girl, plus. I was 125 percent human.

◆ ◆ ◆

After a year of living with the lump, I was set to pitch for the Purple Bobby Sox softball team in our August semifinals. My dad had been so pleased with my sporty success that he'd volunteered to be a coach for my second softball season. We were, by far, the best team in the league, and I was confident we'd win the title. I was going to make this happen; I'd hit six home runs so far, and I was shooting for more.

That morning, on the way to the game against Red, I stopped at Big 5 with Traci so she could buy some new cleats. As she tried on shoes, at the back of the store I saw the row of gleaming aluminum bats lined up like metallic candy. They had cushy black foam grips and flashy logos in bright colors—Super Slugger, Batting Ace. I pulled out a shiny green bat, wrapped with baby blue tape. It was heavy and long. It felt solid in my hands. It was bigger and heavier than anything in the team's equipment bag. It was a boy's bat. *I bet no one else on the team could handle it,* I thought.

I had a wad of allowance money, almost the whole summer's worth, in my pocket.

I bought the bat.

I struck out at every opportunity that game, my swing following the ball by seconds. After my third up, and my third strikeout, I looked at my dad, standing by the dugout. He mimed a slow, lazy swing with eyes closed and shook his head.

My sluggish batting brought the whole team down; we surprised ourselves by losing three to five to a team we'd beaten twice during the season. We didn't even make it to the championship game.

Of course I blamed myself. It was stupid to buy a new bat on the morning of a big game. It was stupid to shoot for home runs instead of base hits. And the bat was too heavy; the testicle, the source of my strength, had failed me. My dad didn't say a word on the drive home after the game.

I soaked for a long time that night in the bathtub. Every ten minutes I drained a bit and refilled the tub with piping-hot water. The beige bathroom walls gleamed with the steam. And here, moping, floating just under the white bubbles, a new thought entered my brain. I didn't know why I hadn't thought of it sooner. That lump was very likely not testicular at all—it was probably tumorous. *What if I wasn't part boy, but instead . . . had cancer?*

My imagination took off then, in the way only a child can, one whose life has been fortunately sheltered from tragedy. I imagined in dramatic cinematic style the visits to the hospital, my bravery in the face of terrible odds. I saw a tall, kind, dark-haired doctor with a furrowed brow speaking quietly to my mother. My father was outside the room, pacing some long, dimly lit hospital corridor. Cut back to the room: There was I, my hair a little bit curlier, sitting on the bed, melancholy but beautiful in a pink satin robe.

The kids at school would all send me cards, of course. Traci would visit; she'd promise to come over to my house every day after school once I got better. Chris Snodgrafft might even stop at my hospital room—maybe when I was sleeping to spare me the agony of actually talking to him. But as I snoozed, my head resting delicately on the satin pillow, he'd come to the edge of my bed and sigh over me; around us the machines would be gently beeping, softly bathing the room in something like candlelight. Chris would vow to be my boyfriend as soon as I got better and returned to school. His big brown eyes would fill with tears and missed opportunity.

And then—oh, the funeral. The candles, the flickering that would illuminate the stone faces of saints and gargoyles and a white-haired, white-powdered, mournful priesty kind of guy (never mind that we were Jewish, and barely that). There would be somber music, organ of course, and my mother's and father's faces full of tears; even my sister would be crying. Actually my sister, Jennifer, would be crying hardest of all, regretting all those times she refused to let me borrow her green shirt with the roll-up sleeves, or screamed at our mother that I was bothering her, or simply banished me from her room. Oh, there would be so many tears.

I was crying myself then. In the steamy bathroom, salty tears ran down my cheeks and into the tub. I got out, toweled off, and put on my pajamas. I sat on my bed, shaky and exhausted.

I would miss so many things. My parents. Playing softball, even if it was my fault we'd lost the game that day. Traci. My sister. I'd miss the baked apples with brown sugar and vanilla ice cream that my mom made after practices. And there was so much ahead: I'd never get to pitch in the Bobby Sox Major League. I'd never get to wear a bra like Jennifer. Would I even get to wear the new corduroy knickers I'd bought for the first day of seventh grade?

I sat on my bed and sobbed.

I would have to tell my mother.

She came into my room to say good night, and found me, red faced, still on the edge of the bed.

"It's okay, honey," she said. "You had a great season. You came in third in the league. That's something to be proud of."

"Oh, that's okay." I sniffed. The concerns of that younger, healthy, frivolous girl-child seemed far from me now.

My mom kissed me on the top of the head and turned to go.

"Wait . . ."

She turned, raising her eyebrows at the urgency in my voice.

"I have to tell you something."

"Okay." She drew out the word, a half smile on her face.

I scooted myself back on the bed, so just my feet stuck out over the edge. "I have a lump."

"A lump?" The half smile wavered, uncertain.

"There." I pointed at my lap. "Down there."

"Down *there?*"

I nodded.

"A *lump?* What kind of lump?"

"I don't know," I mumbled. "A bump lump."

I stood up and dropped my pajama bottoms so my mom could see the lump in my underwear. I turned to the side.

She looked at me and then bent down to examine my crotch. She straightened again and patted around in her denim skirt, checking to see if she had any similar bumps. Finding none, she bent down to scrutinize my crotch again, gently poking the lump with her finger. "Does it hurt?"

I shook my head, bravely, I hoped. "Do you think it's something really bad?" I swallowed.

Her face was scrunched up. She wasn't crying. She looked more confused than distraught. *That,* I figured, *would come later.* "I don't know," she said. "I'll call the doctor."

♦ ♦ ♦

Two days later I found myself, pants down, standing in a large, cold room with a strange man examining my groin. He was seated in a rolling office chair, set low so his forehead was at my belly button. He was skinny and dark haired, but he lacked the charming bed-side manner of the doctor in my tragic fantasy. For one, his hands were cold. He made a few *hmm* noises as he pressed and prodded, asking me about pain. Then he began speaking to my mother.

"We should do something about this fairly soon," he said. I couldn't concentrate on his words, though; I was still standing there, jeans around my ankles, the doctor's face in line with my lumpy part. The room was drafty. The skin on my upper thighs was goose-bumped. It's impossible, I discovered, to pay attention to the conversation in the room when you are the only one present with your pants down. I wondered, *Can I pull up now? Or would that be rude? Does he need to be looking at my girl parts as he discusses this with my mom? Or can the doctor go on memory?*

"Better to schedule it and get it taken care of," the doctor said. My mother was leaning against a wall of gray cabinets. She nodded. I felt so exposed. Below me, I could see white speckles of dandruff in the doctor's hairline. He'd turned toward my mother but now glanced over as if to include the very topic of discussion in the conversation.

"All right, then," my mother said. She picked up her purse. The doctor rolled his chair back to shake my mother's hand, and I ducked down and grabbed my underwear.

◆ ◆ ◆

I knew it was bad when my mom stopped at the grocery store on the way home and, as I waited in the car, bought me a brand new issue of *Glamour* magazine (even though she had a subscriber copy coming in the mail, which my sister and I would have normally fought over) *and* a box of chocolates. All for me. They weren't See's, but still . . . this was as extravagant as my mother could be on a Tuesday afternoon at John's Market.

I had imagined the graceful dignity with which I would approach my infirmity, the moving and wise way I would carry myself. But the doctor put a hole in my plans. I was not prepared for shame.

"It's just a tear in your stomach wall," my mother said as we drove the rest of the way home. She was repeating the words the doctor had used. I'd already eaten three of the chocolates. "Your intestines poke out. The surgeon will just sew it up, like patching some pants, and you'll be fine." Her cheery voice didn't fool me.

At least with a genetic aberration or a terminal disease, I was a heroine. But instead, I had a hernia. This was just purely embarrassing. The kind of embarrassment you should be able to die from.

There was something wrong with me *down there*. It was as shameful as it could possibly be. This was the early 1980s, back before Bart Simpson introduced the phrase "Don't have a cow" to the American lexicon; back then, the current go-to expression was "Don't have a hernia." Or, even better, "Don't bust your gut." I was the shining example of what could go wrong if you were fundamentally, primordially, awfully uncool. Your groin area popped out for all to see.

There'd been an older boy at Wade Thomas Elementary School two years before who'd had, it was whispered, a hernia. Henry had been in the fifth grade and was out of class for a week. The two toughest Wade Thomas boys, Vincent Estes and David Griswold, had snickered when Henry returned to school. "Look at him!" Vince crowed as Henry crossed the lower parking lot toward the classrooms. "He had a *her*-nee-ah!" Dave said, giggling. "He busted his gut! His balls were too big!"

"Hernia, *Hen*-ry-ah!" Dave laughed.

"Hen-*ree*-ah, di-ah-*ree*-ah!" Vince added.

"Diarrhea! Diarrhea!" They both laughed out of control.

Henry's saving grace was that he was almost two years older than the other kids, having stayed back for third and fourth grade. He was as big as some of the teachers. He was also prone to violent fits of rage during which he had to be locked in the vice principal's office. Not even Vince and Dave teased Henry to his face.

Shortly after the hernia incident, Henry left for a special school and we never saw him again. I was just about to start the seventh grade. And I had neither size nor age nor violent attacks on my side.

My mom scheduled the surgery for the next month, so I'd have time to get into the swing of things at Red Hill Junior High School. I told Traci that I had to get "an operation on my hip." This was six inches from the truth.

But seventh grade was a whole new ball game. Traci ended up in a different homeroom and shared most of her classes with Anna Souter. I, on the other hand, had homeroom with a bunch of unfamiliar kids who'd come from the elementary school across town.

During the summer, Traci's parents had separated and were going through a raucous divorce. Traci now spent half her time at her dad's new apartment two towns away; she had to drive with him to school in the mornings super early and then leave right after class. There was no way she had time anymore to hang out with me in the afternoons. My house wasn't even on the way.

I sensed, too, that there was something more than inconvenience driving us apart. Traci was now the child of divorced parents. She had an older brother who smoked pot and he had even been arrested once. She was worldly in a way I couldn't understand. She used a curling iron every morning to style her hair and had started wearing eye shadow. Somehow the popular eighth-grade girls all knew her name. Traci was marching, with her feathered hair and powdered blue eyelids, into a world that was, for me, still very far away.

At lunch the week before my surgery, she dealt the final blow. "Why do you always *do* that?" Traci asked as we were sitting down on one of the benches that lined the breezeway between classrooms. "You *always* put your sandwich on my bag. I'm sick of it."

"What?"

"Can't you put your lunch on your own bag?"

I looked down. I *had* put my lunch on the brown paper bag that she'd flattened and placed on the bench space between us. I hadn't known this was a bad thing to do. I pulled my sandwich and can of Coke back and put them into the paper bag in my hands, the one that had been labeled with my name in red felt-tip marker by my mom.

"You just act so young sometimes. Anna says you should still be in sixth grade." She stood up. "I'm going to meet her on the lower field."

And she walked off.

She was right, I guessed. I was almost a year younger than most of the kids in my class. I hadn't known it was a sign of immaturity to put your lunch too close to someone else's. But there was a lot I didn't know; I didn't know how I'd managed to tear a hole in my stomach wall. I didn't know why I'd just lost Traci as a friend. And so now I was left, horror of seventh-grade horrors, to eat my lunch alone.

I employed the bathing suit strategy for this emergency too: *Keep moving.* I roved past the lunch yard, down the breezeways, and across the sports fields. I kept my distance from the other kids. Without glasses, I couldn't tell which three students were huddled in the door well of the history room. I didn't know if they noticed my walking past for the third time, alone, while there were still ten minutes left of recess. If I couldn't see them, maybe they wouldn't notice me. At least I didn't know which students had cold, hard evidence that I was a loser.

◆ ◆ ◆

The night before the operation, it was quiet on the pediatrics floor of the hospital. I was the oldest patient there, in that ill-defined place between childhood and adolescence. I was sharing a room with a four-year-old named Lucy, who spent all her time sleeping. My mother brought me more chocolates and stayed until as late as she could watching *Laverne and Shirley* and *Three's Company* with me. She had to leave at 9:30, though, and then I was alone.

Just after *Love Boat* finished, two women appeared, sliding open the curtain that separated me from Lucy and then closing it behind them. "We're here to shave you," one of them said.

I nodded, as if I had known this was coming. But icy fear spread across my chest. One woman moved to the foot of the bed; the other stayed at my side. They wore greenish-blue hospital scrubs, aprons, and plastic caps on their heads. The closer one had round gray eyes and arched eyebrows that disappeared into the scrunchy band of the cap. She looked at me questioningly and then gently lifted the sheets and my gown. She was wearing plastic gloves on her hands.

They had shaving cream and razors. I went very still and closed my eyes. I pretended I couldn't feel the coolness of the shaving cream. I ignored the soft, steady grating sound of metal slicing off my one badge of puberty. I pretended that I was asleep and was having an odd dream about space-alien ladies in shower caps.

It was over in a few minutes. They were gone after covering me back up and closing the curtain with a metal scrape of hooks. I held the sheet just under my chin, immobilized. Finally I slipped out from the bed and padded to the bathroom, locking the door. I took a deep breath and lifted my hospital gown.

My skin was raw and red, sort of numb from the shock of being exposed. After spending the recent years with a nice, dark covering, the spot was now bald. It looked awful. I had only tufts of hair at the bottom, like one of those creepy Amish men with a beard only along the jawline.

I wondered if I could avoid looking at my body below the waist for the rest of my life. I worried of course that it might never grow back—who's to say that couldn't happen? I was alone in a cold, dark wheelchair-accessible bathroom in the pediatrics ward of Marin General Hospital. I had no friends. I had no pubic hair. I'd lost the softball championship that summer. And I had no secret superpower that made me stronger than the other girls. I couldn't even keep my guts on the inside of my stomach.

◆ ◆ ◆

After getting home from the surgery, I had a four-inch bright red wound, stitched with ugly dark threads and edged in blood. It was covered with white gauze and medical tape, and I wasn't supposed to touch it. I couldn't even look at it. I did as little moving of or gazing at of the lower part of my body as possible.

I walked with a limp and with my shoulders hunched, as I compensated for the cobweb of pain radiating from my crotch. I also wasn't supposed to carry anything heavy and couldn't do PE for six weeks. Back at school in the afternoons, I sat in the school's dark library while the rest of my class headed to the red dirt track and concrete basketball courts. My absence from PE prompted a lot of questions from a wider circle of kids—not just Traci, but my new friend Michelle Miller and even the inner-circle popular girls.

They asked more probing questions than I was prepared for. "What exactly was wrong with your hip?" asked Anna Souter as she lingered one afternoon in front of the library door.

Despite my propensity for shame, I've never been a good liar. "It's not exactly my hip . . . " I started. "Just my side."

"What's wrong with it?" she asked again.

Anna had ash-blond bangs that feathered back from her forehead like wings. She was dressed for PE in navy sweats and a striped Adidas jacket.

"I had a tear in my stomach. In the lining." *That sounded pretty medical,* I thought. "The doctor had to sew it up."

Traci strolled over. "C'mon, Anna," she said. She'd decided to entirely ignore me at school. "We've got basketball today."

◆ ◆ ◆

At lunch the next day I sat at a bench with Michelle, peeling a banana. Anna, Traci, and the most popular girl of all, Kirstie Loomis, sat at a picnic table in the center of the yard. They laughed over something, and Kirstie handed Anna half of her salami sandwich.

The monitor, Mrs. De La Cruz, patrolled the yard in her shiny black trench coat, keeping watch that no biodegradable items were tossed in the bushes to "draw the bees." In her view, she was the single trench-coat line between us well-meaning but sloppy students and swarms of South American killer bees, certain seventh-grade slaughter. Her job required constant vigilance. I put my banana peel back in my paper bag.

Tommy D and Chris S walked past. "How's your hip?" Tommy shouted. Chris laughed. It had been probably a year since either one of them had spoken to me.

"Fine," I muttered.

The trio at the picnic table laughed again and then all stood up, gathering their lunch leftovers and bags in a crumple of paper waste. Mrs. D eyed them; Traci dutifully dropped the garbage into the can as they walked toward my bench.

"Really? Your *hip* is fine?" Tommy taunted.

"Anna says there's nothing wrong with your hip," Chris chimed in. "She says there's something wrong with, ah . . . something else."

Now the girls gathered behind the boys. A semicircle of superior coolness faced me. "I asked my dad—he's a doctor—about you," Anna said importantly. "And he said what you have isn't a *hip* problem . . . " She smiled. "My dad said what you have is a *her*-nia!"

Tommy and Chris laughed. Michelle, who'd been kindly carrying my backpack from class to class, cocked her head in surprise.

Anna Souter would go on to be considered the prettiest and most popular girl in my class at Sir Francis Drake High School. She would double-date to the senior prom with the boy who had dumped me a few weeks earlier, breaking my heart in that shattering first-time way. If I had known all this then I might have been too discouraged to summon my inner, and recently repaired, strength. Then again, it might have spurred me on.

"So what?" I said. I blinked. I forced myself to stand as straight as I could, even as I felt the stitches pull. "Yeah, I had a hernia. Like that's a big deal."

Fury warmed in me. It burned away my shame, extinguishing it in an instant as if it were fueled by pure oxygen. The hernia wasn't my fault. I couldn't help it. What a strain this was, being ashamed, believing something about me was all wrong.

The faces before me were in a half circle. They were so close. I had never looked this carefully at the popular kids before; I guess I'd been certain I already knew what I'd see. Kirstie crossed her arms and then Traci did the same. Traci mimicked exactly how Kirstie stood, with her weight all on her right leg, hip jutting. Tommy's leering grin made his unfortunately buggy eyes stick out further. Even Chris Snodgrafft had a pink pimple emerging on the center of his chin. And Anna: Anna's smile exposed little chunks of white schmutz, salami sandwich parts, stuck here and there all around her braces, upper and lower.

I had clarity of vision for the first time in my life. I saw I wasn't so awful after all. If I were all wrong, then so were Anna and Traci, and all the others, too. We all were, or we all weren't.

"I'd *hope* your dad would know what a hernia is." I snorted. I even laughed. "You did say he was a doctor, right?"

It was easier than I could have imagined. I saw my opportunity: the unknowing look on all of their faces. They weren't any surer than I was.

"Does your dad diagnose *all* the kids at school for you?" I went on. "Do you sit around at dinner and he says, 'Oh, that Traci Peterson is crazy. And Kirstie Loomis has head lice?'"

It was enough to divert attention. Spread the attitude around. It was a conversational version of *keep moving*.

"I wonder what kind of problem he diagnoses for you?" I said to Anna.

Tommy laughed. Anna opened her mouth, closed it, and stepped away from me.

"Let's go down the hill." Traci pulled at her arm.

Just that tiny upwelling of confidence was enough to avert the public shaming I'd feared for so long. None of the kids at school ever mentioned the hernia to me again. And even if they had, I was no longer afraid. I'd found a new voice, discovered a new stance to take in the world. All it took was a moment of clear vision—and some guts.

Stretch Marks: Pregnancy & Other Bum Deals

Bump Doesn't Begin to Describe It

SAMANTHA SCHOECH

Some months ago, while lying legs agape in a tiny pair of disposable paper undies as a gum-smacking twenty-three-year-old ripped excess hair from my nether regions by means of hot wax and muslin, I was given one more thing to consider when thinking about the impending birth of my twins. In addition to worrying about preterm labor, tearing, ripping, a C-section, an epidural, the possibility of pooping on the table, and varicose veins of the vulva, I have learned that I should also worry about having an unkempt bikini line during labor. "A lot of women come in just before they give birth," she said as she slathered and ripped. "They don't want to be all hairy for the doctor."

I am seven months pregnant with twins. I have cellulite in my armpit and something that reminds me of a mushroom growing under my right breast. It has never occurred to me that a little pubic hair—or, let's be honest, a lot—might gross out a doctor whose life's work is dependent upon poking around in yonis. But apparently it might and I should take care of it.

I want to state for the record that I am against Brazilian waxes. When I subject myself to the humiliation and pain of a stranger fresh from cosmetology school abusing my soft parts, it is to create a nice-looking triangle, something meant simply to keep strays within the confines of my underwear and bathing suit, something you could take home to mother. A Brazilian, for those of you who haven't watched porn, read fashion magazines, or had sex with a woman under thirty in a while, is the process of taking it all off—labia, butt crack, all of it—except for a tiny landing strip running the length of the *mons pubis,* a trim little mustache that belongs squarely in the "why bother" column of life's little details. I find them insulting and, frankly, scary. After all that I do, the creams and lotions and colors and cuts—I dye my eyelashes, for Christ's sake!—I am now supposed to have an aesthetically presentable crotch? It pisses me off; it really does. It makes me want to put on a pair of Birkenstocks, eat a pie, and just give up on the whole looking-pretty chore.

Giving up on looking pretty, I have learned, is not a good choice. As the gum-chewing waxer brought home to me once again, vigilance in that department has become synonymous with power and self-respect. Women facing childbirth gain confidence by taking prenatal yoga, reading up on pregnancy, and getting a nice Brazilian wax before contractions start. Impeccable grooming is the new Lamaze. So I am considering a final wax before birth. I hate it, but who wants to have the only scraggly crotch on the maternity ward? Not me.

Before I got pregnant, and it took me a long time (I was barren as a stone for three years before hitting the fertility jackpot with twins), I looked forward to a time when I would be able to forget for a while about my looks. First, enormous weight gain was inevitable, and second, it seemed there were more lofty concerns to be had during pregnancy. The health of the baby, perhaps, or the mother ship/Earth Goddess/womb warrior thing that I supposed would overtake me and trump all more frivolous concerns.

I used to roll my eyes when my pregnant friends complained of being fat. "You're not *fat.* You're *pregnant!*" I would state indignantly, as if they had somehow failed to notice the subtleties of the situation.

And so I looked forward to pregnancy as a time when I might finally be able to stop scrutinizing myself, as a time when all that gentle self-love that more well-adjusted people have toward themselves would come flooding in like so many pregnancy hormones and I could relax. Finally. My thighs would swell and my butt would spread and I wouldn't care. After all, it would be natural and, in its way, beautiful. For the first time in my life I wouldn't have to feel guilty about not looking pretty. It was reason enough to want a child.

But then it came, elusive pregnancy, and lo and behold, after a few weeks of elation and disbelief, I went back to being the same person I was before—vain, self-critical, and angry at my body for myriad injustices. I ate more and slept more, but my personality didn't change. If anything I became more upset with my physical failings. I had a custom T-shirt made that read I'M NOT FAT, I'M PREGNANT just in case the subtleties of the situation were lost on anyone else. I just couldn't seem to give myself the break I was looking forward to. Fortunately, other people did.

When you are pregnant people tell you all the time that you look cute. Sometimes they use the word *adorable*. I understand that there is something sort of cute about a big round belly containing a baby, but it can't be just that. People say it all the time. People who have never commented on my looks now tell me I look adorable. My boss, an impeccably dressed woman of a certain age with long legs, a lush mane of hair, and the ability to size you up with a nearly imperceptible eyebrow raise, has even made the comment. I often find myself dressing for her in the mornings, trying and mostly failing to achieve that elusive "put-together" look she is so good at. Recently, I showed up to work in yet another slightly ill-fitting maternity outfit, something made of T-shirt material that I was too lazy to iron, and my boss, wrapped in tasteful cashmere the color of merlot, told me, for the first time ever, that I looked cute.

It makes me suspicious. For one thing, I am one of those unfortunate pregnant women who has gained weight in her face. Sometimes, when I catch my profile in the mirror, I see not myself but one of those thick peasant women Van Gogh and other Dutch artists were forever sentimentalizing. For another, because of a pregnancy-induced stuffy nose combined with the fact that one of my babies rests contentedly against my lungs, I have become a mouth breather. Wheezing, neckless women in pilled knit gauchos are not generally considered cute, so I suspect that the world has conspired to try to make me feel as if I look cute because it is so, so sad just how uncute I actually look.

Occasionally, people out there remind me of this. Recently, while browsing in an insanely overpriced baby store where I would never, ever buy anything lest my Depression-era Ukrainian Jewish grandmother rise from the grave to give me a *patsch*, I came across one of them. She was a lockjawed mother-to-be in a mocha-colored velvet tracksuit trying to figure out which white $1,500 crib would best suit the baby who had yet to make an appearance on her waistline. She tossed her hair a lot and blew at her bangs in exasperation. She thought she might go shabby-chic but was torn because what if she changed her mind and wanted something more modern? Her bored husband rocked glumly in a $2,000 glider nearby and she admonished his inability to help her make a decision by saying loudly so that everyone would hear, "When you are handling millions for your clients you have no problem making decisions. I don't know why you collapse now."

As I walked by them on my way to the sale bin, the saleslady she had monopolized managed to turn away for a minute to address me. "Oh, and when are you due?" she asked, eying my swollen midriff. I hate this question. I hate it first because I am huge and look much closer to my due date than I actually am. In my desperate attempt not to seem like a pathetic cow, my answer is always rushed and apologetic. "Not-until-June-but-I-have-twins-so-I-look-really-big," I say, smiling and patting my enormous belly. This brings me to the second reason I hate this question: When you tell people you have twins many of them feel free to tell you how unlucky you are. Sometimes people are awed and happy for you, but more often they expel a little puff of air through lips pursed to look like assholes before saying something such as "Oh, dear God!" or "Wow, I'd hate to be you." The scowling crib lady with the money-manager husband simply looked at me wide eyed and muttered, "I was gonna say!" with a there-but-for-the-grace-of-God head shake and a hand absentmindedly smoothing her flat belly.

I stood there among the German-engineered strollers and the hand-stitched $900 baby blankets feeling like the physical embodiment of gluttony and slovenliness. The *poor* physical embodiment of gluttony and slovenliness. I wanted to defend myself. "My nutritionist says I'm right on track with my weight gain," I could shout. Or "Twins are double the fun!" Instead, I wandered off, my eyes stinging, to self-consciously look through a basket of baby linens other women had rejected.

♦ ♦ ♦

When you are thirty-six and carrying twins and your blood clots a bit too easily, you are considered a "high-risk" pregnancy. Like being infertile, this feels like a failure. It carries with it all sorts of worry and lots of conversations about what could go wrong. It means you are monitored and scrutinized and sighed at a lot. It means you can't give birth at home or travel to Mexico or have sex. It also means you can't exercise.

I come from a place where people tend to be very good looking. The confluence of affluence and lots of time outdoors produces many, many fit blond people with excellent fashion sense. It is the land that invented the soy latte and the supermarket sushi bar. Pilates is a given. Saying you don't do Pilates is like saying you like to spend your weekends smashing bunnies—simply unthinkable. Being fit, and looking fifteen years younger than you are, are par for the course. As the writer Joyce Maynard, who lives nearby, said to me, "I would be so embarrassed if I didn't exercise."

Pregnant women are given no special dispensation. We are expected to spend $200 on designer maternity jeans and enroll in something called "Baby Boot Camp," an exercise regime for new mothers meant to erase any signs of motherhood from your body as quickly as possible. We should keep up our mountain biking, or, if that should prove too difficult, we should walk and swim and elliptically train for miles at a time. And, of course, it goes without saying that we should be doing our prenatal yoga, preferably while wearing adorable matching maternity separates made from organic spandex.

When I run into other pregnant women, one of the first things they ask after when am I due and do I know what I'm having, is if I am exercising. Usually they pick their regime of choice and ask if I'm doing that. "Are you walking/swimming/biking/doing yoga?" they ask, hoping to make a lifelong bond over the joys of physical fitness. "No," I tell them, sadness in my voice. "The doctors won't let me. I'm high risk." They look at me with pity and a bit of skepticism (could there really be a reason in the world not to work out?), and I feel lazy and inept despite my medical orders. What I don't tell them is that I have always been a reluctant exerciser. I do it, but minimally and only because I privately harbor a hope that my husband's friends will think I'm hot. I am secretly thrilled that I am not allowed to exercise. Given a choice between mountain biking and lying on the couch staring off into space, I choose the couch 100 percent of the time. Still, this doesn't stop me from feeling inferior when I talk to the glowing chosen people of pregnancy with their tiny bumps and their hardened glutes.

◆ ◆ ◆

As it turns out, the meeting of egg and sperm has not only not made me less vain, it also did not magically make me a more laid-back, wholesome person. It's true that except for the slow disappearance of my jawline, I don't mind the weight gain so much (gaining enough weight is a crucial part of bearing healthy twins) but neither have I given up on my looks the way a true earth mother would. In fact, the body that seemed to betray me so consistently as I tried and failed to get pregnant all those years now seems to be lording it over me in an entirely different but equally aggressive way. It is not my stalwart partner in this baby-making business, supporting me through what is an astonishingly difficult physical endeavor. It is my adversary, alternately taunting me and letting me down.

This is not the first time in my life when I've felt as if my body were the enemy. Getting my first period filled me with shame. I am convinced that my uncooperative high school skin is what stood between me and the homecoming crown. When I was fifteen and frolicking on the beach, carefree in my bikini, my boyfriend at the time stopped dead in his tracks and said, "I can't believe you have cellulite already!" sending me into paroxysms of self-loathing, a feeling now so familiar I consider it family.

When the pimples subsided (they never really gave up and I now have a mild case of "adult acne"), dark, wiry hairs took their place on my chin. I endured hours of electrolysis to keep them at bay and then noticed that my pubic hair had started a steady march down my thighs, threatening to create the dreaded knee-to-knee snatch. I began waxing. Keeping up with my body's little jokes of aesthetics is like playing Whack-a-Mole. Stoned. With one arm. No sooner do I deal with one betrayal than another one crops up. Figured out how to tackle ingrown hairs, eh? Well, let's see how you deal with skin tags!

I remember looking at my mother's face when I was a child and puberty had not yet taken its toll. I scrutinized her close-up, noticing the enlarged pores, the broken blood vessels on the sides of her nostrils, the fine, downy mustache, the faint wrinkles, and felt a flush of superiority. I made a pact with myself. I would wash my face every day, thereby avoiding the little marks of life that I mistook for character flaws or laziness, and so would maintain my unmarred complexion. I would never have broken blood vessels or enlarged pores or a mustache. I would be pious and vigilant and beautiful (I must add here that my mother, despite her flaws, has always been considered a beauty).

It didn't take me long to figure out that I had little control. By sixth grade a rash of tiny pimples spread across my forehead and I became an easy target for those girls with less active oil glands. Once, in the library where I was diligently working on a report about China by copying large chunks of text from the *Encyclopaedia Britannica,* the meanest girl in our class, a girl with creamy brown skin and white, white teeth, approached me from one of the other tables of report writers. "We're taking a poll," she said, grinning. "Can I count the pimples on your forehead to see who wins?" It horrifies me to admit that I said okay and sat there, burning with humiliation, while she quantified my failed promise and brought to light what I saw as my own character flaw—my inability to be perfect.

◆ ◆ ◆

But it's been a long time since puberty, and although I have battled the usual suspects—weight fluctuation, the occasional monster chin zit, stretch marks glimmering like ribbons on my hips—I have also enjoyed a couple of decades of relative good looks. My friend Tara and I play this game called "best self/worst self." My best self looks like Kate Winslet. At my worst, I'm Linda Tripp. I've turned a few heads in my day, but I'm no supermodel. Still, nothing prepared me for the mysteries of pregnancy, for the suddenness with which you lose all familiarity with your own body.

There's the fun part: gazing at your bare belly in profile, admiring its smooth roundness, the way it looks so damn *pregnant*, feeling the babies kick; having people tell you to eat more. And then there's all the other stuff, the stuff that hurts and the stuff that makes you ugly. A list: acne, areolas like saucers, snoring, the inability to get out of bed without a plan for how to do it, exhaustion, putty ankles, numb fingers, shooting vagina pain, nipple cheese, fat calves, toenails you cannot cut yourself, dizziness, rampant cellulite, sausage fingers, and a thick neck. Symptoms vary from woman to woman, but you get the idea.

Lots of wise women will look at you when you are pregnant and tell you to enjoy it. "It goes so fast," they say wistfully. But I think they must be confused. I think they must be confusing pregnancy with the lovely ripeness of youth, which, like an ice cream binge, goes quickly and unappreciated. In my opinion, pregnancy is not something to be mourned. I cannot wait to breathe easily again, to sleep on my back, and wear to a pair of pants that doesn't slide down my waistless trunk. I am looking forward to seeing my feet and being able to shave my own legs. I am seriously dying to take a walk on the beach or through the park or even across the parking lot without feeling the ligaments in my lower abdomen stretch.

I realize I will never completely have my body back. I may lose the pregnancy fat, and maybe even the broken blood vessels sprinkled across my chest like bright red stars will fade, but my body will belong in part to my children for the rest of my life. They will climb on it and sleep on it and suck at it and pee on it. For a time they will depend on it for their very survival. I am looking forward to this part. Maybe I'm naive. Maybe pregnancy will seem like a breeze once these kids are outside of my body, but for now I can't wait. I am looking forward to devoting my imperfect body to people so utterly without judgment, who couldn't care less whether I've waxed my bikini line or exfoliated my elbows or done Pilates. I'm thinking I have at least ten good years before they start scrutinizing it for flaws and signs of weakness. Until then, I will be perfect in the eyes of others for the first time in my life. And then they will notice their own bodies and start inspecting mine, cataloging the things they think they can avoid by the sheer force of will. They will, in their youth and inexperience, misread it, taking my physical flaws for character flaws, for evidence that I just didn't care enough.

Scrambled Eggs

MOLLY WATSON

*E*verything I've said I would never do has come to be something I have, indeed, done: Once, long ago, while enjoying the hospitality of family friends in Malibu, I pledged I would never live in California (beautiful as it was, how could a nice Minnesotan girl like me live someplace where I was led to believe wool sweaters were superfluous?); I now live in San Francisco. As a graduate student slogging through dusty French archives for six years, I knew it was worth it because I would never be leaving academia; immediately after earning my degree, I took a major career left turn into magazine publishing. And, even back when I was in my early twenties and far from ready to plan a family, I was sure—absolutely sure, I tell you—that I would never undergo fertility treatments.

Why, I would ask, would someone go through all of that when there are "so many children who need homes?"

And I had stuck to it. I had stuck to it when I didn't get pregnant after trying—really, really trying, trying until it wasn't as much fun as it used to be. I stuck to it as I kept detailed charts of my womanly cycles: my waking temperature each morning, the consistency of my cervical mucus, the texture of my cervix, anything and everything that might help pinpoint those magical moments of possible conception and, as time went on, help diagnose why I wasn't pregnant yet.

I had stuck to it as friends started having babies. And I was happy for them. Truly. I thought maybe being around babies would jump-start my system. I found myself holding babies and thinking, *Get it, uterus? This is what we're up to; this is why you're around. Get on it.*

I had stuck to it when my husband and I decided to adopt. I had stuck to it as we filled out applications, sent in deposits, and attended orientations for private, public, and international adoptions. I had stuck to it as we debated the various merits of adopting a Vietnamese boy versus a Guatemalan girl versus African American siblings from around the corner.

I had stuck to it until I realized, like a bolt of lightning one day while walking home from the store, that I would forever be able to adopt, but if I wanted to be pregnant and birth a child, now was my best chance. *Now.* Now kept changing in actual time, but it remained constant. Now was the best time to even bother trying. Now, now, now.

So on Thursday, January 17, I visit my ob-gyn. I tell her about my plans to get pregnant. I also tell her that for years I've neglected to use birth control (oh, yeah, and forced carefully timed sex alternating with abstinence on my husband). I pull a stack of paper out of my bag—these are the charts I have so carefully kept.

"Let's see here," she says. "You're thirty-one and have been trying for almost three years?"

"Yes," I say as I hold out my charts for her to see. "You can see on these that I have a really long luteal phase, which is frustrating because I . . . "

"We need to get you in for some tests," she says as she waves her hand at my lovingly kept charts, the paper trail of my efforts to assert a measure of control over my disappointing biology. The physical proof of my desire to get pregnant becomes so much fodder for the recycling bin.

Before I can pull the paper sheet back over my waist I have the following: a prescription for Clomid to regulate my remarkably irregular periods, an appointment for a hysterosalpingogram to see if all my tubes and valves are working, a referral to a fertility specialist, instructions to have tests for every sexually transmitted disease known to humankind, and a bandage over the draw-point for a vial of blood the doctor will send to the lab to check my hormone levels.

Funny, when, at age twenty-nine, I'd mentioned to the same doctor that I hadn't gotten pregnant after trying for almost a year, I was patted on the back and told to just keep trying, stay patient, and relax. At thirty-one, the situation has changed.

◆ ◆ ◆

Thursday, February 21: I find out what a hysterosalpingogram is. A technician shoots dye up into my uterus and takes several x-rays of its journey. Everyone is pleased by how far the dye goes and the path it takes. I am pleased that they are pleased, especially since I was given a Valium before the procedure. They have to clamp my cervix in place, clean it with a brush, and then put a tube through it to inject the dye. So really the Valium seems the least they could offer. The whole thing is like having a Pap smear—the same way having a tooth pulled is like brushing your teeth. The Valium doesn't so much ease the pain as make me not care about it.

As everyone *oohs* and *aahs* at how free-flowing my lady parts are, I can't help but wonder: *Aren't all these places exactly where we hope an egg, embryo, and eventual baby will be? Should we really be targeting x-rays at them? Don't dentists put that lead apron over us precisely to avoid causing reproductive damage? Is that dye such a good idea? Where does the dye go now?*

I am hushed and sent with a sanitary pad to change back into my clothes. So that's where the dye goes, I realize, all over my underwear. Yet the dye never shows up. It ends up that, since I'm in the happy position of having unblocked, free, and open fallopian tubes, the dye has spilled out into my abdominal cavity. As I double over with cramps that are "normal," I'm told that the dye is "perfectly safe" and "water soluble." Water solubility offers me no comfort whatsoever. Bleach is water soluble. Round-Up is water soluble. Most cyanide compounds are water soluble.

• • •

Tuesday, February 26: My first appointment with the fertility specialist. Dr. Z assures me that my hormone levels are "perfect" and that I am an ideal candidate for fertility treatment. It's as if I'm applying to college all over again: Yes, I am told, you would fit in nicely here. What lovely hormones! What open tubes! What a fine young uterus! And look—it's free of fibrous growths! Very impressive!

He instructs me to continue with the Clomid and, at day ten in my next cycle, to start taking an ovulation test every day. When it comes up positive, I am to call a special number, at which time I will be told when to arrive at the office the next day—with husband in tow—for IUI, intrauterine insemination. Artificial insemination refers, I learn, to cases in which the sperm is donated by someone not intending to be the diaper-changing father, just the sperm-giving father.

• • •

Monday, March 4: Yet another in a long line of negative pregnancy tests followed by my period's arriving within hours. It is as if I can menstruate only after peeing on a stick.

• • •

Sunday, March 17: We arrive for our first IUI, as directed, at 8:00 AM on a Sunday. Although the building is open, no one is there. Correction: A security guard is in the lobby. But when we go to the fifth floor for our appointment, the office—like all the other offices—is empty.

"Why isn't anyone here?" I frantically, though rhetorically, ask my husband.

"I don't know, sweetie. I'm sure they'll be here. They said to come to this floor, right?"

"Of course it's this floor," I snap back. "This is where his office is. What other floor would we go to?" I'm thinking that maybe it isn't this floor. *Oh, my God,* I think. *Where the hell are we supposed to be? Is the doctor anxiously waiting for us somewhere? Should I wander the halls calling his name?*

"Do you have a number we can call?" Steven asks while pulling his cell phone out of his coat pocket.

Did the doctor not get the message to come in at this unusual hour and day? I start to breathe heavily and my mind races; this might be our last chance to get pregnant. What if some schedule goof-up ruins our only opportunity to have a baby?

We frantically call every number I have for our HMO. When I do finally get a live person on the line, she can't call the doctor, she can't confirm the appointment, she doesn't know what I'm talking about, she can't do anything useful at all. All she can do is assure me that if I was told I had an appointment, I probably have an appointment and the doctor will be there.

"It is raining out," the nonhelpful but not unkind phone lady says. "Maybe there's a lot of traffic and he's running late."

Steven goes downstairs to interrogate the security guard. As I stare out the picture window in the empty waiting room, tears flow down my cheeks. Deciding to go ahead with the fertility treatment did, I realize, give me a sense of purpose. The extent to which I have no control over my ability to have a child is, once again, painfully evident. I am as powerless as ever.

He returns with no news. The security guard knows nothing. Yes, people come into the building on Sundays. No, not that many. And no, no one else has been in today yet.

When the nurse finally arrives—ten minutes late—she does not appreciate how upsetting this unannounced schedule change has made me. She, therefore, also does not appreciate how happy we both are to see her. She pauses midstep as we rush toward her when she steps off the elevator. She seems perplexed by our enthusiasm for her presence and treats us like slightly obsessive fans: with minimal but kindly address. She calmly asks us to please sit down so she can open the office. She assures us the doctor is on his way. She escapes behind the office door.

Along with a sample cup and directions to the private bathroom, Steven is given a "Consent for Sperm Donation and Use" form on which he must decide whether he would like any leftover sperm "disposed of by being flushed down the drain," returned to him, or "other." What "other" might be, I dare not guess. He must also sign a statement that reads, "I understand that my donated sperm must be treated before it can be used for insemination purposes. During the course of such treatment, an unknown amount of sperm may be destroyed." I've never known guys to be that interested in what happens to their sperm, but I guess some of them are deeply concerned.

As I lounge in the stirrups, with a lovely little paper floral number draped across my knees, Steven, seemingly no worse for wear after his trip to the bathroom, tries not to notice that I am in the stirrups and that another man is about to insert something in my vagina. The doctor and I try not to notice that Steven has just jacked off in the bathroom while we waited for him. The doctor leaves to "prepare the sample," returns about ten minutes later, sits down between the stirrups, and casually asks if Steven works with a lot of chemicals. No, we answer, why would he ask? "I thought that might explain this motility problem," he says. The sperm count, as we knew from previous tests, is fine. The motility, according to the doctor's look-see at this morning's sample, is not at all what one looks for in sperm. A high percentage of them are "inert."

"But we only need one, right?" Steven asks.

No, it ends up, you don't need just one. See, the sperm work like a team. They each release an enzyme that helps weaken the wall of the egg and allow that one key player to enter and make baby magic. That one sperm needs the help of the group to get in is why sperm counts matter. Horrible analogies run through my head as the doctor announces: "This is a real Hail Mary pass, but since we're all here, let's give it a try, shall we?" He hurls the pass on in.

♦ ♦ ♦

Friday, April 12: The Hail Mary pass did not work. After several negative pregnancy tests and yet another ultralong cycle, I get my period. I dutifully mark an *x* in my planner. The days of my planner are marked with small penciled numbers, as they have been for more than two years. The day of each cycle—which range from twenty-three to forty-two days long—is duly and painfully noted every day. Number one through five or six of each cycle is followed by an *x* noting my period. I hate those *x*'s.

♦ ♦ ♦

Saturday, April 27: We go back for a second round. Maybe, we are told, that sperm was anomalous sperm. Maybe today's sperm will be better sperm. It is not. Today's sperm is just as bad. As I cry in the stirrups, Dr. Z throws another Hail Mary pass, since, once again, we're all there and set up for it anyway. He tells us that we are excellent candidates for in vitro fertilization, IVF, test-tube babies. "That is really the only way to address these kinds of sperm issues," he says.

"Go to a research institute," he recommends. "I know all these guys and the pressure to have good numbers is so high at some of these private clinics that they will implant more embryos than they say they will. They don't do that at research centers."

Four months may sound like enough time to process the drugs, the turkey baster, the barrage of paper robes, the surreal tests, but it wasn't. The leap from turkey baster to test tube is huge—to me and to our savings account. Test tubes, it ends up, aren't covered by our insurance. So I am now faced with the prospect of doing something I find ethically questionable, spending a lot of money to do it and, to top it off, worrying about shady doctors to boot. And Steven, bless him, is unwilling to either push forward or pull back. The decision, he says, is mine.

◆ ◆ ◆

Monday, May 13: At my consultation appointment at the fertility research center, Dr. F is remarkably personable as he explains the IVF procedure clearly and simply. Overall 30 percent of the center's patients conceive, but given my age and "other particulars"— by which I believe he means my free-flowing fallopian tubes and fine hormone levels—he would guess our chances would be significantly higher. So I start a cycle of birth control pills—the irony of which is painful.

"It's the best way to regulate your cycle before treatment," he explains. "Plus, it gives your ovaries a nice rest before being overworked."

Well, I think, *at least my ovaries will get a break.* Although, quite frankly, I haven't been so impressed with their work of late.

I also start a round of prophylactic antibiotics, like the kind they give cattle on feedlots to keep them from developing infections. "We don't want any undetected microorganisms interfering with implantation," the doctor says. *No,* I think, *we certainly don't.*

♦ ♦ ♦

Monday, July 8: The great ovary vacation is about to end. Today I have a baseline sonogram: the real start of the IVF treatment. Steven sits on a stool at the foot of the exam table. I point out that is where the doctor will need to sit. He jumps up as if someone has just asked him to do the exam himself. When Dr. F arrives, he has some trouble finding my ovaries since they've had such a nice break from the month of birth control pills.

Perhaps I should explain how this sonogram is done. If you are picturing a flat-headed wand being rubbed over my belly, think again. These sonograms are done from the inside, with a dildolike wand up my vagina. It's a strange enough procedure; having my husband witness it is surreal. Although no more so, I guess, than having had him watch the "Hail Mary pass."

The doctor, clearly trained in keeping the chitchat going to distract everyone from the dildo in the room, treats us to a running commentary of his explorations of my insides. "Oh, there they are," as he points to the screen, pointedly placed to focus our views away from my genitals. "These ovaries have had a nice rest on the oral contraceptives. They're very small. That's good. And see these spots? Here and there and there? Those are the follicles. Let's see; let's count them up." He counts fourteen. This is far below the twenty to thirty estimated at my consultation visit.

"But that's a good thing," he explains. "We don't want too many eggs. In your situation"—by which he means my young age and awesome hormones—"we worry more about hyperstimulation than we do about getting enough eggs."

Hyperstimulation may sound good, sure, but it is an unfun situation in which playing God at making babies backfires and your body retains fluids—lots and lots of fluids. Symptoms vary from "intense discomfort" to blood clots to kidney damage, he says.

"I'm happy to see fewer than twenty follicles," he assures us while removing the wand from my cootch. "We'll keep an eye on things, but things look very, very good." I assume he is talking about my extra-egg production capacities, and not my crotch per se.

He leaves the room, I wipe myself off, and Steven stops staring at the floor. It's 9:00 AM; I need a drink.

◆ ◆ ◆

Thursday, July 11: Before leaving the house this morning I call our nurse. "Hi, it's Molly Watson. According to our protocol I should have gotten my period by now and then start the shots tonight. Um, I'm calling because I haven't gotten my period . . . pretty typical of me. Anyway, I was just wondering if we should still start the shots—I assume we should but wanted to check. You can call our home number and leave a message, okay? Thanks, again, this is Molly Watson."

I come home to a message instructing me *not* to start the shots. My lining is thick enough so they want me to have a "real" period before starting the medication. This is good news, she explains. It is good to have such a thick lining. Once again, I take comfort in my physiology, which, in the larger picture, is so letting me down. They will induce a period if necessary. No need. It arrives practically as I listen to the message.

"Hi," I explain to the voice mail. "This is Molly Watson again. I'm calling because I got my period—so now I'm really not sure of what to do. Should we start the shots tonight? I guess it's too late for you to get back to me. So . . . give me a call tomorrow and let me know what to do. Okay, thanks, bye."

I don't know that I've ever called a stranger to relate the timing of my menstruation in such detail before.

◆ ◆ ◆

Friday, July 12: I play phone tag with our nurse all morning. Finally, that afternoon, we talk. She has checked with the doctor—yes, I should start the shots tonight. When we get home Steven and I set up the medical center in the living room. We break one vial of sterile water and four vials of gonal-F, the drug that will trick my ovaries into producing many eggs this month. I take the water and dilute one vial of gonal-F, bring it back into the syringe, inject it into the next vial, combining all of the diluted vials together into one shot. I cap the needle and rub the top of my left thigh with alcohol.

I had decided I needed to do the easy subcutaneous shots myself. Steven is going to have to do the intramuscular ones that come later. I think I need to get over my fear of needles and face it like a grownup. My hand shakes. "Just do it," Steven says. "Do it in one swift, angled motion. It's easy. Just think, you're doing this for the baby."

I follow his instructions. *I'm doing this for the baby.* I jab the needle into my thigh. I start injecting the medication.

All of a sudden I realize I didn't shoot out the air first. As the medicine is dripping into my flesh, the skin around the needle starts to puff up. I am injecting a ton of air into my thigh along with the gonal-F. I feel faint. Have I just ruined my leg for the sake of the baby? Will a bubble of air now be shooting through my veins, ready to go into my heart or lungs or something and kill me?

I lie down on the floor while Steven calls the doctor's office. His voice gets higher and more desperate as he talks to first the receptionist and then the nurse, asking them to page the doctor.

But down on the floor I realize I feel fine. The swelling in my leg is going away. I walk to the bathroom, yelling, "I'm sure I'll be fine, nothing's wrong, I'm fine" in a pathetic martyrlike way. I come back to the living room and Steven announces that I need to be rushed to the hospital. He's so casual about it I know he's kidding. My hypochondriac husband would in no way take an emergency trip to the hospital lightly, calmly, or even standing up. It ends up that you really cannot hurt yourself doing these shots. All the same, we decide that Steven will administer all future shots.

♦ ♦ ♦

Monday, July 15: Steven admires the precision with which I dilute the gonal-F. We definitely have the routine down. I arrange all the supplies on a Scandinavian cheese board Steven gave me for my birthday once and carry it to the living room for the procedure.

I'm not even focused on having a baby anymore. I'm focused on the preparation of the shots, the timing of the shots, the frequent visits to the doctor and the lab, and generally creating ritual around this insane process to give myself a sense of command over the uncontrollable.

♦ ♦ ♦

Tuesday, July 16: I have the second sonogram and blood drawn. The follicles look good. Several on each ovary are getting big, and many many others are waiting in the wings, hoping to catch up.

◆ ◆ ◆

Wednesday, July 17: I think I feel my ovaries. I feel two heavy fist-size weights on my sides above my hip bones. It is the weight of them that I feel and the movement of that weight. They sort of slosh around in there, like the untethered organs they are.

◆ ◆ ◆

Thursday, July 18: There are twenty-seven eggs now. That's a lot of eggs. Dr. F says he would not be surprised if I do feel my ovaries—they are twice their normal size and will get even bigger. Since I'm relatively thin, he also said that before the retrieval I might even be able to see them when I lie down. Freaky.

◆ ◆ ◆

Saturday, July 20: Dr. F declares there is an "80 percent chance" that the retrieval will be on Tuesday. The eggs are getting pretty damn big. He counts twenty-seven, decreases my dose, and orders me back Sunday morning. Because Steven needs to abstain for at least forty-eight hours before the fertilization, but not any longer than seventy-two hours, we make a point of having sex. My ovaries are taking up so much room that all that moving around gives me cramps.

◆ ◆ ◆

Sunday, July 21: The eggs are *huge* and there seem to be more than thirty of them. At home we get a message in the afternoon from the nurse: HCG injection at 11:00 PM; transfer Tuesday at 11:00 AM. I am extremely nervous about this shot, a literal shot in the ass. I'm worried the pain will be horrible and I won't be able to handle the nightly ass-shots of progesterone for the next six to eight weeks. Steven seems nervous too, but he keeps a calm facade and tells me he's fine. We set an alarm for 10:45 PM because we're both so tired we worry we might fall asleep. But not to worry; we are wide awake. We turn to page seventy-six of our IVF protocol booklet. As instructed, I lie down on the bed. Steven consults the very basic diagram of a human backside and compares it to the one laid out in front of him, trying to identify the meatiest part of my ass to stick the needle in. The lack of control (I can't even see what's going on!) drives me nuts and I have a bit of a freak-out while Steven further contemplates my heinie. But he calms me right down. Using the satellite time from our cell phones, the shot is given at precisely 11:00 PM.

I hardly feel it.

◆ ◆ ◆

Monday, July 22: Throughout the day I keep getting paranoid, worrying that something is wrong, that the eggs have been released, that the retrieval tomorrow will go horribly awry. I can't even think about the possibility of a baby's coming out of all of this. I'm just focused on the immediate next step: Tomorrow we go to the hospital and the doctor "retrieves" the eggs and fertilizes them. Tomorrow is the D-day of the IVF cycle.

◆ ◆ ◆

Tuesday, July 23: As he looks at the steam—no, wait, is that smoke?—coming from under the hood of my car, Steven asks, "Honey, do you think this is a sign?"

"A sign?!" I shriek. "A sign of what?!?!"

"That, you know, we shouldn't do this, that something is wrong. That the fates are against us."

Are the fates with us or against us? It's a good question, I suppose, but I'm too far into this thing to give it a second thought, much less listen to any last-minute philosophizing, especially the medieval superstitious philosophizing Steven tends to indulge in when under stress.

We try to raise the hood, but it's too hot to touch. We stand back, staring at the car.

"What the fuck?" I yell to no one. "What the fuck?!" And I burst into tears.

"Honey, we'll just call a cab," says Steven as he fishes for his cell phone in his pants pocket. "It's going to be fine. They'll wait for us."

"They might, but the drugs are timed. If we don't get there . . ." I can't even finish the sentence. If we don't get there on time my ovaries will release the eggs into my fallopian tubes where they will be unretrievable and, if experience proves correct, utterly useless.

"I can't just stand here," I yell. "There is no way I can just stand here waiting for a cab that may or may not show up in time. We're not that far; let's just start walking. Maybe a bus will come; let's just start walking." I start up the hill. Steven locks the car and starts up after me.

It's true that we are almost there. We are about halfway there from our house. My car has gotten us across the wide, flat, eminently walkable Mission District. It has failed us just as we turned onto one of San Francisco's famous hills. The hospital is on the other side of the hill. So close, and yet so steep.

I can feel my ovaries jiggling as I run-walk up the hill. Although the doctor has assured me that the eggs cannot be dislodged through physical activity, it doesn't feel that way. I can't help but think that bouncing them around like that will upset the delicate reproductive possibility in these precious thirty-plus bubbles of baby potential. What's more, the jiggling hurts. It gives me cramps and makes it hard to walk, much less run. The only good thing about being able to feel my ovaries is that I know exactly where they are. So I grab my sides in an attempt to immobilize my engorged gonads and head up the hill.

"Should you be running?" Steven asks.

"I'm not running!" I scream. And I'm not. I'm speed walking at best, but only in its most awkward form, since I'm holding my arms as still as possible to hold my ovaries as still as possible. I can hardly breathe, what with the dozens of eggs and my stomach vise and the steep hill. That's the thing about San Francisco hills: They may look steep, but they are even steeper when you are on them. But I must go on. I will get these eggs to the hospital. The Selfish Gene has taken over. I am single-minded in my pursuit of reproducing part of myself. I will speed crawl over this hill if I have to. . . .

"It isn't much farther," comes Steven's voice in my ear. He is right beside me. "We're almost to the top of the hill."

I'm huffing and puffing as if I'm running a marathon, not shuffling and lurching up a hill.

"Can you see a bus?" I ask between heavy breaths.

"No," responds Steven while continuing to hold his cell phone to his ear. He's on hold with the cab company and glancing behind us for signs of bus, cab, or magic carpet.

We make it to the top of the hill. We can see the hospital in the distance. That distance is much greater than I envisioned as I huffed up the hill. My tears start all over again.

"We'll never make it," I say, crying.

"Of course we can," says Steven. "We made it up the hill! It's not that far; it just looks far. You can make it. Let's go." He grabs my hand and starts pulling me down into Cole Valley, past picture-perfect Edwardian houses that are normally shrouded in fog but shining and bright in the full sun against a clear blue sky. It is the kind of day when anything seems possible. It is the kind of day that makes a nice Minnesotan girl decide to live in California.

"Okay," I gasp as I follow him down the street. Downhill, of course, is easier than up. I can kind of run, and we make better time.

The *Chariots of Fire* theme plays in my head as Steven trots alongside me and I continue to hold my sides and run as smoothly as possible. We get to the bottom of the valley only to realize that the last few blocks are uphill again.

"You can do it," he says. "It's just a few more blocks. This is nothing."

"Go ahead," I breathe out. "Run ahead and tell them we're coming."

"Honey, we're only ten minutes from the door, max. I don't need to go ahead. We're not even late." Thank God we left early. My uptight punctuality has finally paid off.

"Just go," I insist. "You can run so much faster than I can. I'll feel better if you go ahead."

Steven sprints ahead. I enter the Surgery Center only a few minutes late. I am sweaty and breathless but triumphant and proud.

Steven, the nurse, and I gather in a small changing room, where I don a paper gown, robe, and slippers. Steven and I kiss and hug, and I'm led to the procedure room—small and dim, like a facial or massage room, but with stirrups on the table. I lie down and the nurse puts oxygen up my nose; the anesthesiologist starts the meds with a needle in my hand. He starts the pain medication, which

I feel going up my arm in a cold stream. He tells me that he had numbed my hand to keep it from stinging. I thank him profusely, like a drunken person. Dr. F comes in and asks how I'm doing. I say fine, and that the ceiling's moving around. They are pleased to hear this. The last thing I remember is his inserting the speculum.

When I wake up I'm in the recovery room with a new nurse and the anesthesiologist. I basically feel okay but a bit sore. The anesthesiologist mentions that he's going to Hawaii next week. I ask which island. All are pleased that I respond to real-time conversation appropriately, so the anesthesiologist takes off.

Dr. F comes in to deliver the good news: They got forty-two eggs.

"Plenty to freeze!" he exclaims.

The nurses agree: That's a lot of eggs.

◆ ◆ ◆

Wednesday, July 24: Fertilization report: Of the forty-two eggs, thirty-one are mature, and of those, twenty-two fertilized "normally." Twelve are frozen today—embryos frozen on the first day behave just as though they've never been frozen once they're thawed. Like flash-frozen fish. Ten are developing in a dish. Whatever doesn't get implanted in me and still looks good on Friday will also be frozen. We are, the nurse explains, in a very good position.

◆ ◆ ◆

Friday, July 26: Such high hopes crushed like so many grapes. Our nurse calls us back to the surgery room for the transfer and we are met by a sad-looking Dr. F. The embryos, it ends up, are not of the "best quality." Our best ones are rated four on a scale of one to six, with five and six being really very bad. They will freeze only those ranked one to three. Dr. F wants to put three in. He explains why, showing us pictures and exclaiming to my worried-looking husband—"It's not the sperm!" My eggs, it ends up, have a lot of "abnormalities." They leave us to discuss the three-embryo idea. As they leave the embryologist asks us (through the sliding window between the room and the lab) if she can tell us something. This clinic has never had a case of someone my age becoming pregnant with triplets. She encourages us to go with the three-embryo option to maximize our chances of having even one of them take. She rattles off some statistics and closes the window.

We look at each other and realize we need to do the three.

Dr. F returns and does the transfer. Steven watches the whole thing on sonogram. It all takes about five minutes. Before leaving, Dr. F gives us a picture of the three embryos he transferred.

On the way out the door, I can't help it; I just start crying. Steven takes me out to a terrace at the hospital. There is nothing to say. I just cry and cry and Steven holds me for almost half an hour. I stop and look out at the great view of Golden Gate Park, with the ocean in the distance and the sun shining brightly. Steven keeps his arm around me and we stand there silently. I am despondent and crushed. But I am glad that I married this man, happy to be at least *trying* to have a baby with him.

"We should head home," I say because there is nothing we can do. Nothing we can say.

"Okay, sweetie," Steven says. And then he utters those magic words that we all need to hear most whenever they aren't necessarily true. "Everything is going to be okay. It's all going to be fine."

We stop for carnitas tacos on the home. *That*, I think, *should tempt at least one of those embryos to stay.*

Biting into the taco, I think it's a good thing I took the optional Valium before the procedure. It isn't like me to realize when there is nothing to say.

My mom calls to hear how things went. Her voice gets high and tight the way it does when she's upset but doesn't want anyone to know.

"Well, honey, I think a little abnormality is just great," she says. "Why, everyone I like is a little abnormal. What's normal anyway? Abnormality is interesting. You want some abnormality."

I tell her our chances of getting pregnant with this round of eggs just plummeted from 80 percent to 40.

"Forty percent isn't bad at all. What are the chances of anything happening?" I can hear her grasping at straws now, but my drug-induced calm helps me appreciate her efforts to cheer me up. "Why, it's a great chance when you compare it to plenty of things, like, well, like meeting Steven. What were the chances of the two of you ever meeting? What were the chances of that?"

Good friends come to dinner that night and point out that while it is reasonable to be upset, this may well end up being a great day, even the best day of our lives so far. We have a lot of people rooting for us.

◆ ◆ ◆

Tuesday, August 6: I have a blood draw for a pregnancy test. An HCG level above twenty is positive; my level is eighteen. The under-twenty result can mean one of two things: An embryo implanted long enough to trigger hormone production, but it didn't take in the end, or an embryo implanted a little later than normal. We are hoping for option two. Eighteen is almost twenty, right?

I thought I would have an answer today. This is not an answer: This is more uncertainty. All I can do is retest in three days. Maybe on paper I've waited only eleven days for this result, but in the bigger picture of my quest to become pregnant, it seems as if I've been waiting years. All the days when I thought I might have been pregnant, all the trips to Walgreens for another pregnancy test, all the anxiety and planning that have taken place feel as if they have led to this test result. And there is, for me, no real result yet. Once again, I feel my lack of control acutely.

♦ ♦ ♦

Friday, August 9: Not only has my level doubled, it's in the nineties. It is unreal and just right: I am finally pregnant. It all *has* led to this result. Yet I have had no more control over this than over any other aspect of my body in the quest to pregnancy. But the outcome is finally what I wanted, and I'll happily take it. I would like to think that after all of this effort I will be grateful throughout the pregnancy, that I will treasure this blessed time, that nausea and cankles and blotchy skin and sleepless nights with a kicking baby inside me won't cause me to complain. I would like to think that after everything I've done to get my body into this new state I will stay appreciative. I would like to think that I will be a gracious victor in this fight to get my body to do as I want it to, especially since I know that while I won the battle to become pregnant and have a child, the ultimately futile war to get my body to do as I like is far from over.

♦ ♦ ♦

Tuesday, November 12: Today we have the regular four-month sonogram—just as in any other pregnancy—in which they look for defects and reassess the due date based on various fetal measurements. The tests come out normal. We feel like a normal couple too. Until the technician tells us that key measurements of the fetus show that the conception date must be off—we assure her that it is not. We're pretty goddamn sure of the conception date, thanks.

• • •

Four years later: I'm sitting at our dining table reading the paper when my son asks to look at pictures of himself as a baby—a newly acquired pastime. We pull out his first photo album and it opens to the first page, which has always clung to the cover before. There is a black-and-white photo of three embryos, like something from a biology textbook. I had forgotten putting it in this album.

"What's that, Mama?" he asks.

I hardly know where to begin.

Two Things I'm Really Good At

VERONICA NICHOLS

Somewhere out there, the Miscarriage Woman roams. She is everyone's second cousin's baby sitter's aunt. She's your friend's assistant manager, or the lady from the post office, or daycare, or church. You may not know her. But the Miscarriage Woman is out there, and she knows all your relatives and half of your friends. I'm not kidding! The story is always the same: The Miscarriage Woman loses four or six or eight pregnancies, and no one knows why, until one day the clouds finally part and she carries to term—then she has three more.

I think, just maybe, she's total bullshit. She's similar to the couple who try for years to conceive with no luck, throw in the towel and take a vacation, and then come home to discover a miracle has happened. Surely, you've heard this one? They finally conceived because they *relaxed*.

Yeah. *That* couple. Everyone knows about them. And I bet they know the Miscarriage Woman.

The nurse in the emergency room knew a hybrid version. "We had a doctor up here. His wife went through at least half a dozen rounds of in vitro, but the little suckers wouldn't stick. And if they implanted, she'd miscarry."

"Oh, fuck that," I said, sniffling.

"What?"

"In vitro. I'd take the money and travel. Go to Europe," I whimpered. My husband, Jeoff, chuckled and rubbed my knee.

"You might be better off," the nurse said, and shrugged. "But, anyway, this wife, she's had it. She gets done with what she's decided is the last round of treatment, goes home, and pours a glass of wine. And the doctor-husband freaks out.

"'What are you doing?' he asks.

"The wife tells him, 'None of this is working! I give up. If I want a glass of wine, I'll have a glass of wine. I'm done!'"

"And that's the one that stuck?" I asked, expecting the predictable as I ripped through another sandpaper-grade hospital tissue.

"Of course," the nurse said with a smile. "So, go home and have a glass of wine. You'll be fine; it's mostly hard because you've gotten used to the idea. Now you have to rearrange your head. And, really, they're more trouble than they're worth. I have three. They're no fun after third grade or so."

Jeoff shook his head. "Three is too many."

The nurse nodded. "I don't know what I was thinking. But you're both young. You'll be fine."

She handed me a sheet of paper full of emergency information, with one of those junior high school diagrams of the female reproductive system, the drawing that looks like a cow's head, printed in the center. IF YOU LOSE A GALLON OF BLOOD OR YOUR UTERUS FALLS OUT, CALL THE EMERGENCY ROOM; LIKEWISE, CONSULT A PHYSICIAN IF YOU START TO SMELL LIKE TWO-DAY-OLD ROADKILL.

All of the Just Relax stories hinge on the notion that if you employ just the right Jedi Mind Trick, if you master the Force, and Really Want It while also Not Wanting It Too Much, then magic happens. Mind over matter. Find your center. Invoke the power of prayer. Seek the Goddess. Manifest your own destiny.

Great. Because, as a woman, I don't get told often enough that my problems are all in my head, and that the cure for what ails me is simply a matter of willpower.

I didn't have that glass of wine. Alcohol and potentially dangerous bleeding are not two ingredients that I'd like to mix.

Instead, I went home and hated my uterus. I hated the womb of doom. I hated the bleeding and the pain. And I hated the crying over the blood and the pain.

Hating one's own uterus is a damned shame.

◆ ◆ ◆

When the pregnancy test showed up positive, I'd had a giddy cascade of unconditional body love. Finally! For the first time since fourth grade I felt like shouting, "Being a girl is awesome!" I immediately pardoned the fat on my ass and the roll on my tummy, because now, instead of sabotaging my best efforts to look cute in capri pants, that fat protected the baby. My breasts no longer hung around mocking the whole notion of button-up shirts—they *activated*. They sprang into action. Suddenly, the muscles and cells, the sinew and bone, the flesh I was carting around went sci-fi. Long-dormant functionality lumbered to life. I have all these bits for a reason. *Who knew?* The world went topsy-turvy and jumping on the scale rocked. Gaining weight meant health and progress. Every ounce meant things were okay.

Then I started bleeding, and it all went wrong.

Now, I curled up in bed crying at baby food commercials and hating my uterus.

Now I housed the fetal killer. The *hostile environment*. My uterus . . . the betrayer. Or maybe my blood committed the crime! Maybe antibodies or hormones gone wrong had poisoned the baby. Maybe my eggs were all half cooked. Maybe my hypothalamus failed to regulate, or I had fibroids and microscopic tumors. Maybe mercury in the water contaminated my organs, or gamma radiation ripped the fetal DNA asunder, or voodoo hexes floated up from unknown bayous as part of secret family curses passed through the generations. It may have been a lack of vitamins. Poisonous lunchmeat. Too much pepper.

Maybe it *was* all my head's fault, after all.

I didn't know. No one knows. No one even bothered to pretend that she or he could find out.

And, given that no one knows, and mostly, no one really cares—there are only two miscarriage clinics in the country—me, and all the other women who miscarry, we really have two options: shock and bodily self-loathing.

Lucky for me, those are two things that I'm really good at; I've had years of practice.

First item up for vicious criticism? The breasts. They expanded during pregnancy, going up a cup size, to a whopping triple D. I might not have qualified for those weird fetish videos in which the women have boobs as big as a man's head, but I was certainly feeling bustier than I'd ever hoped to.

My mother had no sympathy.

"I told you so," she said, wearily. "A cup size for every pregnancy. I was a C before I had you."

"No, that's *not* what you said," I protested. "You said a cup size per kid. I thought it had something to do with breastfeeding."

"Maybe they'll go back down," Mom generously suggested.

"Oh, get real. It's been a month. They're here to stay. My ass already shrank; I can get into my old pants. But my bras are too small."

"I tried to give you those bras—you should have taken them. Bras are so expensive in the larger sizes." Bear in mind that my mother probably hasn't been a triple D in fifteen years, and, really, inheriting piles of my mother's fifteen-year-old worn-out undergarments just isn't . . . sexy. But, yeah, we have one of those relationships in which I genuinely think I have to justify not wanting her old underwear.

"So, does this mean that if I try this again, they're going to get bigger? That they'll keep inflating and inflating if I keep trying?"

"Genetics are a bitch, hon," Mom said. "You should have seen your great-grandmother."

"She was pregnant fourteen times," I muse. "That we know of."

"Exactly," Mom said ominously.

So, yeah. They're huge. They may get bigger. I have the boobie gene. *Fantastic.*

Then there's the part when I turned anemic. 'Cause nothing is sexier than navigating life with ever-expanding breasts road-mapped with scary blue veins, legs in an alluring shade of "ghost-white with bruises of unknown origin," and purple under-eye circles. Actually, add the dark bags to the puffiness from the crying, the acne breakouts from the hormonal roller coaster, and the mild dehydration from suddenly redevoting myself to consuming caffeinated beverages, and suddenly I looked *older.* I looked as if the whole process had taken something out of my face. I looked tired all the time. Sadder. Haunted, even. Which, ya know, is just what I needed. On top of being the incubator of death, she of the mighty Sahara womb, I was visibly, noticeably, one step closer to my own physical demise. Even when I smiled, I looked as if I were faking.

So I went out and bought "brightening" moisturizer. It shim-mers, it smells like citrus, and it's gritty. I'm not sure what's in it, but last time I looked into such things, moisturizer isn't supposed to exfoliate. In addition to the face-scraping lotion, I brought home moisturizing face cleaner, toner full of some sort of acid, whitening toothpaste, fruit-scented mousse, and curlers.

None of this crap ever works. I know. But a girl's gotta try, right?

The exfoliating moisturizer (whose brilliant idea was that?! Blame Johnson & Johnson) made matters worse, leaving me with irritated fuchsia splotches. My gums bled from the toothpaste. The curlers tangled up in my hair, ripped strands out, and, ultimately, left me rocking a Bride of Frankenstein 'do. Clearly, I am not the Estée Lauder target audience. I am, even on the best of days, moderately beauty-product challenged. And these were not the best of days.

I decided a haircut would help; maybe my straight long hair dragged my features down. I would go to a salon where, presumably, the woman at the helm would have a clue and she'd perk me right back up. That's the kind of ridiculous insanity magazines and checkout ladies tell you to go for in these situations. "Pamper yourself. Eat gourmet ice cream. Buy shoes. Go to the salon. Spend your way into a proper state of distraction."

So . . . I trekked to the local salon.

One word of advice to those of you seeking new salons: Anyone who cuts hair under the harsh and unflattering glow of fluorescent lighting simply does not care about how *you* look. She may gossip with you as if you're best pals. She may have all the right equipment. She may smile and nod in understanding when you tell her what you want done to your head. But by the time you hop in the swiveling chair and realize that you're stuck staring at yourself in lighting that highlights all your worst features, it'll be too late . . . she'll already be back there hacking away at you with joyful abandon.

There's a difference between a haircut that takes some getting used to and a haircut that's karmic retribution for some sort of terrible dinner party you threw in a former life. When you get the shocking haircut, your husband is silent when he sees you, taking in the change. He's not sure if it likes it, but he's willing to give it a go. When you land the hair of karmic retribution, you walk into your husband's workplace and he *laughs at you.*

"It's, um. . . . " My husband actually smirked. "It's really short."

"Yeah. It's not like the picture I brought to her."

"Did you want it that short?" Jeoff asked incredulously. "What did you want?"

"I wanted it short. But the picture was sleek and cute. I wanted sleek and cute. Not poufy. Not this. That woman is blind and works in bad lighting." I poked gently at my hair's dizzying new height.

"It *is* a little poufy." Jeoff smirked again. "It's very soccer mom."

I ignored the twist in my gut at any notion of myself as a mother. "I'm twenty-seven years old. I can't conceivably qualify as a soccer mom. I think all the soccer moms are empty nesters now, anyway. Soccer moms are *so* nineties."

Jeoff scanned my head dubiously. "Okay, so you're not a soccer mom. But, it's older. It's an older haircut."

I frowned. "I look like a lunch lady in Texas, don't I?"

"You don't look like a lunch lady," he protested.

"Maybe it'll be better when I wash all of the pouf out," I speculated. "I mean, surely I can make it work. It can't be as bad as I think it is, can it?"

That's another thing about the karmic retribution haircut; it's so bad that you go into denial.

Eventually, I washed the pouf out and discovered that I'd ended up with something far more sinister than the lunch lady haircut.

I had Laura Bush hair.

All I needed was a Valium prescription and a nonthreatening job title, and I could infiltrate Republican headquarters without a second glance.

So the makeup idea bombed. The hair idea bombed. Not easily deterred, I decided I needed new clothes. I wanted nothing to do with empire waistlines or maternity-paneled pants. I would celebrate my involuntary recommitment to a child-free state. I would wear cute shoes, tight pants with buttons, and impractical white shirts. I wanted clothes that weren't built to stretch. If new motherhood no longer loomed months away, then I sure as hell didn't want to dress like someone prepping for labor pains and dirty diapers. When confronted with the fact that I wouldn't be paying for baby stuff in February or starting any college funds in the near future, paychecks burned a hole in my pocket.

Babies? What had I been thinking? Had I lost my mind? With a baby in tow, I couldn't spend recklessly on stuff I didn't need. I liked to drink and smoke cigarettes and dance to loud music. And I liked to watch R-rated movies without a second thought and read in dead silence for hours on end. And suddenly, I wanted to do all of these things that mommies can't do while wearing fabulous new clothes. So I went shopping.

I soon discovered that it was the goal of every jeans manufacturer in this glorious nation that my ass be visible when I sat down. I knew this because I couldn't find a pair of jeans with full ass coverage, and that sort of thing can't be mere bad luck. It *had* to be a highly organized low-rise conspiracy.

"Did you find anything?" my incredibly patient yet visibly bored husband asked, hovering outside the dressing room.

"Did you know I have back fat?"

"You *don't* have back fat," Jeoff sighed.

"I didn't think I had back fat, either. These pants come with *free* back fat."

"That doesn't make any sense."

"Of course it doesn't make sense to *you*. You are a man. You can buy jeans that don't stretch. You can buy pants that hang off your hips. Some of us don't have that luxury," I whined.

"I'm sure they make pants that don't stretch."

"Oh, yeah?" I taunted. "Go find me a pair, O Superior Shopper. I dare you. Once you get over a size 7 or 8, you're stuck with stretchy pants. Then you're forever pulling them up after you sit, because they slide down. And they *create* back fat."

I poked my head out of the dressing room.

"You don't *have* back fat." He looked at me in that particular way men have of looking at a woman when they think she's strayed too far into Crazy Town.

"Look!" I turned around and lifted my shirt to my waist. "See? It's making me lumpier."

"Probably just the wrong size. And you're just not looking in the right place. You should check the stacked displays at the back for stuff that doesn't stretch. Stop picking the jeans on the hangers."

"I checked the stacked jeans. They stretch."

He shook his head and took off to find mythical nonstretchy pants. I went back to the dressing room and continued the jeans quest.

"Hon?" he called out a few minutes later.

"Yeah."

"They all stretch."

"I know."

"That's lame."

"I know."

"Now what?"

"Well, how do you feel about ass cleavage?"

I don't think that my giant-breasted great-grandmother had to worry about this kind of thing. But, realistically, she had to wear all sorts of weird foundation garments, and surely the vulcanized rubber confines of Playtex girdles generated more back-fat lumps than stretch denim. According to family history, though, my great-grandfather had no aversion to her fat lumps. She gave birth fourteen times, but only seven of those babies ever took their first breath. My great-grandmother was *hardcore*. She likely hated her uterus quite a bit more than I can wrap my pampered twenty-first-century head around.

Maybe.

I'm not sure which sucks more, honestly—the uterus that won't work at all or the uterus that works a little too well. Sometimes a miscarriage is a good thing, and sometimes it hurts worse than the breakup you only ever survived through the grace granted to fools and drunks. You cry, a lot. And you want to smack the next person who tells you to just keep trying, when she's never been there in the midst of the pain and blood and wondering if you need to go back to the hospital.

But still, the Miscarriage Woman roams. She's the woman with the splotchy face, the tired eyes, and the nightmare haircut. The clothes that don't fit, the eyes that dart quickly away from small children, and the smile that's a little fake on some days. Yet, her ass is out there. She's mind over matter. She's one Jedi Mind Trick away from crying in public on bad days. She might not trust the power of prayer. She might not be the embodiment of the Mother Goddess. She might not assume you can make your own destiny. And the center she thought she had may be empty after all. She's out there, putting a new coat of paint on the broken-down machine. The Miscarriage Woman is trying her hardest not to be full of shit. She's trying not to want things too much.

The Breakdown: Aging & Illness

Now You're Just Like Flannery O'Connor:
A Few Things Not to Tell the Newly Sick

MARY O'CONNELL

1. "Look at this deformation!"

The doctor will have a sonorous, outdoorsy name: You will envision a kind earth mother MD, her lab coat strung with daisy chains. But when she walks into the examining room, trailed by a Russian medical student, you will find that her beautiful name is something of an antonym to both her appearance and her demeanor. After a curt and perfunctory introduction (a nod, a quick hello, not bothering to reply to your perky, sickgal greeting: "Nice to meet you!"), she will get to work, examining your swollen joints and conferring with her student.

"Look at this deformation!" she will say, bending back your thumb. Here, you will yelp like a Pomeranian on crack.

Behind her back, the medical student will offer a conspiratorial eye roll.

"And look at her ankles," the doctor will say, offering a quotidian tongue cluck. "That's bad." She will yank away the top of your paper gown to check your heart and your ribs. She will address you with a sigh and a flustered "Okay."

Time to smile! Because *okay* is a pretty nice word. *Smile big!*

"This is presenting like either rheumatoid arthritis or lupus. We'll need to do some tests."

Now it's your turn to say it: "Okay." The doctor will look at you with a deep frown that ruins her forehead, waiting for more. So, you'll go ahead and add a jangly "Thanks!" Blink away the very thought of tears: Blink blink! Blinkety blink blink! Grin insanely.

The medical student will press his lips together in a sympathetic smile as the doctor lowers her head and starts writing on your chart. Keep up the insane grinning until the medical student looks at the floor, freaked by the Lake Wobegon tableau: The Midwesterner Receiving Bad News.

2. "You must feel like your body has betrayed you."

The wind will stir the blossoms from the pear trees, floating out tiny white flowers like April snow. Daylight saving time will give you sunshine after dinner. You will be newly married, happy with your handsome husband and your small brown dog. But spring has sprung, baby. Your hands will swell like pink boneless hams; your anklebones will become a memory. You'll comfort yourself with this delusion: I have the flu, the word *flu* sweetly suggestive of 7-Up hissing over cracked ice, lemon-lime popsicles, a nest of blankets on the couch.

Even though you have the flu and it's getting harder to get your fingers to curl around a fork, you will agree to meet a friend for Saturday brunch because the world is born anew: pink and green and white; because you enjoy brunch—mango pancakes and pastel tulips in a clear glass vase on the table.

But your friend hovers a forkful of omelet next to her mouth as she steals a look at your hands.

Move over in your chair ever so slightly—the connective tissue in your hip joints electric and firing—so that the tulips will block her view of sorry little you trying to cut up your concrete pancakes. Admit that you have the flu, a weird harsh flu, a flu you hope will go away soon, like yesterday, ha! There will be a prolonged silence during which your friend will stare into the cinnamoned foam of her cappuccino. Her voice will be cathedral-clear and sympathetic when she finally says, "You must feel as if your body has betrayed you."

Wonder if your body is tricky that way, not only painfully swollen but hell-bent on double-crossing you. Perhaps even now your organs and limbs are in cahoots, planning on having sex with George Clooney though you have expressly forbidden this activity. Your body! You were far too trusting, childlike in your belief in its essential skeletal innocence. *Sucker!* Pretty much everyone else could tell that your body was biding its time, waiting for just the right opportunity to screw you over.

3. "You still have your great big brain."

Your tests are in, you have a diagnosis, and one thing you do not have is the flu. You would like to keep this new information to yourself, but there is the standing-up problem: You are not yet thirty but you rise very slowly, your legs staying bent, your body lurching awkwardly forward as your hands brace the chair, the table, anything. It feels odd and self-aggrandizing in an off-kilter way—here's some big news about me, people—to disseminate this information, but then people do seem to wince and wonder about the standing-up problem, about the way you have to hold your glass with both hands like a baby bear.

You tell a friend by telephone, not a brunching faux-friend, but a pal from the playground days, a comrade in the arts. You say,

"God, this is all so weird." He sounds choked with tears when he blurts, "Well, you still have your great big brain."

As if your skull is a holy repository for your true and expansive genius, as if you are Stephen Hawking demystifying the cosmos, not Josephine Average who spends a good amount of time pondering this equation involving new pants and your ass: *Does angle of pockets + low-cut waist = (a) Inherent foxiness, (b) Try again next time, or (c) Won't shred his heart but not bad for a non-returnable clearance item?* You will have no desire to experience the deep and mystical revelations of illness with that great big brain of yours; you believed it was your destiny to solve the ass equation.

But you will understand that it is sometimes hard to find the right words. And when you hang up the phone you will lightly run your fingers over your pulsing temples, the base of your neck, the crown of your head.

4. "Oh, my God! Now you're just like Flannery O'Connor!"

Equation two: Because many women are writers and many women have autoimmune disorders, some women who are writers will also have autoimmune disorders!

But you will live in the same town as the acclaimed writer who had lupus; you will have attended the same graduate school; you will have perhaps sat in the same chair and looked out the same window, watching fresh snow fall upon the banks of the Iowa River.

A fellow graduate student will go ahead and say it. Her eyebrows will rise high, higher, higher still—plucked half-moons in the middle of her forehead—and she will take a short, sharp breath and say, "Oh, my God! Now you're just like Flannery O'Connor!"

There is one and only one possible response to this comment, and that response is: "Except for the fact that I am not a genius."

This comment will make her chuckle; she will nod vigorously in agreement. This vigorous nodding will strike you as bitchy and unnecessary, for everyone is a crappy writer in comparison to Flannery O'Connor.

You will say: "Also, I do not live on a farm with my mother and paint pictures of chickens."

She will nod, not so vigorously.

You will say: "Also, I am not a major racist."

Her face will flush and her amazing eyebrows will draw together in disgust: "Are you kidding me? Do you really assume that Flannery O'Connor was a major racist just because she was a white woman from Georgia?"

Shrug. It will send hot blue waves of pain down your back, but shrug again. Shrug vigorously.

5. "You must be worried that you will end up in a wheelchair."

You will talk real estate with your hotshot friends at their backyard barbeque. They are revamping their sprawling Victorian and blather on about crown molding and bamboo flooring until you wish that you could sleep like a horse, standing up with your eyes open. You and your husband will be jealous of this couple with their good luck and big money and hipster conspicuous consumption: their big old charming house, their brand-new Volvos in the driveway. And so you will put on a scolding smile and clasp your hands in front of you like Mother Teresa. Your voice will be warm as candle wax and your breath will smell sweetly of communion wafers when you say, "When we buy a house I think we'll probably get a little bungalow. Maybe a cottage since there are only the two of us."

The woman will squeeze her eyes in pity. "Of course you will." She will gesture to the back of her four-story house. "We have all these *stairs*. And you must worry that you'll end up in a wheelchair."

Her husband will fiddle with the strings of his tie-dyed apron; the burgers will sizzle, helpless above the flame. He and his wife will share a meaningful look: *I love you.* Their pitying exaltation will be nearly tangible: You are sick and they are not. Then again, they are jackasses and you are not. Perhaps it is a draw.

But the next morning at the grocery store you will see a blind woman in a wheelchair speaking to her attendant. (You assume the other woman is her attendant, for of course you rule out the possibility that the blind woman has a friend to shop with.) They will be in the cookie and cracker aisle discussing Wheat Thins and Triscuits: Which has less saturated fat?

Your great big brain will cook up this thought: *Wow! At least I don't have it that bad. Not nearly that bad!* A certain lightheartedness will ensue as you hobble off to the dairy section.

You had thought yourself saintly in your new affliction, but the blind woman in the wheelchair will open her cupped hands and show you your very own little heart of darkness there among the Saltines, the goldfish crackers, the bone-hard bagged pretzels.

6. "You must be nervous about having a baby."

It's that time of life when a young (not-really-all-*that*-young) woman's fancy turns to reproduction; you will find yourself at many a baby shower. Your best friend's shower will be a late-night, raucous affair. The gifts will include a baby quilt embroidered with martini glasses and a baby T-shirt with the Ramones logo. A good time will be had by all until your best friend's psycho aunt takes a bite of her fudge-frosted cupcake and lets loose with a long *mmmmmmm.* She will roll her eyes to the heavens, perhaps thanking God for the orgasmic deliciousness of the cupcake before she turns to you and says, "Oh, honey. You must be nervous about having a baby."

Your heart will do a death drop, a scream-roller descent as you shrug and sip your fruity punch.

She will not be referring to any biological clock anxiety. What she means is precisely this: You must be nervous that you will have a baby but be too ill and fatigued to take care of it.

This idea will have already kept you up many a night, a new world of grief trimmed to one sick little sentence. You will realize—Ladies and Gentlemen, we have a winner!—that this is the worst possible thing to say to a young woman who is newly sick.

You will despair, and you will despair needlessly.

For your body has a few marvelous tricks tucked up its uterus. Your body will redeem itself beyond measure. You will give birth to a baby girl, and then a baby boy, children who you will be able to take care of just fine, thank you very much, children who will show you such a pure-hearted universe that you will believe in things you once found inane: that the earthly body is but a shell, that the soul ascends, and that love is everlasting.

The Seven-Month Itch

PATRICIA BUNIN

*T*he itching started during dinner at the Ritz-Carlton. Instinctively I reached up to scratch my head before remembering that my hair now moved. That is to say, it moved separately from my head. The lining of my wig was scratchy against my bare scalp.

When I had tried on wigs in the shop, before starting my chemo, I still had my own hair. "See how comfy that is?" the wig consultant, twenty years my junior with hair down to her tush, had said as she patted the synthetic hair over my own hair. She never bothered to mention how different the fake hair would feel against my bald head.

"You okay, honey?" my husband, George, whispered as I held my hand tentatively in midair, sort of like a wave gone awry. I didn't know exactly what to do with my hand that was being drawn like a magnet to my itchy head. Terrified that the whole wig might come off in my hand if I succumbed to my impulse to scratch, I held my right hand on my lap with my left. I fought the urge to scratch as long as I could . . . about forty-five seconds . . . before I shot up from the table, knocking over a glass of water, and ran, water dripping down my dress, to the hotel powder room.

Crazed with the need to scratch, I ripped the perfectly coiffed wig from my head, threw it on the table that held the fancy guest towels, and started scratching with both hands. It felt so good that it took me a few moments to notice that I was not alone. A woman in a black suit, triple strands of pearls at her throat, and silky gray hair swept into a fashionable knot, tried not to stare at me. She was artfully applying her lipstick in the mirror directly over my wig. My eyes moved swiftly from her face to the sight of my bald head, reflected in the mirror. "I seem to be having a bad hair day," I said. She smiled and disappeared through the carved oak doorway.

I stayed calm. Evidenced by the fact that I was standing bald in a ladies' room with a wig before me. George, my mom, and dear friends Zandra and Paul had arranged the dinner in my honor. It was my "coming out" party, my first time in public with my newly revised body since my breast cancer surgery. Earlier, as I prepared for the celebration, I had felt like a teenager dressing for the prom. In my favorite dress, a short and sassy rust-colored knit number, with my new wig and prostheses, I felt moved to put on eye makeup for the first time since my cancer treatment began.

"It's starting to feel like normal again," I told George. "Even if many of my body parts can now be boxed up for the night."

Sinking into one of the green-and-white-striped silk slipper chairs that faced a full-length mirror, I toyed with the idea of sticking my head in the sink to feel cool water against my scalp. Instead I indulged myself in another scratching session, my hands going after my head like a cat on a scratching post. The itching gradually eased and I started thinking about the role my hair had played in my life.

Sometime in my midtwenties I had started "accentuating" the red highlights in my brown hair with a little help from my hairdresser. Pretty soon it was bye-bye brown; redheads rock. At about the same time a few gray streaks started appearing in my mother's pretty, dark hair. "Get rid of them," I admonished her. I didn't want to have a gray-haired mother, especially since she looked so young. And wash away the gray she did. Never to this day (she's now ninety, and she still looks young) have I seen a gray hair on Mom's head.

As the years passed, happy as a redhead, I supposed that I would carry on the family tradition I had imposed upon my mother with nary a gray hair gracing my head. "Me go gray? No way," I told every hairdresser. That was my motto until a life-altering event changed my mind . . . and my hair color. In addition to the expected gray hair, midlife brought me an unexpected change: Cancer. In both breasts.

Strangely enough, the decision to have a double mastectomy was not all that hard. Once I knew my breasts were diseased, they became the enemy and I didn't want them anymore.

My hair, however, was a different matter. I am small boned and thin. While no one had ever said I had a "great rack," I was defined in younger years by my long thick red tresses, and in later years by my shorter pixie-style thick red 'do. I wanted my hair. I needed my hair. I loved my hair. When I was told that chemotherapy was vital to my full recovery, and I would definitely lose my hair, I, err . . . wigged out. Literally.

◆ ◆ ◆

The search for the perfect wig began in fashion magazines. Only a good idea if you happen to look like a fashion model. "Wow," I said to George as I flipped through the pages containing one gorgeous hairstyle after another. "How do you think I would look as a blond?" In a word, terrible, I discovered a few days later in the Wig Wam, where hair hung on hooks, like meat in a butcher shop. I detached some long blond curls, selected mainly because the hook was low enough for me to reach.

"Close your eyes," I admonished George and my mom. I wanted them to get the full effect, after the wig was on my head, rather than seeing me put myself together like a puzzle. "Do blonds have more fun or what?" I asked, trying to strike a sexy tone as I strutted toward them. The answer was in their expression. Or rather lack of expression. They stood stone still, smiles pasted on their faces, afraid to speak. I took a long look in the full-length mirror. Staring back at me was a washed-out, wannabe hooker.

If I were ridiculous as a blond, black was no better. As I had already established, gray was not an option. Long was ludicrous. I even tried an orange-red curly *I Love Lucy* style. Let's just say I'm no Lucille Ball. Several days and many wig shops later, I finally found what I wanted.

"Do you have any wigs that are like my own hairstyle and color?" I asked the consultant at the North Hollywood salon. This salon was unique in that it specialized in hair solutions for chemotherapy patients and specialty wigs for the movie studios (how's that for a combo?—you gotta love L.A.). Bingo. She brought out an auburn number that was just slightly darker than my own hair. Placing it carefully on my head so that the fake pixie wisps covered my real ones, she explained that I should have my hairdresser trim the wig while I still had my own hair. That way we could get an exact match for the bangs and other details.

"Exact match." That's what I wanted. Here, amid the glamour of movie megastars, and endless opportunity to create a new persona, I discovered who I really wanted to be. I wanted to be me.

Soon I was on my way home, wig on head, supplies, including faux-hair-care shampoo and a cute set of bangs that I could glue into hats, in hand.

"I guess all I ever wanted was my own hair," I told George that night.

• • •

I found it the next morning. On my pillow. The first strands of hair had begun to fall out during the night, exactly eighteen days after my first chemo treatment, just as my oncologist had predicted. In the beginning I viewed losing hair as being a victim. Then one day my oncologist said, "Look. The chemo is working; your hair is falling out." And in that moment it became a less difficult means to a very worthwhile end.

Rather than shave my head, I opted to let my hair fall out naturally. Getting used to the change a little bit at a time worked better for me, process-oriented creature that I am. At the end of each day Mom and I swept up hair from the floor, measuring who had lost more hair, me or my cat. Gomar Kitty's tabby black and silver strands soon began to pale against the piles of my red hair.

I took a cue from my aloof feline friend and decided that losing my hair was no big deal. I began wearing a white knit hat to breakfast every morning to keep my hair from falling into my food. Mom, who stayed with us for five months to help me through my treatment, took this idea to another level. When she called me in to lunch or dinner, she'd say with a laugh, "Don't forget to dress for dinner." That was my hat reminder.

Soon I was practically bald except for a thick clump of red that stuck up about an inch from my head and curled forward. George said I looked like Woody Woodpecker. He started each day singing, "HaHa-HaHaHa . . . it's the Woody Woodpecker Song." Even as I pretended to be mad at him, I couldn't stop laughing at how funny I looked. To this day, eight years later, if I wake up in the morning with my hair sticking up on the top of my head, we burst into song.

When the last strand of my hair finally fell out, George gently touched my head and said, with a tenderness I will never forget, "You know, Baldy, you have an elegantly shaped head."

◆ ◆ ◆

Elegantly shaped or not, when the hair was gone, I wanted my head covered. The dinner at the Ritz was the official kickoff of many itchy events to come. Restrooms became my personal spas. No longer sink shy, I developed the ritual of "run and dip." During a business lunch at a restaurant, I would excuse myself to go to the ladies' room when the first signs of an itch appeared. I could pull off my wig, dunk my head in the sink, splash with water, pat dry, scratch, replace wig, and touch up my lipstick in seven minutes flat. Dining with friends, I'd just laugh and say, "Gotta go scratch."

Sometimes the itch would come on so suddenly that getting to a ladies' room was not an option. I kept a large purple straw picture-frame hat in the car to hide behind if I had to scratch on the run. Once at a fancy wedding in a private club, I ducked behind a coatrack and stuck my head in some woman's fur wrap, scratching my head with one coat sleeve while I stuffed the wig in the other. Panicked that she might return to retrieve her coat while my head was still in her sleeve, I imagined myself having to scamper away on my hands and knees trying to pass myself off as some strange furry wild animal. After the fur incident I started to rely on hats and scarves as much as possible. Some women can wrap scarves around their heads and make them into works of art or fashion statements. Unfortunately, I am not one of them. The babushka wrap was more my skill level, a style that, let's face it, really isn't a style. I progressed from tying the scarf under my chin to behind my head, a slightly more fashionable look, especially if you wear bangs.

Now bangs are another whole story. I taped. I glued. I super-glued. Once, in desperation, I even stapled the bangs to my scarf. But the results were not good. They kept falling off and turning up in odd places. My supermarket cart. On the gas pedal of my car. *What's next?* I wondered. *My beef stew?* When they turned up in the toilet, I decided to flush fake bangs from my life forever.

"Hand over the hats," I said to Mom as I was hiding behind the door of a Macy's dressing room, my wig already balanced on a dress hook. I owned many hats, but nothing seemed to make the statement I wanted. Studying myself carefully in the mirror, I realized that maybe George was right. I did have an elegantly shaped head.

Stuffing the wig in my tote bag, I left the dressing room, bareheaded, and asked a startled saleslady to direct me to the earring counter. Mom got it immediately. She had been with me when I told the oncologist about my itching problem. He'd replied, "Wear big earrings and show off your nice head."

Mom picked up a pair of large hoops with dangling stones in my favorite lavender and purple. When I slipped them through my pierced ears and gazed in the mirror, I felt feminine, even without hair.

I wore the earrings out of the store as I walked my bald head to the car.

◆ ◆ ◆

About seven months after my chemo treatments ended, little sprouts of hair starting popping through my scalp, like grass from seed. When my hair grew in, it was . . . you guessed it . . . gray. Soft and shiny with beautiful salt-and-pepper curls. "I love it," George said. Amazingly, so did I.

That, however, is not the end of the story. A year later, when the curls went straight and my hair lay in gray flat layers on my head, I chose to become a redhead again. It's just that this time, it was a choice, not a necessity. Will I ever go gray? Maybe someday.

Ain't No Forehead
Smooth Enough

MONICA HOLLOWAY

I turned forty-three last year, and even before I'd blown out my candles, a transformation had begun. To be clear, I understood that forty-three wasn't *that* old. But for me, it was the year my body really got away from me—the year I lost all reasonable elasticity and crossed over from being young to being middle-aged.

I had other issues about aging, of course, but thinking about them brought on anxiety so profound that it kicked my some-what-under-control obsessive-compulsive disorder into high gear. If I'd asked myself—*Did I accomplish what I thought I would at the halfway point of my life?* or *Am I truly happy?* or *What have I done in these forty-three years that is worthy of a gold star?*—the next thing I knew I'd be sitting on my kitchen floor organizing the cabinets under the sink for the fourth time in three days or scrubbing the teakettle until the bright blue enamel began flaking off onto the sponge.

So instead of concentrating on *who* I was at forty-three, I fixated on *what* I was—and *what* I was wasn't what I used to be.

I remembered my grandma telling me when I was fourteen, "It's just terrible being in this eighty-two-year-old body. Every morning I open my eyes and am ready to throw my legs over the bed and jump up like I always did, but then I try to sit up and realize this old body won't let me. It's distressing."

Until that moment, I had assumed the mind integrated with the body. I'd assumed that as people grew older, their attitudes changed along with their bodies and that old people knew and accepted their slower, wrinkled bodies in exchange for their hard-won wisdom.

That was not the case, Grandma assured me. First off, no one wanted to hear her wisdom. The world was too busy asking her to step aside so they could squeeze by her and race through their lives. No one had time to ask for advice. Not that Grandma remembered much of the wisdom she'd accumulated. She had trouble remembering to turn off her own oven.

Being claustrophobic, I imagined aging to be like finding yourself trapped inside a puckered, age-spotted, sluggish cocoon. Right then, at fourteen, I decided to resist aging. I didn't want to grow old anymore, not ever.

◆ ◆ ◆

Now that I was in my forties, it was true that I still felt thirty. It was also true that I stood in front of a rack at Bloomingdale's fingering the adorable pleated wool miniskirts trying to convince myself I could still pull it off. But every time I saw some appealing, groovy outfit and began to picture myself in it, my internal age monitor thwacked the side of my head. *You must be joking*, it said. *Go find a pair of elastic-waist pants and a nice panty girdle to wear underneath them*. I finally understood why my Aunt Sandy wore panty hose under her shorts. Spider veins, a sagging ass, and stomach support, that was why.

◆ ◆ ◆

Once, my seven-year-old son was sitting in the back seat of our Jeep when a bee flew in his window. (His comfort level with bees was on a par with the Wicked Witch and water.) He began shrieking and trying to smash the bee with his purple notebook. I pulled over, turned around, and nailed that sucker with one wallop of Christiane Northrup's book *The Wisdom of Menopause*, which I carried in the car but never read. Feeling smug (and athletic), having saved my precious offspring from a fierce insect attack, I turned around only to catch a glimpse of my sagging chin in the rearview mirror. I immediately and instinctively positioned my hand under my chin and rapidly patted it back up to where it belonged and very recently had been.

But it wasn't just my chin. I had two vertical creases in front of both ears. When I told my older sister, who was forty-seven, she calmly replied, "Oh, that's just forty." *Just forty?* Ear crags? What other middle-age realities was she keeping from me?

Certainly she needed to tell me what was going on with my eyelids. When I put on eye shadow, I had to manually stretch my wrinkled, puffy lid out to smooth on color that was very subtle and light because, as the woman at the Estée Lauder counter recently told me, patting the top of my hand, "Darker colors don't look good on older women." Instead of telling her to go fuck herself, I bought a trio of light brown, gold, and beige shadow for $43.

Makeup wasn't helping me much, though, because my eyes were not bouncing back from that sleepy morning look as they once had. They remained swollen and droopy all day and into the evening. Looking as if I had pulled an all-nighter was a permanent state. I tried opening my eyes really wide but the fold of skin snuggled back over my eye the second I relaxed it. My sister called it the "Ruth Semback."

Ruth was our neighbor in Ohio when we were growing up; her eyes sagged so badly she had to have skin removed four times in six years. When she spoke to you, it was anybody's guess as to whether her eyes were open or closed.

I didn't want to look like Ruth. I didn't want to look forty-three. I highlighted the gray in my hair, waxed the fuzz off my face every three weeks, dyed my eyebrows so I'd *have* eyebrows, and scanned the endless parade of catalogs that arrived in my mailbox for the latest fashions, which might hold the clue as to how I could look hip, without accidentally (and tragically) diving into Britney Spears territory.

It was hopeless. Nothing currently fashionable was suitable for my age. When I was in high school and had a stomach you could bounce a dime off, the style was high-waisted jeans and gauchos. Today, the waistlines sat below the belly button and some of them were barely above my graying pubic hairline. Just when I needed a pair of high-waisted jeans to cover and support my bulbous belly or gauchos to hide my thick, dimpled thighs, "low-rise" jeans and Daisy Duke shorts were all I could find unless I sewed my own or shopped at Sears. When I mentioned this to my mother-in-law, she said, "Older women should wear their pants backward. No asses and huge stomachs." This didn't make me feel better.

◆ ◆ ◆

One Saturday, I walked into my hair salon to have my hair cut and colored. When my stylist of seven years turned around, she looked odd. I panicked because I couldn't figure out what the hell had changed. She looked like herself but not really because her face was swollen and taut and her cheeks appeared to be elevated, as if a tiny scaffolding were shoving them up from below.

To cover my shock I managed to say, "You look great," lying out my ass.

She leaned down, "I had my eyes done." She was thirty-eight years old.

"Wow," I said. "You're so brave."

What the fuck was I talking about? Brave was *not* getting your eyes done. Brave was letting nature take its course. The change in her face had thrown me so much that I continued my lying streak. "Well, you look refreshed and *so* young," I added to the shit pile.

There was something more to it than her eyes, but I couldn't put my finger on it. Her nose looked wider and then there were those cheeks, which were disconcertingly high and perky. She began tinfoiling my hair. We made small talk. I stole glances at her in the mirror. Before she blow-dried me, she bent down to confess that she'd also had butt fat injected into her face.

"You're kidding," I said, horrified and intrigued.

"Yes, he lipoed my ass and injected the fat into my cheeks. Can you believe it?" She smiled, her cheeks rising to freakish heights.

"I had no idea," I managed. This was not a lie since no reasonable person would conclude that someone's ass fat could make the long trip to his or her face.

"So when people say I'm glowing, I secretly smile because I know it's really my butt fat glowing," she said with a laugh.

"So hilarious," I said, disgusted and hungry for every detail, including the doctor's number—just in case.

For the next four minutes, while she sprayed and positioned each strand of my hair, I stared at my own aging face, at the semicircle of wrinkles under my eyes and the lines on either side of my mouth. I looked back at Eva, her face smooth and tight. I appeared tired but I wasn't. She looked weird but awake. I couldn't decide which was worse.

I arrived home with hair that didn't look a day over thirty-five. In contrast, my face looked much older. It was not only wrinkled but extremely dry *and* oily at the same time. I had acne that rivaled my puberty outbreaks. Premenopausal acne was what my facialist casually called it. *Premenopausal,* holy shit. I had whiteheads, blackheads, oil slicks. My face needed to be veiled.

I was also sporting unidentifiable spots and moles. First, there were the tiny red bumps scattered across my stomach, popping up on my back, and trotting across my forehead. I didn't know what they were until one day my boss pointed between my eyes and said, "I would get that mole removed."

"What mole?" I said.

"That red one." She pointed again.

I didn't know moles were red. I worried those red dots might be a rare form of cancer best left unidentified under the pretense "what you don't know won't hurt you."

My boss wrote a phone number on my message pad and the next thing I knew I was heading to Beverly Hills to visit her expensive dermatologist. In one visit, he froze off ten red moles. The problem was that they regenerated like gecko tails. I now had a standing appointment in Beverly Hills.

He wasn't removing just red moles. Every time I departed, I left behind skin tags, brown bumpy warts, and unidentifiable bumps he'd frozen off my face. Walking down Wilshire Boulevard, I felt like a million bucks despite the dozen or so round Band-Aids dotting my face and body and my plunging checking account balance. This was war, and it took money or a credit card with some room on it to win a war (or at least to keep up with the enemy).

If my physical decline had begun even six years earlier, I wouldn't have had the money to pay the dermatologist. My husband and I had married twelve years ago with less than $200 between us. We rented an apartment in Los Angeles, where he began his television writing career, and I was an assistant producer on the television show *Unsolved Mysteries.* (Not knowing at the time that the biggest mystery I would face would be, "Where did all the collagen go?") Twelve years later, we had a little extra, and it was all going right into my face.

Los Angeles had been kind to us in some ways, but living there wasn't helping my struggle to age gracefully. I often found myself walking behind women who looked twenty-five in their Joe's "Twiggy-style" jeans (yes, that's really the name), their curly blond hair bouncing around their perfect shoulders, enormous leather handbags stuffed under toned and tanned arms, only to be scared to death when they turned around. Their faces were a cosmetic surgeon's wet dream. So many L.A. women in their late sixties had been pulled and injected with so much Restylane that they resembled wax figures. That confusion kept everything off-kilter. After a while, it was hard to remember what sixty really looked like.

• • •

My friends weren't escaping the aging thing either. My friend Olivia called one afternoon in a panic.

"Get a handheld mirror," she screamed into the phone.

"What?" I said, holding the receiver away from my ear.

"Just get a handheld mirror and come back to the phone. Hurry!"

I raced to the bathroom, grabbed the mirror, and padded back through the house. I picked up the phone. "I have it."

"Put the mirror on the counter and look down at your face," she instructed. "See what it does."

I laid down the mirror and when I looked at myself, the skin on my face bunched forward and my eyes became slits surrounded by deep wrinkles like those of a shar-pei. "Oh, my God," I shouted, my armpits instantly sweaty. "Dear God, no," I repeated, unable to stop gawking at the dried-apple face in the mirror.

"I know," she said. "I already told my husband that I'll never be on top *ever* again."

After the shar-pei incident, I began to worry even more about my sagging face. I was sitting in the auditorium at my son's school when another mother said, "Are you in a bad mood?"

"No," I said, confused.

"You look like you're either in a bad mood or you're really thinking hard about something." I still didn't know what the hell she was talking about. I was peaceful, refreshed even, having just returned from an afternoon concert in the park.

That night, I looked up at the mirror while I was brushing my teeth and saw what she had seen. Two deep wrinkles had appeared between my eyebrows, one horizontal and one straight up and down. She was right; I looked distinctly pissed off.

◆ ◆ ◆

For Christmas, I gave myself Botox injections right between the eyes. I was sorry it was fabulous, because injecting poison into my head seemed pretty stupid. But when those wrinkles completely disappeared, I felt high on life—giddy and young and miniskirt ready. It was the most radical age-defying thing I'd done so far. And it was massively expensive—$400 a pop. But I was a Botox miracle—my injections held up for six months. I went twice a year even though some of my friends went every three months. I wanted to embrace the beauty of Georgia O'Keeffe in her last years, her gorgeous, wrinkled face and hands, but I was afraid that without exercising great restraint, I was in danger of emulating Mary Tyler Moore or Joan Rivers instead. Those women looked like aliens but they didn't look old. Surely, I could be courageous and just embrace the whole aging thing. But with Botox already in my forehead, I had to admit that a Georgia O'Keeffe ending was drifting farther away.

Just about the time I and my Beverly Hills dermatologist out-smarted my wrinkles, I began sprouting hair like an adolescent boy. The hair on my head was behaving itself but the hair every-where else was having a party. I changed my if-I-won-the-lottery fantasy servant from a chauffeur to an on-call waxer. I might not have had a mustache in the morning, but when I checked in the evening, I could be sporting a full-on Frida Kahlo.

I was at Serenity Spa in the San Fernando Valley to get some of my newly sprouted hair waxed when my technician persuaded me to do my bikini area.

She handed me the tiniest paper roll. "Here you go."

"What am I supposed to do with this?" I asked.

"Put it on," she said. It didn't look as if it fit any part of my body—maybe my thumb?

"Where?" I asked.

"Put it on instead of your underwear and I'll be right back," she said, closing the door behind her. I unrolled the paper and there was a miniscule strip of white and gold-flecked paper with a string on each side. I slipped my panties off, shoving them into the pocket of my jeans so my technician wouldn't see that I wore large stretched-out cotton underwear, and put on the scrap of paper. It covered nothing. I lay on the table feeling embarrassed and ridiculous.

The technician swooshed back in the door. Suddenly she turned around and saw my fully exposed vagina. The look on her face was as if she'd seen Mia Farrow's offspring from *Rosemary's Baby*. "Oh, dear, this all has to go," she declared, gesturing wildly over my crotch and making a clicking sound with her tongue.

"All of what?" I asked, worried.

"All of this crazy hair. It's not *clean* to be so hairy," she scolded.

There were many things I didn't know, but I *did* know that I was in no way "crazy hairy" in my crotch. My sister called my pubic hair "Hitler's mustache" because it was so skinny and well maintained.

Nonetheless, she attacked the area with fervor and scalding wax, causing great pain and redness. And it wasn't just the front and the sides she waxed. She lifted my leg and actually went after the most intimate place of all.

"No, don't do that," I told her.

"We have to do it. This is not healthy," she said with a glint in her eye.

"Leave it alone," I said, trying to put my leg back down.

"It'll just take a moment," she said, with a vise grip on my leg.

When it was over, I was completely bald front to back. What was supposed to be a bikini wax became a shearing. I wondered what my husband would think. *Would he find it sexy? A nice change? Peculiar?*

When I got home, I ran to the bathroom and pulled down my jeans. My crotch was red and swollen. I turned and looked in the full-length mirror. A Rodney Dangerfield joke immediately came to mind. "You know you're getting old when your testicles tell you it's time to mow the lawn."

I didn't have testicles but my labia could've told me it was time to mow the lawn. My husband was in no way going to find *that* sexy.

What happened to my cute vagina? The last time I saw it without hair (in fifth grade), it rocked. Now it was elongated and droopy, swaying below my body. Was this normal? I considered a crotch harness.

◆ ◆ ◆

My husband had done well in the entertainment industry, and we recently attended the Emmy Awards. I had my hair and makeup professionally done and wore a beautiful long beaded gown. He won an Emmy that night and we danced at the Governor's Ball. I felt young and sexy.

But when I got the pictures back, there was a forty-three-year-old woman wearing *my* beaded gown staring back at me. I saw a woman with jowls and arm fat bulging ever so slightly over the hand-sewn straps.

Even at my very best, even with help from Hollywood make-up artists and hairstylists, even with Botox, I looked my age. Of course I did; how could I not? Why did I keep forgetting what I really looked like? Why was the image in my head so different from the one the world saw?

I'd decided to come to terms, really soon, with who I was and what I looked like. I wanted to accept and (I hated this word) embrace who I was becoming every day. I couldn't roll back the clock. I taped pictures of Diane Keaton, Helen Mirren, and Judi Dench to my bathroom mirror. These women were glorious—gorgeous and sexy. Beside them, I taped Mary Tyler Moore's hopelessly stretched-out mouth and Lisa Rinna's bee-stung face and lips. I looked at them every day and decided I'd try to do the Diane Keaton. I'd find the right clothes somehow, and I'd be groovy and sexy even with my crotch harness.

And I'd start right after my next Botox appointment, which was in two weeks.

Acknowledgments

We'd like to extend huge, heartfelt thank-yous to all our contributors, whose humor, honesty, and talent shine in these pages. Thank you to Nina Collins and Matthew Eblonk for all their work on our behalf. To Jill Rothenberg, who saw this project the way we did and helped it become a reality, and to Laura Mazer, who took the baton and ran without stumbling even once. Thank you to Laura Donahue for sharing her teaching stories.

Friends and family contributed in numerous ways—mostly by being smart and funny and wonderful. Thank you to Connie Biewald, Laura Brown, and Brooks Philips for listening during the proposal stage and to Trent Stewart for reading a draft. Also, thank you to Wendy Honett for enthusiastic, energetic publicity. *Muchísimas gracias* to Mary O'Connell for getting on board early and enthusiastically and for helping us sell this book. Thanks, Peter Fish, for your general smarts and for sending us Laura. Thanks, Wayne Schoech, Catherine Pilfrey, and Joseph Schoech, for title ideas and good summertime company. Thank you to Spencer Toy for making us look good in pictures. Last but not least, a thousand thank-yous to the husbands, Pete Mulvihill and Jim Gothers, who always maintain that our jeans do *not* make our butts look big.

About the Contributors

Adrianne Bee's hang-ups about her appearance began at age five when a Safeway cashier told her she was a darling little boy, perhaps because she wore her brother John's hand-me-downs and had an asexual bowl cut courtesy of her father, who was no Vidal Sassoon. She survived puberty and now works as a journalist in San Francisco. She is writing a memoir focused on her relationship with her brother, who passed away in 2003. He taught her to laugh at any curve life throws her way.

Marie "Riese" Lyn Bernard's work has appeared in *Nerve.com, Conversely, Clean Sheets, CollegeBoundTeen Magazine, The Sarah Lawrence Review, The Michigan Daily, ElitesTV.com, The Best American Erotica of 2007,* and *The Best Women's Erotica of 2005.* Check her out and read her blog, This Girl Called Automatic Win, at www.marielyn bernard.com.

Laura Catherine Brown is the author of *Quickening,* a novel. Her short story, "Leftover Gonal-F," appeared in *Before: Short Stories about Pregnancy.* A recipient of the Walter E. Dakin Fellowship at the Sewanee Writers Conference, Laura has been awarded residencies at The Virginia Center for the Creative Arts, Vermont Studio Center, Ucross Foundation, The Ragdale Foundation, Norcroft Writing Retreat, and the Hambidge Center. Her job as a graphic designer supports her writing habit. She is working on her second novel. In her spare time she examines her flaws.

Patricia Bunin lives in Altadena, California, and works as a public relations consultant. She writes regularly for the *Pasadena Star-News* and contributed to a previous Seal anthology, *Tied in Knots: Funny Stories from the Wedding Day*. She is working on a humorous book about her experience with breast cancer.

Jennifer Carsen is a freelance writer who divides her time between New Hampshire and London. She specializes in the areas of food (of course), fitness, relationships, and travel writing and has just launched a website for the down-to-earth, non-Bridezilla bride (www.weddingchickie.com). Her work has appeared in *Chicago Health & Beauty* magazine and other publications, as well as in a previous Seal anthology, *Tied in Knots: Funny Stories from the Wedding Day*.

Laura Fraser is the author of *The New York Times* best-selling travel memoir *An Italian Affair* and the weight-loss industry exposé *Losing It: False Hopes and Fat Profits in the Diet Industry*. She lives in San Francisco.

Sarah Hart lives in a cottage in the middle of a wood in Hertfordshire, England, with her partner and cat. When she's not badger watching or foraging, she writes, counsels others, and facilitates personal and professional development workshops for women.

Monica Holloway is the author of the memoir *Driving with Dead People*. Her first published work appeared in the anthology *Mommy Wars,* and she has also been published in *Parents* magazine. Despite what she says about her sagging body parts, she highly recommends life after forty.

Kim Wong Keltner is the author of the *San Francisco Chronicle* bestseller *The Dim Sum of All Things* and its sequel, *Buddha Baby*. Her next book will come out in spring 2008.

Beth Lisick is a writer and performer from the San Francisco Bay Area. She is the author of the books *Monkey Girl, This Too Can Be Yours,* and most recently, *Everybody into the Pool,* which was named one of the Top Ten Nonfiction Books of 2005 by *Entertainment Weekly.* With her friend and collaborator Tara Jepsen, she made the award-winning short film *Diving for Pearls,* in which most of their screen time is spent entirely in the nude.

Roseanne Malfucci spent three years after college balancing work at a family violence nonprofit with publishing an independent magazine and learning to deejay. Recently, this native New Yorker went solo to hustle a living off her three passions—music, language, and the "humanist arts." This is her first essay to be published in a book.

Laura McNeal is the coauthor, with her husband Tom, of four books for young adults: *Crooked, Zipped, Crushed,* and *The Decoding of Lana Morris.* She lives in Fallbrook, California.

Jennifer D. Munro's work has appeared in three Seal Press anthologies: *Secrets and Confidences, Shameless,* and *Literary Mama.* She's also been published in *Zyzzyva, Calyx, Under the Sun, Room of One's Own, Best American Erotica,* and other journals and anthologies. She received an Artist Trust GAP Award and a Hedgebrook fellowship. Her website is www.munrojd.com.

Veronica Nichols lives in Northern California with her husband, three cats, too many computers, and way too much time to think. She's obsessed with women's history and the stories of female saints; she's now writing a feminist retelling of the life of St. Mary of Egypt. She blogs at http://ninepearls.com.

Mary O'Connell is the author of the novel *Shakespeare for Freshmen* and the short-story collection *Living with Saints.* She lives in Lawrence, Kansas, with her husband and two children.

Nancy Rabinowitz, a 36D, lives with her husband and young twins in New York City. She has written for television clients such as HBO, Lifetime, A&E, and ESPN Classic for the past fifteen years, and she has had essays in *Brain, Child; The Imperfect Parent;* and in the anthology *The Knitter's Gift.*

Mae Respicio is the author of the photo-history book *Filipinos in Los Angeles.* She is a recent recipient of a PEN Rosenthal Emerging Voices Fellowship and is at work on her first novel. Her favorite kind of week is a combination of five days sunny and two overcast ones.

Tara Bray Smith, who grew up in Hawaii, is the author of the memoir *West of Then: A Mother, A Daughter, and a Journey Past Paradise.* She lives in Düsseldorf, Germany.

Molly Watson is a staff food writer for *Sunset* magazine in California. Her work has also appeared in *The New York Times* and *The Week.* She is writing a book about women and their wedding dresses.

About the Editors

Samantha Schoech is the coeditor with Lisa Taggart of *Tied in Knots: Funny Stories from the Wedding Day*. Her short stories and essays have appeared in many magazines and books. She lives with her husband, Pete, and their twins, Magnolia and Oliver, in San Francisco, where she is an editor, writer, and maker of smashed peas. Her goal weight is 140 pounds.

Lisa Taggart is the author of *Women Who Win: Female Athletes on Being the Best* and is a senior travel writer for *Sunset* magazine. She lives in Santa Clara, California, with her husband, who agrees with her that she takes in the world in an astonishingly myopic, distorted way.

Read more at their website: www.mirthgirls.com.

SELECTED TITLES FROM SEAL PRESS

For more than thirty years, Seal Press has published groundbreaking books. By women. For women. Visit our website at www.sealpress.com.

Full Frontal Feminism by Jessica Valenti. $14.95, 1-58005-201-0. A sassy and in-your-face look at contemporary feminism for women of all ages.

Tied in Knots edited by Lisa Taggart and Samantha Schoech. $14.95, 1-58005-175-8. A collection of smart, original, laugh-out-loud wedding essays by women.

Woman's Best Friend edited by Megan McMorris. $14.95, 1-58005-163-4. An offbeat and poignant collection about those four-legged friends a girl can't do without.

Dirty Sugar Cookies by Ayun Halliday. $14.95, 1-58005-150-2. Ayun Halliday is back with essays about her disastrous track record in the kitchen and her culinary observations.

Nobody Passes: Rejecting the Rules of Gender and Conformity by Mattilda, a.k.a Matt Bernstein Sycamore. $15.95, 1-58005-184-7. A timely and thought-provoking collection of essays that confronts and challenges the notion of belonging by examining the perilous intersections of identity, categorization, and community.

Intimate Politics: How I Grew Up Red, Fought for Free Speech, and Became a Feminist Rebel by Bettina F. Aptheker. $16.95, 1-58005-160-X. A courageous and uncompromising account of one woman's personal and political transformation and a fascinating portrayal of a key chapter in our nation's history.